C000157951

This is a modern book for modern times. Basi defies conventional wisdom – that call centre employment is either India's post colonial revenge or globalisation's way of destroying national identity – and in true feminist tradition, privileges the experiences of the women themselves. She explores the lives, experiences and aspirations of young women working in call centres in New Dehli outsourced from the UK and examines the ways in which they negotiate patriarchal expectations of management family and culture, actively constructing new identities which work for them in the new India. This is a compelling account of fast changing industry which Basi captures with sophisticated theoretical analysis as well as a woman's eye and understanding.

Ruth Pearson, Director, Centre for Development Studies,
University of Leeds

Tina Basi makes an invaluable contribution to discussions on globalization and postcolonial subjectivity through a captivating study of women call centre workers in India referencing their lives inside and outside the workplace. The focus on identity and agency ensures the emergent picture is one of complexity and contradiction, exploitation and empowerment, challenging singular depictions of docility prevalent in the literature to date.

Diane Perrons, Gender Institute, London School of Economics

Women, Identity and India's Call Centre Industry

This book examines the concept of globalized identities and the way in which agency is exercised over identity construction by women working in India's transnational call centre industry.

Drawing on qualitative empirical data and extensive original fieldwork, the book provides a nuanced analysis of the experiences of Indian women call centre workers and the role of women's participation in the global labour market. The author uses social, cultural and historical factors to create a framework for examining the processes of identity construction. Within this framework, the book explores the impact of the call centre labour process on the social landscape of urban centres in India and the way in which this has impacted upon transformations and shifts in society in relation to gendered, sexual and generational relationships. Highlighting the significance of identity in a globalised world, the author argues that identity acts as one the most powerful constructs in transforming global 'scapes' and flows of culture and economics.

This book will be of interest to academics working on South Asia, gender and labour studies and issues of globalization, identity and social change.

J.K. Tina Basi holds a PhD in Gender Studies and Sociology from the University of Leeds. Previously a freelance ethnographic researcher with Intel's Digital Health Group in Ireland, she has also established a consultancy, Mehfil Enterprise, conducting corporate ethnography in media and technology related industries. She is currently working on a new ethnographic research project about spirituality.

Routledge Research on Gender in Asia Series

1 **Women, Identity and India's Call Centre Industry**
   J.K. Tina Basi

Women, Identity and India's Call Centre Industry

J.K. Tina Basi

Routledge
Taylor & Francis Group

LONDON AND NEW YORK

First published 2009
by Routledge
2 Park Square, Milton Park, Abingdon, Oxon OX14 4RN

Simultaneously published in the USA and Canada
by Routledge
270 Madison Ave, New York, NY 10016

Routledge is an imprint of Taylor & Francis Group, an informa business

© 2009 J.K. Tina Basi

Typeset in Times New Roman by
Taylor & Francis Books
Printed and bound in Great Britain by
MPG Books Ltd, Bodmin

All rights reserved. No part of this book may be reprinted or reproduced or
utilised in any form or by any electronic, mechanical, or other means, now
known or hereafter invented, including photocopying and recording, or in
any information storage or retrieval system, without permission in writing
from the publishers.

British Library Cataloguing in Publication Data
A catalogue record for this book is available from the British Library

Library of Congress Cataloging in Publication Data
Basi, JK Tina.
   Women, identity and India's call centre industry / JK Tina Basi.
      p. cm. – (Routledge research on gender in Asia series ; 1)
   Includes bibliographical references and index.
   1. Call centers–India. 2. Women employees–India. I. Title.
   HE8789.B37 2009
331.4′813811420954–dc22   2008045887

ISBN 978-0-415-48228-8 (hbk)
ISBN 978-0-203-88379-2 (ebk)

Dedicated to the memory of Barbara Powell,
for calling to the rebel within and daring me to try.

Contents

Figures

Acknowledgements

This book has been a real labour of love. Beginning with academic research that saw me transition from Regina to Leeds to Delhi to London, it's been quite a journey. Along the way I shed a lot of skins and experienced the reality of being a cosmopolitan citizen wearing labels and badges in multiple, and sometimes simultaneous, contexts. There were many people who helped along the way and I offer my thanks.

My supervisors Sasha Roseneil, now at the Birkbeck Institute for Social Research, and Ruth Pearson, in Politics and International Studies at the University of Leeds, were not only patient and supportive, but also truly inspirational. With Sasha and Ruth you never bring your 'B' game and the rigorous challenges they offered often pushed me past my comfort zone. I doubt I can come up with the words to appropriately acknowledge all that they did and continue to do, so instead I follow their lead and pay it forward. Max Farrar at Leeds Metropolitan University offered me a job in the final few months of my PhD and has remained a source of support and encouragement in all things professional and all things personal too, and, of course, John Roberts, thank you, for making me laugh through all of it and reminding me never to take myself too seriously.

The Economic Social Research Council funded my PhD research and my year of fieldwork in India. Radhika Chopra at the Delhi School of Economics and the staff and members of the Centre for Women's Development Studies, the Centre for the Study of Developing Societies and SARAI, all based in Delhi, were gracious and helpful in pointing me towards archives and sources to fill in the gaps around my interviews. Of course this book would not exist if it weren't for those interviews and I thank the women whose stories I've been allowed to share: Sangamitra, Indu, Ritu, Anshu S., Swati, Rashi, Preetika, Anshu P., Neha, Jennifer, Pooja, Nidhi, Amrit, Urmila, Sonali, Gurmeet, Seema, Anyuta, Shvetangana, Reetika, Dipti, Nimisha, Reena, Smita, Chanelle, Harshdeep, Yashica, Upasana, Nisha, Monica, Namita and Sunita. Thanks also to India Today Group for granting copyright permission to use two of their cover photos.

My life in India was enriched by three very important people: Charu Nagrath and Rishi Levi revealed to me an India I never knew to exist – I have never been the same since; and Randeep Chandyoke, thank you for EVERYTHING – I really owe you – I wouldn't have survived in the depths of Pahar Ganj if you hadn't found me. Pratibha Sawhney and her family provided a warm and safe home on Hanuman Road, in Connaught Place, as well as offering up countless opportunities to discuss and experience life in Delhi, especially Banita and Harpreet, who were both working in call centres at the time. Kapil Sharma was an amazing gateway to the call centres and his help in negotiating that entry as well as the introduction to late night socializing was crucial in gathering the research for this book.

I am eternally grateful to my parents, Balbir and Tarsem Basi, who didn't always understand 'the dreamer's desires' but supported me nevertheless. They were at the starting line and pulled the trigger by telling me, 'This is not how we Indians do things.' My mother has continued to show me how to put feminist theory into practice in all that she does and my father has unwittingly taught me even more. My wildly disparate and global support network stretches across Canada, England, India, Japan and Australia and includes: my family, Harvinder and Kavinder Basi, Gordon Sanghera, Elizabeth Shand, Isabella Sanghera and Sandish Benning; and my friends, Tony Elliott, Dev Kashyap, Garrett Schmidt, Jaime and Nik Reban-Jones, Dave McGrane, Lara Bonokoski, Tara Smith, Lucas Stepp, Michelle Mikkelsen, Amy Hodge, Shanthini Cowley-Sathiakumar, Brad Thatcher, Ant Walker, Ben Pheloung and Simon Wilson.

Finally, I acknowledge, with my deepest gratitude, Annemarie Elsom and Jeska Rees, who have been enormously influential in the writing of this book – in reading drafts of chapters, debating some of the key issues and areas of argument and, most importantly, in creating a home and space that nurtured and fostered lively debate and provoked change.

Abbreviations

ACD	automated call distribution system
ATL	assistant team leader
AVP	assistant vice-president
BJP	Bharatiya Janata Party
BPO	business process outsourcing
BTM	bhenji turned mod(ern)
CIO	Computer Information Office
CRM	customer relations management
CTI	computer telephony integration
CWDS	Centre for Women and Development Studies
DOT	Department of Telecommunications
FDI	foreign direct investment
GOI	Government of India
HR	human resource(s)
ICT	information communications technology
IDS	Incomes Data Services
IMF	International Monetary Fund
IT	information technology – the merging of computer technology with communications technology
ITES	information technology enabled services
ITES–BPO	information technology enabled services – business process outsourcing
IVR	interactive voice response
MBA	Master's in Business Administration
MNC	multinational corporations
NASSCOM	National Association of Software and Services Companies
NCR	National Capital Region
NGO	non-governmental organization
NRI	non-resident Indian
NTP	New Telecom Policy
PG	paying guest

PIO	person of Indian origin
TL	team leader
TNC	transnational corporation
VOIP	voice over internet protocol
VP	vice-president

Prologue

Well, I just wanted to know everything about British culture. Here I've learned how to groom myself, how to talk to people, a lot of things. Here you are talking with Britishers, not Indians, and they don't show their emotions very easily. Britishers, man, they like speaking with Indian people – it really touches your heart. It makes you think, I'll do anything for you.

A year back, my boyfriend was asking me, 'Why do you need to work in a call centre? Why can't you do normal job 10–16?' That's why he didn't marry me. We met at a Christmas party. We started as friends and then we got serious. And he wanted to ask me … well, he had some questions about my lifestyle, the way I carry myself, my working timings, everything. For that reason he got married to somebody else. He tells his wife that he met me through a call centre and that I live here and live alone, without any family and he needs to take care of me. Normally, we have our off days and holidays together and we go out – and he has conveyed some other message to his wife.

I used to party a lot, when I was very new in this place. I love boozing, smoking, and parties; clubs and discs. Akhil used to take me because he didn't like me hanging around with other guys. He would call and say, 'Where are you?' and I'd say, 'I am with my friend, we are going to Delhi Devils,' and he would be, like, 'Who are you with? Let me know the names, blah blah blah,' and got too possessive. I quit all of that mostly because of him, he doesn't like me hanging around with these people. He is not a party animal like me.

In call centres, we do feel that we are just out from college. Nobody is so much aware of what background you are from or what age I am. So you feel that you are a fresher, a graduate. You are working so you'll be in a funky mood, a party animal, very outgoing and very fast. No men from my office would like to marry a person from a call centre. Guys only care if the girls are out stationed or live with their parents. When they find out that a girl is out stationed – they have a ball of a time. They can come, they can stay over. Come to her place and booze.

Before you leave your parent's house, you have to have some support and if you cannot convince them, forget it. I can't go back home to my parents now. Back home, they're not into the same things as I am, they're not interested in marketing or communications, they do door-to-door sales. I don't even visit. All my relatives are suspicious of what I do. I haven't actually told them that in fact I work in a call centre.

1 Introduction

'A myriad of well-wishing "little sisters"'

We are rich because the Indians are poor. Now the jobs we stole 200 years ago are returning to India. Last week the *Guardian* revealed that the National Rail Enquiries service is likely to move to Bangalore, in south-west India. Two days later, the HSBC bank announced that it was cutting 4,000 customer service jobs in Britain and shifting them to Asia. BT, British Airways, Lloyds TSB, Prudential, Standard Chartered, Norwich Union, Bupa, Reuters, Abbey National and Powergen have already begun to move their call centres to India. The British workers at the end of the line are approaching the end of the line.

(Monbiot 2003)

George Monbiot stated this week that 'the most marketable skill in India today is the ability to abandon your identity and slip into someone else's'. As a job specification the abandonment of identity seems a rather high price. Indeed, the most accomplished become, like those Thomas Macaulay envisaged in his famous Minute on Education of 1835, 'a class of persons, Indian in blood and colour, but English in taste, in opinions, in morals and in intellect' ... The call centres create new forms of social division, separating these reconstructed young adults from the rest of society. It reinforces social gulfs, alienating people from their traditions, without offering them any place in the values they have to simulate in order to ease the lives of distant consumers they will never meet.

(Seabrook 2003)

India's call centre industry: the sunshine sector, hotbed of sexual liberalism, bound by professional agreements, ripe for discussions of postcolonial subjectivity, evoking the guilt of Empire. This book is a discussion of how agency is experienced by women working in Delhi's transnational call centre industry, seeking out truncated spaces from within which identity is articulated.

Over the last decade we have witnessed a steady rise in the outsourcing of call centre and data entry work from the UK to India, a trend that has proved irresistible to popular commentators.[1] In pairing these two quotations together one can appreciate the contradictory impression left upon *Guardian* readers and the British liberal Left concerning the relocation of call centre work. With one side arguing that call centre relocation is retribution for colonial exploitation (Monbiot 2003), the other retaliates by claiming that commodification of self-identity is too costly to naively identify as reprisal (Seabrook 2003), demonstrating a tension that reflects the contradictions in the agency/structure dynamic engulfing discussions of globalization, labour and identity.

This analysis of Indian call centre workers is itself located within a wider context. The popular perceptions of colonial exploitation (Caulkin 2002; Denny 2003a), retribution (Denny 2003b; Flanagan 2003; Monbiot 2003) and the compulsory commodification of identity (Seabrook 2003) have dominated British media discussions of India's transnational call centre industry. These reports demonstrate an oversimplification of the discussion and the quotations from Monbiot and Seabrook that opened this chapter indicate a sense of guilt emerging from the liberal Left – what Said (1993: 22–24) has referred to as the 'contemporary residue of imperialism'.

Indo-UK bilateral relations evolving out of the context of British colonial rule have created an unmistakable discursive wrinkle within which this discussion takes place: the postcolonial condition.[2] It is difficult, if not impossible, to isolate contemporary social, economic and cultural relations from colonial relations; the postcolonial condition produces subtle hostilities, or subtle forms of racism. This is not to suggest that any reference to socio-historic contexts is to be read as an act of imperialism. Rather, it is important to understand, first, the contemporary discourse surrounding the outsourcing of service work to India and, second, that the very nature of call centre work demands that Indian employees have voice-to-voice interaction with UK customers. This may be up to 300 exchanges per agent per day, and many include references by UK customers to these former colonial contexts. Proclamations regarding the exploitation and the commodification of self-identity are not only presumptuous and without strong evidence, they negate the experiences of Indian call centre workers.

The empirical research for this book is in part concerned with globalization: the globalization of production, particularly in the service sector, and the globalization of cultural identities. It goes some way towards deconstructing the notion that call centre work outsourced to India is simply 'electronic sweatshop' work (Kjellerup 1999; Holman and Fernie 2000) and looks at the way in which such employment has also empowered and given greater agency to those who work in it, both socially and economically. In presenting an ethnographic case study of women working in some of the transnational call centres of Delhi, this book explores how identity is produced through global and national discourses and examines the way in which agency functions in the construction of these identities. Second, it looks at the challenges and opportunities for women brought about by the relocation of call centre work, arguing for a closer examination of social, cultural and historical contexts in researching the globalization of service work. In doing so, it contributes to 'transnational feminist research' by critically examining women's experiences in transnational Indian call centres, linking it analytically to different places, thereby enhancing women's common struggles (Moghadam 2000; Nagar 2002, 2003).

The primary focus of this book is concerned with the construction of women's identities in globalized call centre work. Looking at the way in which women's identities are produced through a number of national and global discourses, the book explores the ways in which women exercise agency over these processes. The second theme builds upon the body of literature concerned with women's participation in the global labour market. This has for some time examined the impacts of globalization and technology on women (Afshar and Barrientos 1999; Elson and Pearson 1981a; Mitter and Rowbotham 1995; Mitter 1999), including women in India (Banerjee 1990; Papola and Sharma 1999), and has recently begun to look at the changing notions of identity (Freeman 2000; Kusakabe and Wah 2004; Gary and Townsend-Gault 2004) and the new technological industry of international data entry and call centre work (Pearson 1993; Freeman 1993). 'Emotional labour' (Hochshild 1983), the management of human feeling during social interaction within the labour process, is most widely performed by 'pink collar' workers (Howe 1977), in areas of the female-concentrated labour force of which call centre work is one. Beginning with the argument that skill definition is saturated with sexual bias (Phillips and Taylor 1980), the research shows sustained patterns of deskilling and feminization in one particular area of the global labour market and contends that certain occupations are defined as unskilled simply because women perform them (Webster 1990, 1993).

The third theme explores the social effects of the call centre industry and labour process on the construction of cosmopolitan identities for women in Delhi. The opportunities and challenges for women in urban centres in India are influenced by changes in the international political economy, but while media reports and academic theories may suggest that the cultural hegemony brought about by Western imperialism is eroding cultural identities and creating a supranational identity, this book argues that a much more complex shift is in fact taking place. This book argues that the theorized slow deterioration of cultural boundaries produced by the Internet and globalization actually creates greater opportunity to access 'mediascapes' and 'ethnoscapes' (Appadurai 1996). Thus cultural identities are viewed as part of a 'cultural interchange process' (Welsch 1999), a process contingent upon 'global cultural flows' (Appadurai 1996). Along with the construction of cosmopolitan identities, new consumption patterns as well as a number of cultural signifiers relating to clothing, food and leisure time have emerged. These signifiers point towards patterns of identification and recognition endlessly constituted and reconstituted through racialized, sexualized, globalized, national and local discourses.

The fourth theme explores the gendered use of space in urban centres such as Delhi and the way in which this has been impacted by the rise of the call centre industry. Drawing upon literature looking at geographies of women's fear, the book explores women's use of male dominated public spaces at night such as 'dhabas' and 'thekas', roadside eating and drinking places. It also looks at the construction of cosmopolitan spaces in urban centres such as shopping malls and cinema complexes that show a rise in sexual liberation and in the increasing significance of socio-economic positioning as opposed to traditional concepts of caste and religion.

The 'Empire strikes back'

> My contention is that without examining Orientalism as a discourse one cannot possibly understand the enormously systematic discipline by which European culture was able to manage – and even produce – the Orient politically, sociologically, militarily, ideologically, scientifically, and imaginatively ... so authoritative a position did Orientalism have that I believe no one writing, thinking, or acting on the Orient could do so without taking account of the limitations on thought and action imposed by Orientalism.
>
> (Said 1978: 3)

Building on Said's (1978, 1993) work, Bhabha (1994) argues that a significant feature of colonialism was in the ideological construction of the Other, resulting in a 'fixity'. He proposes the term 'mimicry', signifying the desire for a reformed, recognizable Other, 'as a subject of difference that is almost the same, but not quite' (ibid.: 122). A discourse constructed around ambivalence, mimicry emerges as the representation of difference that is 'itself a process of disavowal' (ibid.: 122).

Bhabha writes that culture is transnational and translational: transnational because contemporary postcolonial discourses are rooted in specific histories of culture displacement; translational because spatial histories of displacement complicate what is signified by culture, resulting in a hybrid location of cultural value (ibid.: 247). Thus, although colonial discourses have made great efforts to construct a fixed, stable notion of culture and thus cultural identity, it is through this ambivalent dynamic of the transnational and translational that culture is constructed, meaning that all cultures are hybrid and none are fixed.

Based on interpretative literary theory, Bhabha (1994) provides an in-depth critique of the dialectical approach between colonized and colonizer in post-colonial analysis, arguing for the use of 'hybridity' to confront the core/periphery binary. Hardt and Negri agree with this and write: 'social identities and nations were never really coherent imagined communities; the colonized's mimicry of the colonizer's discourse rearticulates the whole notion of identity and alienates it from essence; cultures are always already partial and hybrid formations' (Hardt and Negri 2000: 144). This book argues that call centre workers' identities cannot so readily be labelled 'Indian', as the term is contingent upon a matrix of experiences that precludes one's understanding of what it means to be 'Indian', thus producing varied, hybridized social identities all labelled 'Indian'.

The triumph of Orientalism is due in part to consumerism, as the Western market economy, with the circulation of cultural symbols and its consumer orientation, has produced 'a class of educated people whose intellectual formation is directed to satisfying market needs ... the modern Orient, in short, participates in its own Orientalizing' (Said 1978: 324). With respect to contemporary discussions of Orientalism, I would agree with Rath, who writes: 'I am, in part, testimony to Edward Said's view that as young people from the Orient come to England and America to study they absorb the (Orientalist) dogma themselves and participate in contemporary Orientalizing' (Rath 2004: 343).

Said also raises some important questions about how to interpret Indian and British history in the period after decolonization, offering one view that suggests imperialism has permanently scarred and distorted Indian life, 'so that even after decades of independence, the Indian economy, bled by British needs and practices, continues to suffer. The second view suggests that giving up the Empire was bad for Britain and the '"natives" who have both declined in all sorts of ways ever since' (Said 1993: 163). These concerns remain poignant, as the opening quotations of this chapter show, for the 'contemporary residue of imperialism' rests in the representation of 'natives' in Western media (Said 1993: 22–24). Although it has been argued that call centre work is exploitative of Indians, such work is economically empowering for some women in India. Drawing upon a number of examples, Said argued that Westerners began to rethink the whole process of decolonization, wondering if perhaps the West should have held on to the colonies to remain true to 'civilizational responsibilities and why did their actions of intervention result in a reprehensible sequence of ungrateful bitings'. In short, 'Why don't they appreciate us, after what we did for them?'[3] (ibid.).

Along similar lines, Hardt and Negri (2000) argue that colonizing processes initiated by the British Empire over two hundred years ago, again under the banner of democracy, have been taken up by the new project of 'Empire'. They note that a large part of critical thought from the Left has sought to 'recompose sites of resistance ... founded on the identities of social subjects ... grounding political analysis on the localization of struggles' (Hardt and Negri 2000: 44). However a false dichotomy of the local and the global is produced from this, with the implicit assumption that the global entails homogenization and the local preserves difference, allowing a primordial romanticism to seep in. Hardt and Negri argue that globalization, like localization, should be understood as a regime of the production of identity and difference. Furthermore, strategies of local resistance misidentify and mask the enemy, that enemy which they call 'Empire'.

So what can challenge and resist the essentializing properties of 'Orientalism' and 'Empire'? Movements that have come along such as feminism and the emergence of new authoritative accounts in challenging the representative images of 'the Woman' or 'the Indian' (Said 1993: 376–405).[4]

The 'fleeing' of jobs to India

Journalists and industry analysts, along with dedicated websites,[5] have speculated on the 'fleeing' of jobs to India (Pink 2004) and have documented the rise of the Indian call centre industry, while others have claimed that clerical and back office work in Britain will soon go the way of British manufacturing (Caulkin 2002; Denny 2003a). Elsewhere it has been suggested that Britain's Empire is 'striking back' as claims are made about historical justice in respect of jobs that the British 'stole' 200 years ago (Denny 2003b; Flanagan 2003; Monbiot 2003). A subtle, cultural, nationalist and racist undercurrent can be detected in Seabrook's seemingly ironic writing: 'it was bad enough, the cry goes, when they came as migrants to occupy the mills and factories. How much worse it is now that they can stay at home and filch our jobs and we can do nothing about it?' (Seabrook 2003). At the height of the British backlash against call centres, media reports continued to conclude that high levels of exploitation could be observed as Indian workers were paid one-fifth the salary of a British worker and were 'forced' to change their names and accents for the job.[6]

Although some of these concerns have come from the liberal Left, others have also contributed to the public debate over outsourcing work to India. The cover of the American tech lovers' magazine *Wired* featured an Indian woman stating that tech jobs were fleeing to India and asking, 'You got a problem with that?' American artist Steve Breen's comic strip *Grand Avenue* addressed public concern over relocation with a cartoon featuring a queue of children waiting to see Santa, only to find an Indian man on a screen where Santa should have been sitting. 'I can't believe it', he writes, 'they've outsourced Santa'. In the UK the conservative Right has not been silent in its opposition as newspapers such as the *Daily Express* warn of retribution from former British colonies and the 'fleecing' of British jobs (Flanagan 2003). The British National Party also indicated their stance on outsourcing by producing a tee-shirt that read 'My job went to India and all I got was this lousy tee-shirt'.

Some early studies of UK call centres labelled them 'dark satanic mills' (IDS 1997), 'electronic panopticons' and 'cyber sweatshops' (Fernie and Metcalf 1998), as concerns emerged that the work was monotonous and unskilled (Holman 2002) and was contributing to the ghettoization of female labour (Belt 2002a, 2002b). Kjellerup (1999) branded them 'toxic call centres': places used to 'make money and leave', where bad management practice was the underlying cause of high staff turnover and a sweat shop mentality. Alongside these reports and studies a very recent and growing body of academic literature based in the social sciences and labour studies has emerged, examining the outsourcing of work to India and the expanding Indian call centre industry (Kobayashi-Hilary 2004; Taylor and Bain 2003a, 2005, 2008; Bain and Taylor 2008). Moving beyond the economic effects of outsourcing, or offshoring, others have begun to examine the social effects of relocation and the impact of call centre work on employees' identities (McMillin 2006; Mirchandani 2004a, 2004b; Poster 2007; Cohen and El-Sawad 2007; Cowie 2007).

Indian studies and media reports approached this development from both ends of the critical spectrum, referring to call centre employees as 'cyber coolies' (Remesh 2004) or 'cyber sahibs' (Das 2003), demonstrating an ambiguous reception for relocated call centre work.[7] Others argue that some of the conditioning effects of information communications technologies (ICT) processes in India involve the ways in which working, thinking and being are experienced as social facts rather than social constructs (Cohen and El-Sawad 2007: 1241). For some, the interrogation of the 'cultural transformation of urban Indian labour into global proletariat' goes no further than concluding that whilst 'the outsourcing of labour is integrally connected to the outsourcing of identity, the latter is as much a commodity as the former in transnational flows of culture and capital' (McMillin 2006: 236–41). Elsewhere, academic studies on Indian call centres ranged from work on gender (Mitter et al. 2004; Singh and Pandey 2005; Pande 2005; Ng and Mitter 2005), hybridity (Shome 2006), spatial constraints (Patel 2006), organizational control (D'Cruz and Noronha 2006; Budhwar et al. 2006) and trade unions (Taylor and Bain 2008).

This book engages with some of the theoretical literature concerning feminism, postcolonialism, globalization, identity, women and work, while the empirical research examines the way in which women working in Delhi's transnational call centre industry exercise agency over the processes of identity construction.[8] The women call centre workers of this study are involved in a labour process that is both physically located in India and virtually located in the UK; thus the social processes that impact upon the construction of their identities are both local and global. Ultimately, this book explores the extent to which social processes, both local and global, influence these processes of identity construction and the extent to which the women working in call centres are passive victims, agents of resistance or both.

Through the lens of feminist and postcolonial theory

Gazing through the lens of feminist and postcolonial theory is not so much a choice as it is an unavoidable view, perhaps even an inexorable one.[9] To consider myself, my research or any of the theoretical frameworks used for analysis as external to a feminist or postcolonial context would have been flawed, as much of my experience and knowledge have been constructed within racialized and sexualized discourses (Spivak 1988; Bhabha 1994; Hall 1996a, 1996b; Said 1978). Feminism and postcolonialism are used here as lenses to provide a specific reading of the theoretical contexts and the data analysis; thus the two entwining theoretical contexts have shaped this research project from inception to conclusion and are woven throughout this analysis of women call centre workers' identities.

While a search for theoretical explanations dominates social research with pessimistic suggestions that 'theory is a conclusion in search of a premise', Palan (2004: 14) argues that this not an entirely delusional belief, for theory can be entangled with social constructivism. Thus the historical context of all theory, and all theorists, is significant. Modernist theories have shifted to make room for postmodernist positions that embrace difference; postmodernity sees both continuity and discontinuity in the social condition. It can be thought of as the 'time and space of those who are conscious of living after the metanarrative ... a state of mind [which] critiques modernity, problematizing attempts to develop theories which explain everything, and which ignore difference' (Roseneil 1999: 164).

Feminist theory has long maintained a contention with masculinist discourses that dominate the academy and marginalize women's experiences. Acknowledging the multiplicity and diversity of women's narratives and experiences whilst exploring and deconstructing the categories of woman and gender (Butler 1990), academic feminism has vehemently challenged 'the scientist cloak' and 'objective' research (May 2001: 18).[10] Recently preoccupied by a poststructuralist turn, the transformation of social science in the last decade has turned towards the agency/structure problematic, with a feminist discussion of agency increasingly emerging. Agency and identity provide complex concepts with which we can engage in a discussion of feminist and identity politics. One of the 'optical peculiarities' of academic research on globalization is the notion that the more marginal regions of the world are producers of data for the theory mills of the North (Appadurai 2001: 5). This 'peculiarity' has obscured the subjectivity of 'subaltern' Third World women, promoting the interests of the author,[11] and through the work of feminists such as Mohanty (1991a, 1991b), Anzaldua (1999) and Collins (1990), 'white women ... discovered (that is were forced kicking and screaming to notice) the non-innocence of the category "woman"' (Haraway 1991).[12] Centuries later some of the popular readings of the relocation of call centre work to India continue this trajectory, making seemingly benevolent claims on behalf of 'brown women', deliberately mishearing, ignoring and misinterpreting the subaltern.

In theorizing Indian women's experiences, it is impossible to separate the history of action from the history of ideas:

> For us our very entry into modernity has been mediated through colonialism ... it is important to emphasize that the growth of capitalism and modernity in the West was from the very beginning, linked to India's colonial past so that we do not repeat the modernisation fable that India has lagged behind because we embarked on modernisation late, that our feminism followed on the heels of their feminism, with a time or cultural lag. The point is instead that [we] ... were already living in a world informed by western liberalism, socialism, and feminism as ... defined by the far-reaching changes generated by colonialism.
>
> (Chaudhuri 2004: xii–xv)

Chaudhuri's observations provide the critical springboard for this book, in arguing that the tools used to theorize a Western modernity should be the very same tools used to theorize an Indian modernity.[13] Providing a feminist analysis of transnational Indian call centre work and the way in which the labour process impacts upon the construction of women's identities can therefore be used to glean a greater understanding of the agency/structure dynamic and how it relates to globalizing economic, cultural and social processes and discourses.

However, Indian women's identities are inextricably linked to that of the nation (Jaywardena 1986; Mohanty et al. 1991; Natarajan 1994), as representations of women are often conflated with representations of the nation. The values associated with globalization or modernity signal a shift away from familial, cultural or religious values, establishing a false dichotomy that sees woman used as a signifier for traditional values (Rao 1999). In an increasingly globalized world, women are seen as producers and bearers of national meaning and are therefore commodified by local, global and national discourses (Jaywardena 1986). Woman as signifier for the nation is eternally preserved by the film *Mother India* (1967, dir. Mehboob Khan), in which the newly developing nation struggles with the growing divide between the rich and the poor. Using the family as a trope for unity, the film emphasizes the importance of women's sexuality and modesty (Juluri 1999).[14]

Historically, fundamentalist and nationalist movements have utilized women's identities as a way to promote their values and ideals.[15] When 'group identity becomes paramount, where defensiveness and xenophobia are present, women are controlled' and signs of imposed identity in the form of proper dress are evident (Moghadam 1994: 17). 'Because of their reproductive capacity, women are seen as the transmitters of group values and traditions and as agents of socialization of the young', their roles as wives and mothers are fetishized (ibid.). Also translated as 'westoxication', 'westitis', 'euromania' and 'occidentosis', the term 'gharbzadegi' describes an 'illness, a virus, a "plague from the west", a phenomenon of excessive Westernization that renders members of the community (usually those with a Western education) alienated from their own culture' (ibid.).[16] In India, notions of gender and modernity are used to create a large global female workforce, while simultaneously cross-national ideologies of culture, authenticity and national honour are utilized to put increasing pressure on various communities to morally discipline the very same women (Appadurai 2001: 6).

Women's experiences in the labour market have long been an area for concern, as feminists have argued that skill definitions are 'saturated with sex' (Phillips and Taylor 1980) and that women enter the labour market as already determined inferior bearers of labour (Elson and Pearson 1981a: 24).[17] Over a decade ago, Castells wrote, 'rather than an oppressive "Big Brother," it is a myriad of well-wishing "little sisters," relating to each one of us on a personal basis because they know who we are, who have invaded all realms of life' (Castells 1997: 342). Castells' description is fascinating for two reasons: (1) it immediately locates the discussion within a feminist context which observes a 'global feminization of labour' (Pearson 1998) or women's participation in the 'global assembly line' (Sassen 2001b); (2) the use of 'myriad', 'well-wishing' and 'little' removes the phrase from its originally negative context and reinscribes it within a sexist discourse. Moreover, his description of the 'myriad of well-wishing "little sisters"' connects to the feminized, and often sexualized, descriptions of women working in the transnational service industry,[18] one example of which can be found on the cover of *India Today* (18 November 2002) shown in Figure 1.1.

The woman on the cover of *India Today* is pictured wearing a headset and microphone above the title 'Call Centres, Housekeepers to the World: India's fastest growing industry employs millions and earns billions'. The focal point

Figure 1.1 Cover of *India Today*, 18 November 2002.

of the magazine cover is the woman's eyes. Reducing women to their body parts, like their eyes or breasts or hair, works to reinscribe and commodify body parts within sexist discourses.[19]

In this image, the woman's eyes gaze out, presenting the reader with a submissive look whilst labelled 'housekeepers to the world'. The gaze and the eyes function as metaphors for power relations as the eyes have the power to provoke and women must keep their gazes lowered (Kabeer 2000). These kinds of images are representative both of the shifting call centre worker profile and of the emerging, liberated, empowered Indian woman, both of which have direct implications in the construction of women's identities.

Moreover, these kinds of images have implications for women call centre workers in other ways as well, in that the women interviewed for the research indicated that male customers, both South Asian and non-South Asian, flirted with them over the phone and would sometimes propose marriage. This is, in part, due to the sexualized, Orientalized images of Indian call centre workers, like that in Figure 1.1, similar to earlier sexualized images of secretaries with high heels and short skirts in Britain (Pringle 1989: 175). The notion of 'white man saving brown woman from brown man' (Spivak 1988) is echoed here, in that women call centre workers are victims of exploitation by the multi-nationals relocating their services to India, thus needing to be rescued. These assumptions directly contribute to a sense of the global commodification of women's services (Ehrenreich and Hochschild 2002) and negate the call centre workers' experience, effectively undermining their agency and silencing them.

Embedded within these images is the implicit understanding that a growing feminization of the Indian labour force is taking place – a 'ghettoization' of female labour (Belt 2002a).[20] As the demand for employees with good soft skills rises,[21] the profile of the Indian call centre worker is changing. As Ian, an Irish soft skills consultant and trainer working in Delhi's transnational call centre industry, observes:

> Recently, we were doing a programme where they were trying to recruit 50–50 [women and men]; however, the skill sets required for this was making it 90 per cent women and 10 per cent guys. ... they were only finding women who were meeting the standards for the job. Only 10 per cent of the pass candidates were men, 10 per cent who got through the door were guys.
>
> (Ian, Soft Skills Consultant)

A gendering or 'pinking' of the Indian call centre profession brings it in line with other European call centre studies; however, a significant difference is the way in which social and cultural factors have maintained this 'pinking' (see Figure 1.2). Singh and Pandey's (2005) study showed that of the women working in the call centres 67 per cent were aged 20–25 and 92 per cent were unmarried. McMillin's study (2006) showed that 88 per cent of the workers were aged 21–25, while this study found that 81 per cent of the women

Figure 1.2 Two women making calls.

interviewed were aged 21–26, all of whom were unmarried, the sharp decline in older and married woman demonstrating that call centre work is done by young, single women, the 'myriad of well-wishing "little sisters"' (Castells 1997: 342). This is not accidental as age-related restrictions are imposed upon the recruitment guidelines, as Jennifer, an employee of NCall, discovered:

> I did [apply for work in Gurgaon] but they were only accepting younger women with zero to three years experience. They always mention it in the ad, zero to three years experience. They are very specific about that. So when I would go to the interview, I would tell them that I'd thoroughly checked the ad. You are talking on the phone and the person really doesn't know how old you are. If you are delivering the service properly and doing the work, then it shouldn't be a hassle. I have eight to nine years experience, and I have been working as a secretary all throughout. I have even worked for two years in the Spanish Embassy.
>
> (Jennifer, 38, NCall Employee)

Having faced age discrimination at a number of job opportunities, Jennifer, who lives in Gurgaon, now commutes four hours every day to work at NCall in Noida. At the age of 38 Jennifer does not fit the profile of the female call centre staff, and although she had extensive experience, employers were reluctant to hire someone who might not be comfortable in the fun, college-like atmosphere of the call centre. Moreover, as call centres are full of not only young women but also single women, looking for partners or romantic relationships, Jennifer also experienced an isolation at work as she was shunned by her colleagues. Smita, also in her thirties, but, unlike Jennifer, married, describes call centres as colleges, full of students working and studying at the same time:

> Everybody is just having a good time. There is a lot of flirting happening, but then I guess everybody's young. It's not like any other corporate sector, where you would find a little bit of professionalism along with flirting. It's like an air-conditioned college, except you're getting paid.
>
> (Smita, 33, NCall employee)

From Jennifer and Smita's perspectives there is a general lack of professionalism; indeed, the description of their office as an 'air-conditioned college' demonstrates that they view their colleagues as immature and lacking focus or direction, and that their work experience is as temporary as the relationships they share with one another and does little to foster a sense of motivation or ambition.

Despite this attitude, call centres do provide women with exciting new opportunities for employment. No longer restricted to the average pay or below average work conditions of other professions, call centres offer women the opportunity to work alongside men in a financially rewarding, liberal atmosphere where the values of modernity are readily embraced as they virtually emigrate to other parts of the world and engage in dialectical dynamics.

The creation of employment opportunities for women in India

Historically, women's participation in the Indian labour market is grounded in the agricultural and manufacturing sector and much of the academic literature reflects this.[22] Women mainly worked within familial contexts and, to a large extent, were not educated. Moreover, internal migration for women was primarily over short distances and was, for the most part, for marriage and family reasons. However, increasing educational and employment opportunities have brought about a rise in women's migration to urban areas (Dyson and Visaria 2004), while globalization and mass media exposure have increased the social acceptance of women's work (McNay et al. 2004: 170). For some women, participation in the labour market has also been observed as a way to escape arranged marriages or to perhaps better compete in the marriage market (Mies 1979; Elson and Pearson 1981b: 158).

In the last two decades, India's service sector has replaced agriculture as the dominant sector (Chanda 2002), with the most pronounced growth in the software services and telecommunications sector. India currently leads in offshore destination sites for companies wishing to outsource both information technology (IT) related projects and back office work (ibid.). Internationally, technological advancement in Asian economies has supported a rise in the number of women employed in the call centre sector since the 1980s (Mitter 1999).[23]

Along with the increase in women's employment opportunities, the Indian call centre industry has produced many social, political and economic changes in urban centres and contemporary urban society. With employment as a primary focus, the Indian government has granted legal exemptions concerning women's employment in certain areas, such as amending the Factory Act of 1948, which prohibits women from working at night.[24] Section 14 of the Delhi Shops and Establishments Acts states: 'No young person or woman shall be allowed, or required to work, whether as an employee or otherwise, in any establishment between 9pm–7am during the summer season and between 8pm–8am during the winter season'. Exceptions to this are 'air service companies, cloak room attendants, girl telephone operators, ayaas (nannies), lady house keepers, artists in cabaret and entertainment shows'. This was amended in March 2005 to provide women the opportunity to work at night. Transnational call centres managed to avoid the provision because they fell under the governance of the Shops and Establishment Acts (Patel 2006), although one respondent, a manager, understood exemptions from the act to be contingent upon the transport and safety measures for female employees.[25]

Although these amendments have been made, it has been no easy route for women wishing to work at night as much of the difficulty stems from the lack of social acceptance of night work. Despite this, numbers of women working in call centres looked to increase over time. Currently women make up 40–70 per cent of staff (Mitter et al. 2004; Pande 2005) as firms actively recruit women, with materials and advertisements in newspapers and magazines routinely including photos of women and highlighting the term 'housewives' in effort to attract more women to call centre work ('Women Make the Right Call' 2003).

Women's employment prospects have indeed improved and this is due largely to technological advancement and trade liberalization. The progress and development of call centres in India have enhanced women's possibilities for economic independence and career opportunities and, as Mitter writes, provide 'fresh opportunities and freedom to a new generation of urban women' (Mitter 1999: 18). Linda, a soft skills consultant in Delhi who has been working with British call centres from 1998, observes:

> I think there is going to be a tremendous positive change on the impact of society as a whole because, right now, the Indian woman is very disempowered. One reason is that they are not financially viable. I meet a lot of the participants after I train them and they tell me, 'I feel so good. Yesterday I went there and bought a dress for Rs1000, which I would not have done before.' Earlier, they would think three times before they bought that sari or toy for the child. Socially, I think it's going to have huge impact, a negative impact, more divorces. Because women are going to say, 'Hey, listen, I have my life now, I'm taking my money.' In the urban areas, the call centres have given the women the opportunity to go and work and earn money, and what is probably going to happen is that

they have more buying power, so you're going to have corporates wooing them and advertising becoming more women oriented.

(Linda, Soft Skills Consultant)

Whilst there are numerous academic studies examining the economic advantages and challenges offered by new forms of employment, this study examined the ways in which new forms of employment have offered other kinds of advantages and challenges, particularly those linked in with Linda's comments concerning women's agency and changing roles in the family. As women gain independence through financial security, other social and cultural developments will not be far off. In ethnographic research, 'ethnographic truths are inherently partial – committed and incomplete' (Clifford and Marcus 1986: 7) and what follows is a discussion of how these partial, committed and incomplete truths were gathered.

Building snowballs in the sun

Mohanty argued that the hegemonic construction of 'Third World women' as a homogenous powerless group is both mistaken and dangerous, demonstrating essentialist ways of thinking and paving the way for 'victim oriented analyses' (Mohanty 1991a: 29). The quotations by Monbiot and Seabrook which open the chapter – and indeed much of the work available on Indian call centres – describe such analyses as they bemoan the experiences of the call centre workers, who 'drown their own culture and remake them[selves] in the image of their customers' requirements ... a baptism by total immersion' (Seabrook 2003). That such perceptions were the starting point for my investigation into Indian call centres is a necessary disclosure, for buried within this research are the personal and political motives of the researcher, myself.

The drive to contribute knowledge of 'transnational feminist practices' (Grewal and Kaplan 1994) and to produce 'countertopographies' (Nagar 2002) meant studying women's experiences and struggles for independence from patriarchal constraints that were markedly different from my own. Writing about women of the South Asian diaspora in the UK, Puwar notes that previous studies focused on the first generation of South Asian women simply and overwhelmingly as producers. They were hardly recognized as consumers and, instead, 'pitied for their work conditions and idealized for occupying the most oppressed position in the metropolis' (Puwar 2003: 28). She goes on to say that 'as the daughters of the workers enter the academy ... they are finding that while these studies grant recognition to the labour power of their mothers, aunts, and sisters, at the same time the framework is eskewed [sic] and limited' (ibid.). As a feminist whose mother was employed as a worker in the British textiles industry of the 1970s, Puwar's observations spoke to me and I endeavoured to find an alternative account to the 'victim oriented analyses' (Mohanty 1991a) of call centre workers surfacing everywhere.

From the outset, integral to the concerns of the research were the way in which processes of identity construction were affected by the new technologically enhanced labour processes of call centres and the extent to which women were constituted by social and labour processes or were creative agents forging new identities within an existing patriarchal paradigm. A primary concern in establishing an epistemic framework was the way in which some of the popular discourses surrounding Indian call centres muddied the discussion by regularly describing the jobs in them as 'electronic sweatshop work' (Kjellerup 1999; Holman and Fernie 2000), pointing towards the 'fleeing' of jobs (Pink 2004: 94) and the dumping of 'electronic sweatshop' work.

In India, the concerns were somewhat different in that they were focussed on preserving the modesty, or 'izzat',[26] of women and securing their prospects for marriage (Rathi 2002). Media reports discussed the surge of cosmopolitanism and loss of Indian culture, as well as a rise in sexual liberalism (Rathi 2002; 'Mobiles, CDs, Parties: Call of a New World' 2003; Jowell 2003; Olivera 2003). In this way a predetermined, discursive, gendered framework had developed out of these discussions and had already shaped some of the research aims. One of the dominant themes in UK discussions of Indian call centres was that of 'forced' name or identity changes and accent neutralization (Mirchandani 2004b), which presented a facile entry point for this research project; however, as I will later show, the discussion of name changes was viewed from a significantly divergent perspective by women working in the call centre industry. Built within this discourse were the more subtle Western hegemonic, postcolonial and sexist discourses, layered to produce a particular reading of Indian call centre relocation.

When asked about the ways in which call centres were changing society in India, Smita,[27] a mother of one and self-described educated career woman living and working in Noida, shared the following:

> The average woman in India is on the farm. This question [about the future] is for 1 or 2 per cent of all women who are on the right track: they're growing, they have their priorities clear, they are meeting boys, planning their marriages. But the average Indian woman is still sweeping floors or in the fields. So there are two groups of women but the average Indian woman is still where she was. She's still getting beaten up by her husband. And the husband still has another wife.
>
> (Smita, NCall)

This book was conceived as a feminist research project privileging the voices and concerns of Indian women. However, Smita's comments raise important questions as to who these Indian women are. Who is being exploited? Who are victims of oppression? And whose voices should be privileged? Smita's view that her position as a middle-class call centre worker in Delhi is advantageous questions the British perception that call centre workers are exploited and disempowered. Moreover, it questions the construction of the average

'Third World woman' more than a decade after Mohanty (1991b) first raised the issue. The connection between my own subjective reasoning in choosing a feminist approach to this project and Smita's view on the oppression of Indian women raises many questions about power, positionality, the research process and what constitutes knowledge and truth claims. Feminist contributions to epistemology, ontology, methodology and methods have critically examined the way in which knowledge is produced and the manner in which knowledge claims have been institutionalized. Knowledge itself is a social construct and questioning the construction of ontologies and epistemologies is significant to the process of social enquiry, as it is necessary to look at the forms and processes of *knowing* as well as what is known (Harding 1986: 153). Moreover, there is a tension in using 'situated knowledges' (Haraway 1991) and 'standpoint epistemology' (Harding 1986) to produce a more generalizable understanding of the processes of globalization.

Feminist concerns with the power/knowledge nexus have called into question the methodological concepts of objectivity and value neutrality, or what Haraway refers to as the 'God-Trick' (Haraway 1991: 185). Some feminists (Wolf 1996) have argued that feminist epistemology has presented the social sciences with a powerful critique of positivism and 'value free' research by arguing that the subjective/objective dichotomy is false and that objectivity itself is an excuse for sloppy social research, as it does not make vulnerable the researcher's position or expose the power relations that perpetuate male dominance (Stanley and Wise 1993: 167–68).

Feminist epistemologies present a major challenge to traditional epistemologies in that they are grounded in a political movement for social change. This is problematic as social science is meant to be value-neutral and objective; however, it is through feminist struggles against male domination that women's experiences can be made to yield up a truer image of social reality (Harding 1994). Women's perspectives are from everyday life and women have been assigned the kinds of work that men in ruling groups do not want to do, and as women continue to perform women's work it frees up men to immerse themselves in the world of abstract concepts (Harding 1991: 128). The more women perform 'women's work' the more invisible it becomes, and thus women become excluded from men's conceptions of culture and history. Therefore the privileging of women's experiences, doing research for women and locating the researcher on the same critical plane as the researched (Roseneil 1993) was of significance to this project.

Placing myself in the line of enquiry was important, as ethnographic fieldwork will often have a biographical dimension to it: concerned with 'observing, (re)constructing, and writing lives and experiences of Others', we are simultaneously involved with auto/biographical work of our own (Coffey 2002: 314). As traditional sources of authority are no longer automatically respected and individuals are exposed to a multitude of conflicting perspectives and expertise (Giddens 1990), it is necessary to reveal the researcher's role within the research process (Seale 1999: 164).

Accusations that feminist academics are guilty of 'trading on the women's movement and creativity by publishing stale research papers to further progress in male defined careers' (Stanley and Wise 1983: 39)[28] have made it absolutely imperative to discuss the position and identity of the researcher, as bell hooks cynically declares:

> No need to hear your voice when I can talk about you better than you can speak about yourself ... Only tell me your pain. I want to know your story. And then I will tell it back to you in a new way. Tell it back to you in such a way that it becomes my own ... I am still author, authority. I am still coloniser, the speaking subject, and you are now at the centre of my tale.[29]
>
> (hooks 1990: 343)

To assuage these power incongruities to some extent, the best feminist analysis places the inquirer on the same critical plane as the subject matter (Harding 1987a: 9) to reflexively expose power relations and the way in which they shape knowledge (Skeggs 2002); thus the researcher is presented as a 'real historical individual with concrete, specific desires and interests' (Harding 1987a: 9).

Race and ethnicity are ever-present factors in the field and the negotiation of insider/outsider status was an ongoing dynamic in the research,[30] particularly in how 'white' or Western the research participants viewed themselves and myself to be. In some ways, sharing the ethnic and racial backgrounds of the research participants can prove to be advantageous in establishing a rapport (Beoku-Betts 1994), with access to research subjects significantly less complicated and interviewees responding more candidly (Bhopal 2001). However, 'conscious partiality' (Mies 1983) is not necessarily an 'easy business', as researchers are engaged in performative practices of their own which constitute their identities when representing themselves in their countries of origin (Henry 2003).

Despite my obvious Indian appearance, my Canadian accent and British university credentials lead to a continual 'translation' of my research objectives and my identity as a researcher. Although my loyalty or ability to represent the interviewees was not directly questioned, research participants made continual enquiries as to *why* I chose to carry out fieldwork in India, as they carried out ongoing analyses of the 'stranger's value' (Williams 1996: 92); much less because I was from outside Indian society and more from the existence of a major power disparity. As an Indian woman, I was pressured to conform to local gender norms,[31] giving me a greater sense of how the interviewees experienced their lives.[32] However, such insider status also functioned as a disadvantage in that a woman of European descent would not have been subjected to such scrutiny.[33] My fluency in Punjabi and 'acceptable' clothing[34] created a sense of empathy and belonging with the women I researched; however, my friendship with some of the male workers raised suspicions about my integrity and my authenticity was ultimately determined by the individual women that I interviewed. Approval was not only limited to authenticity but also included issues of honour and respect, as there were concerns that I, being an outsider from Canada and the UK, might misrepresent them, located in India, as 'traditional' or 'backwards'; issues of trust were of paramount importance.[35]

My struggles with articulating an identity put me on a similar playing field to my interviewees with regard to my research aims. The construction of my identity by the research participants as an NRI (non-resident Indian)[36] and Sardarni (Sikh woman), along with the arrival of my parents and two brothers for visits, increased my research opportunities as it provided me a stronger degree of respectability. However, it also presented limitations in that research participants felt that I, as an 'NRI' and 'Sardarni', should not be seen at 'dhabas' and 'thekas'. Though the identities they constructed for me had a direct and consequential influence on the findings, the research field remains a site of complex power relations and it cannot be implied that research participants had an equal amount of power, as ultimately I would be responsible for writing up and presenting the research.

For me, the practising/performing of identities began with the problem of what to wear.[37] Prior to my arrival in India, I had been 'warned' that by wearing Indian clothing and by dressing modestly I would attract less attention and hassle from the men on the streets, thereby making it easier for me to ask for directions and negotiate access within the city. My discomfort with this contrived sense of 'Indianness'[38] was heightened by my return 'home' every evening to the backpacker area of Delhi called Paharganj. Paharganj, located next to the train station and dividing Old and New Delhi, is a narrow bazaar with six-story buildings on either side full of hostels, restaurants, shops and Internet cafés. My desire to blend in as a foreigner with the travellers and backpackers in Paharganj was acute as I attempted to ease the transition and culture shock of moving to India.[39]

Conducting ethnographic observation isn't simply a case of 'hanging around'. The process required that I become part of a social scene, participate in it and be accepted to some degree, as the period of 'moving into' a setting is important in determining those aspects of action which might appear 'strange' to me but may be 'familiar' to the call centre employees (May 2001). Initially treated as a tourist and guest, I began to socialize with groups of call centre employees and was eventually invited to go to bars, coffee shops, cinemas, and attend social events, weddings, birthdays and trips out of town. Although everyone I asked agreed to being interviewed, trying to arrange a time and place proved to be much more difficult.

Fieldwork was conducted over a ten-month period from November 2002 to August 2003. Given the intense media interest generated by Indian call centres, my efforts to make contact with companies or call centres before I left the UK met with resistance and refusal, yielding only two phone numbers of call centre employees in Delhi. Interest from foreign journalists and companies' efforts to protect themselves from intrusion meant that access to the call centres was heavily restricted. A second issue of 'access' was that of travelling outside daylight hours or to places that were 'off limits' to women. Research participants tended to sleep during the day, as their shifts were at night, making it difficult to meet with them during the day. Interviews held in public places such as cafés and bars were regarded with suspicion and sometimes hostility, with staff generally staring, loitering around the table or turning up music to drown out the interview.

Three months after my arrival from the UK, frustrated by the closed doors, I approached the Vice-President of NCall[40] and offered my services as a trainer in British culture and accent in exchange for access to research participants.[41] My role was to provide cultural training for eight hours a day on a two-day module for which all the materials were already available. I trained two groups over four days per week for approximately twelve weeks, with some weeks left for observation and formal and informal interviews with management. The company provided me with a training room which doubled as an office once the training had finished for the day, so that I could conduct the interviews in private. As many of the interviewees and their friends were employed in call centres with UK clients I was able to utilize my position as someone from England to answer questions that they had about the UK and British people. The participants from NCall, approximately half of the sample, form the 'NCall chain', while the ongoing interviews outside NCall form the 'wider chain' of the sample group. All of the interviews were conducted face to face, one on one. The 'NCall chain' interviews were conducted in the training room after the training sessions were finished, whilst the 'wider chain' interviews were conducted in cafés, bars, restaurants and people's homes. Informal interviews both in and outside the call centres, travelling to work and out socializing, have been used to add to the descriptive material and analysis, but, where quoted, the women were largely sitting with only myself.

Interviewing is the art of construction, not excavation (Mason 2002: 227), and the interviews were constructed in a dialogic fashion. Many of the women regarded the interview as somewhat 'therapeutic' (Oakley 1981), in that their concerns were validated and their sense of self worth enhanced. Some of the women took the opportunity to draw on me as a resource for advice on educational courses, CVs, education and employment opportunities abroad, and a few asked me to find them employment as housekeepers or nannies once I returned to the UK.

The semi-structured interviews were arranged around the following themes: exploring, identity construction, decision to work in a call centre, family background, leisure time, nature of the working day, India's political economy and hopes for the future. The final data set included thirty-two open-ended questionnaires and semi-structured qualitative interviews with the sample group and interviews with eight key informants: one call centre consultant acting as a company director; two soft skills trainers operating on a consultancy basis; two male team leaders from call centres; the mother of one of the interviewees; and two human resources managers. After completing half of the interviews, 'theoretical saturation' (Glaser and Strauss 1967: 61–63) had been achieved and there were no more new or emerging themes, so the interviews that followed served to substantiate the already available analytical categories.[42] Additionally, given my access to a wide cross-section of employees at NCall, a short survey questionnaire was used for triangulation purposes (Sarantakos 1993: 155) and to substantiate claims about the profile of call centre employees.

In the years that have followed my research trip to India, the question of class and class identity has been posed many times. When interviews were conducted in the homes of the women, observations were made regarding their socio-economic positioning; however, with interviews conducted at NCall such observations were impossible. Of paramount importance to this discussion is the understanding that call centres offer to the young, educated, English-speaking populace of India the opportunity to become classless. That is not to suggest an ignorance of or indifference to class disparity, but, rather, whereas regional, cultural and religious differences are pronounced and celebrated in the globalized spaces of call centres amongst co-workers, class differences are not. Individuals take up work in call centres to move beyond the class differences that separate them. Issues concerning class were discussed and comments have been included but this study does not aim to present a class analysis of call centre workers. The subsequent chapters present an analysis of their experiences of the labour process, the way in which sartorial strategies are used in constructing identities, and the gendered use of space developing out of the rise of the call centre industry and transgression of male dominated public social spaces. In doing so, the analysis provides a 'thick description' as opposed to a 'thin description' (Geertz 1973)[43] of how the transnational call centre industry creates challenges and opportunities for a particular group of Indian women.

Identity

The substantive literature addressing the concept of identity is extensive; however, there are two theoretical strands offering up different ways of understanding how identity is produced. The first are social theories which look to offer a 'historicized narrative of the development of identity', or self-identity, defined as the 'individual's conscious sense of self'; and the second are poststructuralist cultural theories which are interested in the 'problematic of identity and cultural difference, and in the theoretical deconstruction of identity categories' (Roseneil and Seymour 1999: 2–3). Identity, as it is used in this book, takes its position between these two locations; it can be regarded as the 'individual's conscious sense of self' that has moved beyond identification with others and has itself become 'moveable'; it is not biologically, but historically and politically defined (Hall 1992a: 275–77).[44] Identity is therefore not fixed, but unstable, fluid, often contradictory, and always in process (Hall

1992b). The increased use of terms such as creolization (Hannerz 1992), hybridization (Pieterse 1995) and cultural hybridity (Bhabha 1994) reflects, in its varied and complex ways, this instability and, more importantly, the possibility of the mitigation of globalization processes through the localized production of identity (Kraidy 2002).

This book develops Castells' understanding of identity, which he sees to be a source of meaning for actors themselves, constructed through a process of individuation, or the construction of meaning on the basis of a cultural attribute (Castells 1997: 6–8). He suggests three distinct forms of identity building: legitimizing identity, wherein dominant societal institutions extend and rationalize their domination vis-à-vis social actors; resistance identity, generated by actors who are in positions/conditions devalued and/or stigmatized, thus building resistance; and project identity, wherein actors build new identities that redefine their positions and by doing so seek the overall transformation of society (Castells 1996: 8).

In Bollywood obsessed India, the 'cinematic society' has institutionalized a surveillance code (Denzin 1995)[45] which reveals the power of imagination as a field of social practice (Appadurai 1996), demonstrating how identity functions. As Castells writes,

> The sites of this power are people's minds. This is why power in the information age is at the same time identifiable and diffused. We know what it is, yet we cannot seize it because power is a function of an endless battle around the cultural codes of society. Whoever, or whatever, wins the battle of the people's minds will rule ... But victories may be ephemeral, since the turbulence of information flows will keep codes in a constant swirl. This is why identities are so important and ultimately, so powerful.
>
> (Castells 1997: 425)

Identity as a social construct allows for consideration of discursive practices of race and gender; however, it still affords agency to individuals on local levels through 'resistance identities' and 'project identities'.[46]

Self-identity, 'the self as it is reflexively understood by the person in terms of her or his biography' (Giddens 1991: 53), is characterized by a feeling of biographical continuity, and a person's identity is not to be found in the behaviour or reaction of others but in the ability to keep a particular narrative going. The self forms a trajectory of development from the past to the anticipated future and the individual appropriates his or her past by sifting through it in the light of what is anticipated for an (organized) future (ibid.). The narration of identity, 'narrativity', produces identity through a process of emplotment, configured over time (Lawler 2002: 249–50). The narratives people use to tell their stories are social products themselves, interpretative devices through which people represent themselves.[47] Though valuable, Giddens' argument remains too structured along the lines of ego and overlooks a significant dimension to the discussion of reflexivity, what Lash and Urry (1994: 31–51) describe as the 'aesthetic-expressive dimension': a more embodied sense of reflexivity.[48]

Identity is discursively produced, contingent upon social processes over which individuals exercise agency. However, the power to exercise this agency is contingent upon interdependencies and power balances amongst social actors and social structures. In her study of Indian call centres, McMillin argues that 'jubilation over agency is premature first because agency cannot be equated with freedom' (2006: 235) and second because of the enduring structures of economic and political inequity:

> The liberalised Indian call centre industry makes specific demands on its labour force, regardless of skill level: an ability to withstand long hours of monotonous work, respond quickly to orders, and undergo certain transformations to adapt to the work place environment. Which could mean a change in accent, diction, sleep cycle, and workplace identity.
>
> (McMillin 2006: 235)

Call centre workers, while physically located in India, perform work online and engage with US or UK based customers; much of their daily communication at work is with people who do not share their physical and geographical space but with whom they share diasporic 'cyber publics' formed through online connections and affiliations (Ong 2004). Diaspora theories argue that in the UK second generation South Asians are skilled navigators with a sophisticated ability to manoeuvre between different social worlds, and switching cultural codes is not unlike being fluently bi- or multilingual: 'Cultures, like languages, are codes, which actors use to express themselves in a given context; and as the context changes, so those with the requisite competence simply switch code' (Ballard 1994: 31).

The construction of Indian call centre workers' online and offline identities involve transnational mobility, through virtual migration, bringing with it new modes of identity construction.[49] The diasporic journeys made by the call centre workers are lived, re-lived, produced, and re-produced through individual and collective memory, thus differently imagined under different historical circumstances and certainly not bound to one particular interpretation.[50] Identity is most crucially produced through historical circumstances and discourse, for although agency exists the discursive effects of race, nation and culture on identity formation outweigh notions of agency. Identities 'are the names we give to the different ways we are positioned by, and position ourselves within, the narratives of the past' (Hall 1993: 394).[51] Identity, as an incomplete site of production, can be understood in two ways: first, in terms of a shared, unified, collective experience, a trajectory which begins from the point of the Empire,[52] and, second, in terms of difference, 'ruptures' or 'discontinuities'; which acknowledges the 'continuous 'play' of history, culture and power' (ibid.). This 'profound discontinuity' (Hall 1992b: 292) is a product of the processes of globalization, and whilst globalization is an uneven process that retains some aspects of Western global domination, the local/global dynamic is a duality from which we can begin to explore identity and find truncated spaces from within which to articulate identification.

In some ways this dynamic draws upon hybridity and movement as the maxim of resistance, highlighting how the attribution of transformation and resistance to migrancy, mobility and hybridity has become 'something of a structural or structuring feature' found in certain intellectual Anglo-American discourses (Yegenoglu 2005: 123).[53] Certainly hybridity, a somewhat contentious notion in identity theory, can be understood as a tautology rather than causation; in other words, all identities are hybridized identities. 'Hybridity is an assertion of differences coupled with an enactment of identity, as a process, which is simultaneously assimilationist and subversive, restrictive and limiting' (Kraidy 2002: 205).[54] Hybridity as a concept, though useful in opposing essentialist notions of culture (Bhabha 1994; Kraidy 2002), remains descriptive rather than prescriptive. However, although it can be read as in opposition to the hegemony of Western imperial culture, what is theorized in the West as hybridity remains enmeshed in the gaze of the West (Grewal and Kaplan 1994), for although we may have global imagery, those global images are read through local eyes. 'Not all those eyes are self reflexive ... ' (Anthias 2001: 636).

Given the migration from rural to urban centres, cosmopolitanism offers a more useful way of exploring call centre workers' identities. Rooted in Kant's work,[55] ongoing discussions of cosmopolitanism have created a discourse far more in-depth and exploratory than originally detailed by him.[56] By way of definition, Beck (2004: 132) suggests that 'normative cosmopolitanism' or 'philosophical cosmopolitanism' argues for harmony across national and cultural frontiers whilst academically a 'cosmopolitan perspective' or 'analytic-empirical cosmopolitanism' sees itself as freed from national categories in thinking and research.[57]

Stemming from movements of people, readings of cosmopolitanism contribute to 'multiple identity projects' that see identities as 'fluid and overlapping [and] in which regional and local attachments are negotiated and contested' (Yegenoglu 2005: 110). Diasporas, immigrants and transnational communities all embody a 'cultural cosmopolitanism' compatible with nationalism, which, despite or because of mobility, strengthens ethnic nationalism (Delanty 1999: 368). Cosmopolitanism encouraged the abandonment of dichotomous thinking of 'friend and foe, inclusion and exclusion' in favour of a culture that transcends the 'life-world' (Delanty 1999: 367).[58] It can be read as a process that is transcultural or supranational, not in between but above, described as 'a cultural disposition involving an intellectual and aesthetic stance of "openness" towards peoples, places, and experiences from different cultures, especially those from different "nations" ... it involves the search for, and delight in, the contrasts between societies' (Szerszynski and Urry 2002: 468). However, this reading of cosmopolitanism requires one to have: extensive *mobility*, whether that is corporeal, imaginative or virtual; the means to *consume* en route; a *curiosity*; a willingness to take *risks*; an ability to *map* one's own society; *semiotic* skill to interpret images of others; and an *openness* to other people and cultures (Szerszynski and Urry 2002: 470).

However, there is a darker side to discussions of cosmopolitanism with the emergence of an 'indigenous elite' (Banerjee and Linstead 2001: 709) and, far from promising an integrated world, globalization has produced a new set of class divisions within nations:

> The increased interdependence of social actors across national boundaries [comes] as an unintended and unforeseen side effect of actions that have no normative 'cosmopolitan intent' ... and under certain conditions this type of 'cosmopolitanization' leads to the emergence of global forms of debate and global regimes covering transnational issues ... or 'institutionalized cosmopolitanism'.
>
> (Beck 2004: 132)

The emergence of cosmopolitans as strangers captures the dynamic of modernity and postmodernity in that they have always been located somewhere between closeness and remoteness, and so are objectified and abstracted as a certain type: 'a historical or social interloper'.[59]

While some sociologists argue for a reconstituted sociology that centres on mobilities as processes and metaphors (Urry 1999), Kofman (2005: 85) shows that the concept of mobility can also serve to conjure up feelings of suspicion and hostility. The figure of the cosmopolitan has been critiqued for its emphasis on the frequent traveller trope and it fails to recognize the ordinary cosmopolitanism of working-class and migrant groups; cosmopolitanism is not necessarily based on universalism but is derived locally and nationally using 'cultural repertoires of universalism' available across varying racial and national contexts (Kofman 2005: 86). Today's cosmopolitans are victims of modernity,

> failed by capitalism's upward mobility and bereft of those customs and comforts of belonging, and in this way cosmopolitanism itself is shaped and constituted by dominant power relations. Thus what is interpreted positively in the 'privileged national' is deemed negative and problematic in the 'national outsider' and migrant, drawing upon cultural baggage where the 'rootless and flexible outsider' and today the migrant with 'multiple origins and social and territorial allegiances' is treated with suspicion and hostility.
>
> (Kofman 2005: 86–88)

Kofman's insights are particularly useful in forming an analytical notion of cosmopolitanism for call centre workers. Her argument moves away from the construct of the colourful, universalizing, cosmopolitan embracing 'openness' towards a notion of cosmopolitanism rooted in contemporary culture, a figure that is perhaps more significant for this discussion when considering some of the xenophobic and 'quietly racist' media reports that emerged concerning call centre relocation, not to mention the outright racism directed at Indian call centre workers by British customers. Her understanding is that cosmopolitans can be considered 'victims of modernity' engaged in performative practices.

Butler argues that 'identity is performatively constituted by the very "expressions" that are said to be its results' (1990: 25) and that 'there are ways of occupying the very categories by which one is constituted and turning them in another direction or giving them a future they weren't supposed to have' (Wallace 1998). However, it would be an oversimplification to suggest absolute agency over the interpretations of these expressions, for what lies between utterance and interpretation is Bhabha's (1994) 'Third Space'.[60] For call centre workers, this 'ambivalence in the act of interpretation' (Bhabha 1994: 53–55) represents the virtual space that exists between themselves and the customer. It is in this space that identity is produced.

The 'Third Space' emphasizes two things: first, that until recently the value of culture as an object of study and the value of cultural analysis lay in a capacity to produce cross-referential, generalizable knowledge that signifies a progress or evolution of 'ideas-in-time' as well as being critically self-reflective (Bhabha 1994). Second, it destroys the 'mirror of representation' of cultural knowledge and challenges the notion of historical identity of culture as a homogenizing unifying force 'authenticated by the originary Past, kept alive in the national tradition of the People' (ibid.).

Only when we begin to consider the 'Third Space' as a contradictory and ambivalent space of enunciation can we interrogate claims of originality or 'purity' of cultures. Only when such a space is under interrogation can we begin to interrogate and destabilize notions and categories, such as what it means to be Indian, thus raising questions about the constructions of such notions and categories.

Whilst globalization theorists have discussed at great length the 'tensions' that exist between local and global processes, Butler, Bhabha and Castells instead offer up ways of exploring the mutually constitutive nature of such flows and processes: to focus on the collusion of social processes rather than the collision of social processes.

For call centre workers living in India and working abroad, virtually migrating and speaking with customers every day, life in the 'Third Space' is an acute experience. With only their voices, accents, tone and words, workers must construct an identity that customers find acceptable. Through narratives of difference and disavowal, women working in call centres seek out and utilize truncated spaces to construct cosmopolitan identities that define them as neither the cultural interloper nor the national outsider.

This book offers a glimpse into the lives of a particular group of women, at a particular point in time, all living and working in Delhi, Gurgaon and Noida. It captures the moment that call centre relocation exploded into our lives, and as much as this book is about the economical, cultural and social impact of call centre work, it is also about how call centres function as rhetorical devices to talk about globalization and postcolonial identities. It invites you to think about globalization in other ways and offers a view from below, where the processes of globalization are not necessarily disempowering but also full of opportunities and challenges, producing discourses and spaces that allow women to question social norms and exercise greater agency over their lives.

2 Globalizing India

The rise of the call centre and BPO industries

It is sophisticated subterfuge, though completely legal, that is raking in millions of dollars in foreign exchange for India. Unimaginatively called Business Process Outsourcers or simply call centres, it is now the fastest growing industry in the country – it expanded at an explosive 70 percent last year. This despite a dotcom implosion and a sluggish international economy that slowed up even the country's hot-shot information technology sector. India is now the electronic housekeeper to the world, taking care of a host of routine activities for multinational giants.

(Chengappa and Goyal 2002: 36)

Call centres in India remain a perplexing and confusing area of interest. Contradictory and conflicting reports rarely flesh out the nuanced elements of the debate on the effects and impacts of India's 'new sunshine sector' (Chengappa and Goyal 2002: 36) and seem more interested in discussing whether call centre employees should be termed 'cyber sahibs' ('Cyber Coolies or Cyber Sahibs' 2003) or 'cyber coolies' (Remesh 2004). Polarized perspectives inveigle the Indian chattering classes into wondering whether or not globalization (née colonization) is good for India, whilst obfuscating the larger concerns of how such developments alter and transform the social fabric of India in much more subtle and profound ways. Call centres have quite literally rushed India into conversations about globalization, accelerating its processes, breathlessly taking it all in.

'Globalization' itself is a problematic term, with varying definitions linking it to arguments of 'Empire' (Hardt and Negri 2000: xiv), the 'clash of civilizations' (Huntington 1993) or the much circulated 'Jihad vs McWorld' (Barber 1995). It is perhaps most commonly understood as referring to the increasing economic integration and interdependence of countries and the move from traditional to modern societies via a range of specific processes (Featherstone 1995: 87).[1] However, the view that globalization produces a Western hegemonic culture that will overwhelm other cultures (Robertson 1995) or that India will suddenly become housekeeper to the world is premature and gives rise to a 'double apartheid', the growing disjuncture of the globalization of knowledge and the knowledge of globalization (Appadurai

1999). In this book 'globalization' is used in two ways: the first to make reference to a 'historical epoch, beginning in the 1960s and contemporaneous with postmodernity' (modernity being an earlier period from 1840 to 1960) (Featherstone and Lash 1995: 5); the second refers to a 'compression of the world as a whole ... an increase in global interdependence and the awareness of that interdependence' (Friedman 1995: 72).

Culture and identity play distinctive roles in understanding globalization and its processes. Appadurai's framework for analyzing 'global disjunctures' examines the relationship among dimensions or 'scapes' of global cultural flows: 'ethnoscapes', the 'landscape of persons who constitute the shifting world in which we live'; 'technoscapes', the 'global configuration of technology'; 'and 'mediascapes', 'the distribution of electronic capabilities to produce and disseminate information which is generally image centred and narrative based strips of reality', to name a few (Appadurai 1996: 33–43). Moreover, the global/local dynamic, with its dialectical intersection of 'presence and absence' and the interlacing of social events and social relations 'at distance' with local contextualities, further problematizes the notion of globalization (Robertson 1995: 26–27), particularly through the axes of culture, 'habitually inculcated into people over time ... sedimented into well worn social routines' (Featherstone 1995: 5). 'Culturalism, put simply, is identity politics at the level of the nation state' (Appadurai 1996: 15), and nowhere is this more evident than in the physical migration of call centre workers across India and their virtual migration abroad.

Call centre workers live in both the local and the global in very acute ways, and their experiences provide a unique perspective on the globalization of India and the 'cultural interchange process' (Welsch 1999: 203–04). A veritable explosion of literature on transnationality (Ong 1999), hybridity (Pieterse 1995, 2000) and creolization (Hannerz 1992) has emerged to explore the concept of culture in the discussion of globalization; yet none quite captures the 'transcultural networks' and relationships of the call centre workers. 'Creolization', the interplay between centre and periphery of transnational cultural flows, illustrates how the influx of culture does not enter into a vacuum or inscribe itself on a *tabula rasa* but enters into various interactions with already existing meanings and meaningful forms (Hannerz 1992: 118). The mechanics of differentiation, although fast becoming more complex, are also genuinely cultural, no longer complying with geographical or national stipulations. These 'global cultural flows' (Appadurai 1996) are particularly relevant when considering the role of the nation-state and global cities, transnationalism, consumption, cinematic societies and the Internet, along with the ways in which they feed into the transformative ethnoscapes, mediascapes and technoscapes shaping the globalization of India.

One of the more dominant myths concerning Indian call centres is the belief that they threaten Indian culture. Whilst there is a good deal of evidence to suggest that this shift is taking place on some levels, there is little to indicate that there is some kind of inevitability to it or that call centres are single-handedly responsible for changes in contemporary Indian society. Such arguments resonate with concerns that globalization erodes the nation-state and national identity. However, as noted above, national identity is a construct of global cultural flows. Simply put,

> a nation consists of a collection of people who have come to believe that they have been shaped by a common past and are destined to share a common future ... the belief that closer ties exist among members of the nation than with outsiders.
>
> (Collins 1990: 229)

Although it frees people from bonds of religious or cultural oppression, it could be argued that globalization threatens to annex people into a Western technological and economic monoculture, and increasingly lures people into new dependencies by imposing cultural uniformity, resulting in a colonization of people (Pronk 2000: 51). In the case of India, a national culture has emerged alongside state formation processes in which cultural specialists have 'reinvented traditions and reshaped and refurbished the ethnic core of the people' (Featherstone 1995: 89). Increasingly drawn together in a tighter figuration of competition with one another, nations – and, I would argue, regions – face strong pressures to develop a coherent cultural identity. Thus national culture is not always pure or raw but, in some instances, something that is produced by specialists working within dominating social structures and institutions.

Given the processes of 'individualization' and the erosion of traditional social supports (Beck 1992), it is important to become attuned to the nuances of the processes of globalization and seek to develop theories sensitive to the power potentials of the players in the various global struggles. Local movements, such as fundamentalist groups, women's movements or environmentalist groups, can all have a mitigating effect on the 'homogenizing' forces of globalization (Featherstone and Lash 1995: 3). For this study, this is crucial in two ways: first, women call centre workers play a distinct role in the development of the local/global dynamic, transforming globalization through local practices; second, as women working in the call centres they all experience differing power potential and thus an analytical framework must be sensitive to this. Local knowledges exist 'in tension with the productive structurings that force unequal translations and exchanges – material and semiotic – within the webs of knowledge and power' (Haraway 1991: 195), and these local translations of globalization by women call centre workers add as much to the national narrative as the productive structurings.

Dominant perceptions of local culture suggest that it is (1) a particularity which is opposite to the global and (2) the culture of a relatively small, bounded space in which the individuals who live there engage in daily, face-to-face relationships, with an emphasis upon the habitual and repetitive nature of the everyday culture (Featherstone 1995: 93–94). The local and the concept of 'home' are sustained by collective memory dependent upon ritual performances and commemorative ceremonies, which can be seen as batteries that charge up emotional bonds between people (Featherstone 1995: 94). However, celebrations of the local can also operate in a regressive and fascistic way in that the local can oppose circulations and mixture, reinforcing walls of religion and gender (Hardt and Negri 2000: 362). Understanding the global/local dialectic as a polarized dichotomy is limiting in its analytical scope. Rather than interpreting the global as a homogenizing force, the global and the local must be reinterpreted as 'scapes' (Appadurai 1996) constitutive of one another, resembling playing fields upon which the next transformation of cultural or national identity will be played out.

Global cities provide such playing fields. As some have argued, the denationalizing of urban spaces and the formation of new claims by transnational actors, in this case call centre workers, raises the question of whose city it is. Foreign firms have profoundly marked the urban landscape, reconstituting strategic spaces of the city in their image and contributing to changing the social morphology of the city (Sassen 1998). Transnational call centres in Delhi, constituted via telematics and intense economic transactions, secure the formation of 'transterritorial centres' consisting of multiple and diversifying inter-city links, resulting in a territorialized and deterritorialized sense of space (Sassen 2002: 14).

Call centre workers are regarded by some as the 'mobile elite' who travel in cyber space. While they build their heavily guarded offices, free from the intrusion of unwanted neighbours and the local community, others are confined to the locality, simultaneously helpless as they watch the space they inhabit move from under their feet. Moreover, the local community must accept that modernization means monopolization of cartographic rights; however, as Bauman has argued, 'monopolies are impossible to retain in a palimpsest-like city, built of the layers of successive acts of history' (Bauman 1998: 27–41).

Space is not a reflection of society but an expression of society, or rather it is society; spatial forms and processes are formed by the dynamics of the overall social structure: '*space is crystallized time*' (Castells 1996: 441, emphasis in original). Understanding sociospatial forms as constructions (Sassen 2001b) is particularly useful when moving beyond a focus on transnational effects on cities and moving towards 'glocalized' (Featherstone 1995) interpretations of globalizing trends. The transnationalism of call centre culture can be described as occupational culture with individuals making journeys from a home base, the call centre, to many other places via the incoming or outgoing calls they take (Sampson 2003: 254). Call centre workers are like immigrants, forging and sustaining 'simultaneous multi-stranded social relations that link together their societies of origin and settlement, thereby building social fields that cross geographic, cultural and political borders' (Yeoh et al. 2003: 208).

The call centres' workforce, through their virtual migration, formulate transnational identities that both draw on and contest traditional, national and Indian identities, and simultaneously they experience a sense of 'placelessness' (Yeoh et al. 2003: 209). They are delocalized whilst working and are engaged in voice-to-voice service work, highlighting links to place of origin through accent, amongst other things. They are members of a transnation, a delocalized diasporic collectivity that retains a special ideological link to a putative place of origin (Appadurai 1996).

> The many displaced, deterritorialized, and transient populations that constitute today's 'ethnoscapes' are engaged in the construction of locality as a structure of feeling, often in the face of erosion, dispersal, and implosion of neighbourhoods as coherent social formations.
>
> (Appadurai 1996: 199)

Call centre workers are virtually engaged with other Indians outside India in the construction of an Indian identity, yet these transnational processes are really just situated cultural practices (Ong 1999: 17). As governments and nationalist movements find 'ways of erecting hard edges, slicing through transnational social ties' to define citizenship, transnational subjects and their communities develop innovative strategies to create spaces at the margins, registering agency and voice (Yeoh et al. 2003).

Transnationalism is not only about metaphoric and virtual spaces, as this book will show, it is also about physical spaces both within and outside the call centres. It shapes the built environment and cosmopolitan spaces or 'global cities' (Sassen 1998), demonstrating how globalization impacts upon urban landscapes. In Delhi, evidence of the effects of transnationalism can be seen in the metropolitan shrines to consumerism and the changing patterns of consumption for middle-class Indians.

Globalization has accelerated the rise of consumerism in the Third World by creating and satisfying induced wants (Banerjee and Linstead 2001). Pleasure seeking has become a duty (Lash and Urry 1994); thus consumption has become something which must be understood within a social framework (Featherstone 1995: 24). Consumption is a way of *establishing* differences not merely *expressing* differences:

> The interest the different classes have in self-presentation, the attention they devote to it, their awareness of the profits it gives and the investment of time, effort, sacrifice, and care which they actually put into it are proportional to the chances of material or symbolic profit they can reasonably expect from it. More precisely, they depend on the existence of a labour market in which physical appearance may be valorized in the performance of the job itself ... [furthermore] the self assurance given by the certain knowledge of one's own value, especially that of one's body or speech, is in fact very closely linked to the position occupied in social space.
>
> (Bourdieu 1984: 205–06)

As agents move through and across different fields, they tend to incorporate into their habitus[2] the values and imperatives of those fields, demonstrated clearly by the way the relationship between field and habitus functions to produce agents' bodies and bodily dispositions (Webb et al. 2002: 37). Consumption takes on a uniformity through habituation with practices that are closest to the body, such as food, dress and hairstyling (Appadurai 1996: 67), practices quite easily seen in call centre culture.

To some extent all women call centre workers participate in cultural production and consumption; however, this varies between groups within the call centre, as the power to practice production and consumption is contingent upon interdependencies and power balances. Moreover, a fetishizing of the consumer transforms him or her into a sign in the forces that constitute production, masking the real seat of agency, where the customer is not an agent but a 'chooser' at best (Appadurai 1996). However, this is not altogether true; moreover, it is somewhat limiting in an examination of agency. Although those in the Third World may seem to be manipulated into buying consumer goods which are alien to and destructive of their cultures, they are in fact actively employing consumer goods to express and forge their own unique identities and in this way are expressing their agency over consumption practices.[3]

In India, cultural consumption is most powerfully experienced through the shifting 'mediascapes' (Appadurai 1996) of imported Western television programmes and, of course, Bollywood. Concepts and tools offered up from analyses of 'mediascapes' make a case for using 'cinematic apparatus' (Denzin 2005) as a heuristic device to investigate surveillance and control and the way in which they link to cultural consumption. 'Mediascapes' play an important role in the globalization of India by providing NRIs access to what people are watching 'at home' in India. They present constructions of Indians 'at home' and abroad through Bollywood cinema, as evidenced by the number of films containing song and dance scenes set in Europe and North America (Shurmer-Smith 2000: 175–77).[4] The Hindi film is one of the main ways in which the second and third generation Indian diaspora maintains a dialogue with India and participates in transnational processes of constructing national identity.[5]

Imagination is no longer a mere fantasy, simple escape, an elite pastime or mere contemplation; it is an organized field of social practice and a form of negotiation between sites of agency and globally defined fields of possibility (Appadurai 1996: 31). Nowhere is this more evident than in the Bollywood influenced landscape of Indian culture and society, where film structures and the cinematic apparatus contribute to 'Panopticon'-like surveillance in public spaces and to the social construction of women's identities.

The postmodern self has interiorized the cinematic investigative voyeur's gaze, which itself is more than just a gaze, but rather an exercise of power in its rawest yet most sophisticated form, with women nearly always as the object of the gaze (Denzin 1995: 5–9).[6] Despite the enormous influence of Hollywood on world cinema, Bollywood has managed to resist being devalued or undermined. It is precisely because of this that the role and the significance of Indian cinema culture have been underestimated as it does not easily fit into the theoretical model developed around a First World/Third World dichotomy (Tyrell 1999:

312). One aspect of the success of Bollywood cinema is the quasi-religious iconography of its stars, who come to symbolize the nation itself, as with Nargis, who starred in the film *Mother India* (1967); another is the continued commercial success of Bollywood, both in India and internationally, which has become emblematic of India's resistance to the West (Tyrell 1999: 316–17).

The cinematic society has great constitutive capabilities in negotiating national, cultural and gendered identities. Castells writes:

> Cultural battles are the power battles of the Information Age. They are primarily fought in and by the media, but the media are not the power holders. Power, as the capacity to impose behaviour, lies in the networks of information exchange and symbol manipulation, which relate social actors, institutions, and cultural movements, through icons, spokespersons, and intellectual amplifiers.
>
> (Castells 1998: 379)

Identity itself functions as a powerful tool within these cultural battles and 'ideoscapes' (Appadurai 1996), in the formation of society/state relations (Castells 1997) and the 'cultural interchange process' (Welsch 1999: 203–04). Transnational Indian call centre workers participate in globalizing discourses and processes, by way of their interaction with people living outside India, which in turn produce globalized identities. The production of these identities is contingent upon their access to these globalizing processes and thus serves to create 'disjunctures' (Appadurai 1996) between themselves and those not working in the call centre industry. In this way, identity becomes something that is both constructed by the call centre workers – self-identities – and something that is culturally produced – social identities.

Outside the call centres, participation in globalizing discourses is enhanced by the global forums, groups and social networking sites accessed through the Internet. Undeniably changing India's culture and society through its processes of decentralization, openness and lack of hierarchy for authoritarian or monopoly control (Sassen 1999: 54), the Internet and the subsequent development of the 'network society' reflect the networks of production, power and experience that produce them and are constituted by the interaction between the 'net' and the 'self', or, to put it more clearly, between the network society and the power of identity (Castells 1998: 381–83).

The complex relationship between the net and the self is further underscored by the technologically enhanced relationships emerging from within the call centres themselves. 'Digital diasporas' (Gajjala 2004), 'cyber communities' (Ong 2004) and the creation of online groups of 'various travelling transnational subjectivities that inhabit online spaces' (Gajjala 2004) provide further evidence of growing 'technoscapes'. Far from utopian, online communities are better described as 'ectopian', or outside ordinary space, and 'open to multiple contradictory appropriations by those who create and then traverse their spatial properties' (Luke 1999: 37). '*We are not living in a global*

village, but in customized cottages globally produced and locally distributed
(Castells 1996: 370, emphasis in original) and, as this book will show, 'virtual
communities' are not 'real communities' in that they do not follow the same
patterns of communications and interaction as physical communities do.
However, this does not mean they are 'unreal', as they are interpersonal social
networks, supported by the dynamics of sustained interaction (ibid.: 389).

Transcending distance and of low cost, 'digital diasporas' feed the flows of
transnationalism constituting, and constituted by, changes in and to culture
and identity. One such example of the way in which online groups have been
harnessed is through the development of dating and marriage sites specifically
directed towards call centre workers. The founder of BPOShaadi.com
('shaadi' is the Hindi word for marriage) believes that prejudice directed
towards call centre workers is due to the fact that they tend to acquire a
worldly attitude as a result of their exposure to Western culture, high earnings
and mixed work environments (Dhillon 2008).

The belief that call centres are solely responsible for such profound cultural
changes is somewhat naïve, in that call centres simply extend the experiences
gained at college. Globalizing processes can be found in shopping centres,
cinemas, multiplexes, bars, restaurants, nightclubs, universities – all of which
existed long before call centres rose to such prominence. This chapter now
turns to an earlier time, charting the rise and progress of the Indian transnational call centre industry, providing a backdrop and foregrounding the
meteoric rise of the emerging cultural shifts and transformations that have
rocked the Indian middle-class boat, a part of the story that isn't often told.

Trade liberalization in India

Economic changes in India have historically been linked to the larger context
of constructing an Indian national identity. India's independence from British
colonial rule in 1947, accompanied by the trauma of partition, led to a newly
formed government heavily influenced by social idealism and a socialist ideological paradigm (Athreya 1996). From the Swadeshi protests[7] of the 1940s to
the Green Revolution of the 1970s and the liberalization of markets of the
1980s (Singhal and Rogers 2001), the reforming of economic policy has heavily
influenced the constructing of an Indian national identity (Wyatt 2005).[8]

Cameron and Palan argue that

> the imagined community of the territorial nation-state ... is very rapidly
> giving way to a series of imagined economies which maintain the fiction
> of the state ... but situate it within a radically different set of boundaries
> and notions of social space. The transformation of the state takes place
> through the deterritorialization and denationalization of myths of identity
> and belonging particular to the nation-state of the nineteenth and twentieth
> century.
>
> (Cameron and Palan 2004: 8)

However, in India deterritorialization and denationalization have incorporated myths and identities of belonging, re-narrating the nation and problematizing narratives of global identity (Wyatt 2005). Identity and the imagined economy play crucial roles in the development and globalization of the Indian call centre industry, and given the post-independence, socialist heritage of Indian politics it is difficult, if not impossible, to disengage from a nationalist agenda when historically exploring trade liberalization.

Economic transformations developed rather slowly in India. Although some areas of the economy began to grow, the rapid development experienced in countries such as Singapore, Malaysia and Hong Kong in the 1980s remained elusive until 1991 (Singhal and Rogers 2001), when a series of dramatic economic and trade reforms embracing liberalization were introduced by the government (Das 2000). The assassination of Rajiv Gandhi during an election campaign earlier that year sent waves of sympathy around India that carried the Congress Party to victory (Das 2000: 214). P.V. Narasimha Rao, the newly appointed Prime Minister, ushered in a new era with a loan from the International Monetary Fund (IMF) and new cabinet ministers focussed on finance and commerce (Das 2000: 214). The proposals opened India's public sector services to foreign investors and encouraged Indian suppliers to raise the quality of Indian manufactured goods. In essence, the reforms did away with much of the bureaucracy and ended the unlimited protection laws for Indian technological development (ibid.).

Along with these reforms, the Indian government began to encourage foreign direct investment (FDI) from NRIs and made efforts to highlight and celebrate a history of emigration to the UK. In 2001, the Prime Minister, Atal Bihari Vajpayee, emphasized pride in global Indian success stories:

> From high-tech chip laboratories to curry restaurants, from renowned hospitals to famous educational institutions, from well-known research centres to leading think tanks – *everywhere* you find an Indian who has overcome odds to establish himself through skilled education and hard work. Many of you owe your current success to the quality education which you have received in Government-run institutions, be they Indian Institutions of Technology or medical colleges. My government's policy is to assist the overseas Indian community in maintaining its cultural identity and strengthening the emotional, cultural, and spiritual bonds that bind them to the country of their origin.
>
> (Khadria 2001: 57–58)

Vajpayee's nationalistic right wing Hindu party, the Bharatiya Janata Party (BJP), made great efforts to capitalize on the success of Rao's economic reforms of 1991 and comments such as the one above demonstrate the Indian government's desire to lure FDI from NRI communities, as well as to encourage Indian graduates to work abroad. In 1999, two-thirds of all software professionals entering the UK were from India (Khadria 2001). These concurrent strategies of inviting foreign investment into the country whilst encouraging Indian graduates to gain skills to enhance the Indian economy have, in Vajpayee's words, reversed India's seeming 'brain drain' to its 'net gain'.[9]

The BJP continued with the trade liberalization agenda set by the Congress Party in 'the golden summer' of 1991, demonstrating a focus on economic development, trade and rapid advancements in technology and communication (Das 2000: 213). Throughout the 1990s foreign investment made a positive impact on the software and telecommunications industry, particularly in Bangalore, which became known as the Silicon Valley of India, the hub of software research and development. Though some saw this era as the 'informatization' of India, 'the process through which communication technologies are used as a means of furthering socio-economic development' (Singhal and Rogers 2001: 18–19), others argued that the advancements created further digital divides (Keniston 2004). A newly emerging elite group, the 'digerati', were the primary beneficiaries of these reforms and advances and, unlike old elite groups, this group was not based on caste, inherited wealth or family connections (ibid.). Rather, access to the 'digerati' is through a combination of education and entrepreneurial skills – similarly to the way in which the linguistic divide of India, of those who can and those who cannot speak English, firmly established by the British colonizers and further advanced by Nehru and Gandhi's politics, shaped 'the great Indian middle class' (Varma 1998). The middle class and 'digerati', served by linguistic apartheid, is the strata benefiting most from the recent developments in the IT and telecommunications industry as they accompany the social, economic and cultural changes brought in by economic investment, particularly in the Indian telecommunications sector.

The development of the Indian telecommunications sector

Prior to the trade liberalization reforms of 1991, telecommunications were seen more as a public utility than an instrument of economic competitiveness:

> Monopoly characteristics and political considerations made it a natural preserve of the state, where dissatisfaction of a middle-class customer base could be tolerated in lieu of providing social security to the large employee base of the telecom department ... Disguised unemployment, superfluous labour and low productivity were readily accepted as India's version of social security.
>
> (Dokeniya 1999: 110)

Slow growth in the development of telecommunications was due to: telephones being seen as a luxury rather than a necessity; the dominance of state-run monopolies; the absence of shareholder pressure for efficiency; bureaucratic organization without delegation, initiative or accountability; overstaffed structures; and strong unions of workers with considerable political clout (Singhal and Rogers 2001: 192). From the mid-1980s, however, India became one of the first of the developing nations to begin restructuring its telecommunications sector (Petrazzini 1996) and in 1985 Rajiv Ghandi's administration created the state owned Department of Telecommunications (DOT) to establish policies and grant licences for the development of the sector (Petrazzini 1996).

The DOT was assigned the task of handling import and export licences and ensuring that values of socialist idealism were not abandoned. However, as labour issues played a key role in these developments, Indian employees challenged most of the proposed reforms, fearing that any change in the sector would lead to privatization, generating mass unemployment (ibid.). This effectively slowed the development of the telecommunications sector. Simultaneously, emerging accusations of scandal and corruption pointed towards a monopoly created by the DOT that no one could break, as competition between the DOT and private investors did not encourage the radical economic reforms initially predicted (ibid.):

> Keeping the DOT as a government departmental monopoly while introducing competition in the sector implied that it retained the power of discretion in setting the policy agenda and in deciding the composition and terms of the markets in which it would be one of the players.
>
> (Dokeniya 1999: 126–27)

The proposed reforms were rife with opportunities for scandal and exploitation. Those with the authority to grant licences, the 'license-permit raj' (Das Gupta 2000) and a group of industrialists who came together to oppose the opening up of Indian industry, known as the 'Bombay Club' (Sinha 1996: 31), controlled the state-created and state owned DOT, limiting the opportunity for FDI and slowing down any progress in the telecommunications industry.

The lack of advancement in FDI encouraged the Indian government to unleash a series of radical economic reforms that would liberalize telecommunications and drastically change the country's economy (Sinha 1996). The new reforms were designed to stop the 'permit-licence-quota instrument of socialist development' and end the public monopoly model (Chowdary 1998: 11). Following the process of macro-economic liberalization in 1991, the Indian government adopted the New Telecom Policy (NTP), opening up the basic telecom sector to foreign investment (Dokeniya 1999: 106). The unusual tactic of reform came in the decision to introduce initial competition locally as opposed to nationally, forcing Indian telecom companies to join foreign investors but limiting foreign control to 49 per cent. The government divided the country into eighteen circles, based on state boundaries, and invited separate bids for each circle, emphasizing that only one private company would be allowed for each circle, thereby setting up head-to-head competition with the DOT. This was done to ensure foreign investment and a boost to the country's economy while still allowing Indian companies to remain in control and to ensure that no state would be neglected in the process of expansion and development (Sinha 1996).

These policies played a significant role in the conception of Indian based UK call centres in that reform and technological advancement are necessary for foreign investors. Initially, telecommunications companies in the UK were unable to develop services in India without the participation of an Indian based company that had a strong track record of success (Sinha 1996: 30). These reforms created a push for Indian companies to merge with foreign investors and create new private enterprises. In the mid-1990s Spectramind[10] was one of the first companies to create a base call centre site and invite transnational corporations (TNCs) to collaborate on business proposals with them, thus firmly establishing the roots of the call centre or data entry outsourcing industry. Although similar developments and technological advancements were evident in other Asian countries such as China, Malaysia and the Philippines (Reardon 1999), in India the call centre industry has grown at a rapid rate in a short period of time.

The trend towards call centre relocation to India

The deregulation of telecommunications has had a significant impact on the internationalization of call centre services (Phillips 2002). This is evidenced by the introduction of trade reforms and technological advancements in the Indian telecommunications sector which have produced an increased number of call centres in India (*Economist* 2000a, 2000b). Optimistic predictions of the 'death of distance', the 'end of geography' and 'borderless economies' have often accompanied the research and literature on globalization and ICTs (Huws 1999), and the growth of call centres in India is no exception to such predictive views. However, much of the early literature on Indian call centres focussed on both the economic and political factors for growth[11] and until recently the literature had largely ignored the social and cultural aspects, such as the skilled, English-speaking and highly educated graduate workforce, which have drawn investors to India (Roy 2001: 181; Das 2000: 251).

Call centres can be defined as 'a dedicated operation in which computer-utilizing employees receive inbound – or make outbound – telephone calls, with those calls processed and controlled either by an Automatic Call Distribution (ACD) system or predictive dialling system' (Taylor and Bain 1999: 102). Skill based definitions of call centres are insufficient in that they do not account for the variety of services provided by call centres for clientele, ranging from in-house to outsourced services. Some call centre services require more training and knowledge, for instance those in the financial or IT sectors compared with those providing travel or sales services. Differences in 'volume' and 'value' reflect the managerial concern with the quantity or quality of calls, thereby indicating the skill level required for the job and providing a direct correlation between types of call centres and skilled employees (Taylor and Bain 2003a, 2003b). Types of call centres can be determined by both organizational strategy, such as low cost or high differentiation, or by task, such as advice/solutions, sales and transactions (Wallace et al. 2000, quoted in

Houlihan 2002: 68). The call centres in this study were largely pseudo-relational and median-practice call centres (NCall, NCallB, DelCallB and GCall) and relational and high-commitment management call centres (DelCall, GCallB).

Pseudo-relational and median-practice call centres provide in-depth training lasting from three to five weeks, generally focussed on product knowledge (Kinnie et al. 2000b). Agents are multi-skilled, teamwork is common and the pay scale is at the median for the industry. Contact with customers is intermittent as agents provide services such as mail order and low-value insurance (Kinnie et al. 2000b). *Relational and high-commitment management* call centres provide a highly interactive, customized service to their clientele, with an emphasis on quality and specific company knowledge (Kinnie et al. 2000b). Employees may take only six calls a day and be involved with other tasks such as investigating problems or dealing with correspondence. Employees are offered high salaries, good incentives and may include graduates or those with specific training or skills such as in the IT or finance sectors (Kinnie et al. 2000b).

Although it was GE that garnered most of the attention from British newspapers (Harding 2001; Treanor 2002), with early reports and studies indicating that GE's call centre in Gurgaon, Haryana, was India's first international call centre (*Economist* 2000a, 2000b; Chanda 2002), call centres were gaining interest from foreign developers before GE had established itself.[12] Gayatri,[13] a manager of a median-practice call centre based in Gurgaon, shares her experience in attempting to set up India's first domestic call centre for the customers of STAR-TV, Satellite Television for the Asian Region, acquired by Rupert Murdoch in 1995:[14]

> My first experience with a call centre happened in 1996, which is actually the start of the industry in this country because we had officially already started before GE came in. GE was still in the set-up stage, because they came in at '97. I may have my years wrong, but I know that we set up before GE because they took our agents. So, India's Star-TV, owned by Rupert Murdoch, wanted to set up a call centre, very much like the one of BSkyB. In fact, we were trained according to the BSkyB standards. All the concepts were the same. We had to have an inbound service for customers, telemarketing, outbound services, a customer care centre – the training had to be given, the equipment had to be ordered. But our call centre was going to be for India only. Unfortunately, the project failed because the government did not give the requisite licences. But we had the equipment, we had people trained to do the job, we knew how to manage it to the point where we went out and outsourced our services to other people. 'See, we exist, we don't have any work to do, but we have all the facilities.' Back then, when I used to give my presentations, I carried it around on my laptop; I used to actually define what a call centre was. It would show a person sitting with a headset [laughing], a call coming in, the computer. Literally!'
>
> (Gayatri, Call Centre Consultant)

Gayatri's account helps to locate the beginning of the contemporary call centre industry in India, establishing 1996 as the year that call centres became operational. Although the Indian government denied STAR-TV the necessary paperwork for a domestic customer services call centre, GE was granted the licences to carry out back office, data entry, and voice-to-voice work for a transnational call centre. From this point, two types of call centres emerged: the first, a 'captive' operations site for large Western companies looking to reduce back office costs without outsourcing work to other companies; the second, 'fleeting arrangements between Western clients and subcontractors in India, often brokered by middlemen' (*Economist* 2000a, 2000b). The distinction between these two services is the difference between the *offshoring* of work, using a 'captive' site for back office work, versus the *outsourcing* of work, sub-contracting work to Indian companies while the core of operations remains within control of the parent corporation.

Offshoring and outsourcing have since developed substantially, with analysts hurrying to categorize Indian operations as 'Indian subsidiaries of foreign companies', 'joint ventures between Indian and foreign companies' and 'outsourced Indian companies' (Mitter 1999: 6) – or as captive centres that perform in-house operations for companies, third party service providers, Indian software/IT companies that have acquired outsourcing contracts, and operations run by Indian businesses for domestic services such as with Indian mobile telephone companies (Taylor and Bain 2003a). To some extent all of these descriptions apply, as the call centre industry continues to grow in India. However, of greater significance is the way in which such parameters and definitions are constructed.

The exporting of call centre work from the UK, as well as other sites, to India takes with it the structure and labour processes specific to the call centre industry, which can include flat hierarchical structures, monotonous, repetitious tasks, unpredictable stress levels and performance related bonuses. Analysis of call centres in India based on what is of significance to analysts outside India presents an obscured or incomplete understanding of the labour process. The empirical referent for the analysis of Indian call centres falls short. It is based, quite correctly, on the assumption that call centre labour processes are exported to India and, as such, the tools for analysis must also be exported. However, studies of the Indian call centres are narrowed to reflect the concerns of earlier call centre studies based on findings outside India – not necessarily reflecting concerns found within a specific Indian context.

Although these early studies are correct in suggesting that the Indian call centre labour process can be mundane and repetitious, an over-reliance on these descriptors precludes further investigation as to how call centres may be viewed as positive, exciting and challenging work environments. Furthermore, the propensity for these studies to consider issues raised by media reports concerning forced identity changes and the monotonous labour process is restrictive in that they do not consider cultural changes and the social effects of call centre work such as economic independence for women, male–female integrated workplaces and liberal work environments.

Notwithstanding these negative descriptions of call centre work, the Indian call centre industry is flourishing, owing success in many ways to cultural and social factors such as widespread fluency in the English language, historical colonial relations, lower wages for employees and time differences between India and other countries (Singhal and Rogers 2001: 229). From the late 1990s to 2003, call centre agents earned one-sixth or less of comparable pay in the US and the UK, from approximately USD100 up to £100 Sterling per month (Singhal and Rogers 2001: 229).[15] McMillin's (2006) study found that 56 per cent of the interviewees made Rs5000–10,000/month and 20 per cent made Rs11,000–15,000/month, while team leaders earned Rs15,000–35,000/month.[16] Furthermore, the twelve-hour time difference between India and the US can 'provide a US client with a virtual 24 hour work day, cutting the software development life cycle by half, ensuring speedy deliveries, higher quality, and substantially reduced costs' (Singhal and Rogers 2001: 226). Whilst all of this is ideal for foreign investors to develop back office operations, the creation of a male–female integrated work environment coupled with a liberal, modern work atmosphere which encourages employees to embrace Western clothing and accents has proven to be alluring to young graduates. Clean, air-conditioned work sites with continuous access to the Internet and competitive salaries and bonuses have had an impact on the creation of a labour force rapidly supplying the demand for call centre workers.

The diversity of approaches and findings amongst studies of call centres, telecommunications, informatics and data entry partially reflects a lack of clarity in terminology and definition (Taylor and Bain 1999). British media and academic studies have used the term 'call centres' as a generic term to refer to all service work outsourced to India from the UK. In looking at Indian labour processes, Remesh (2004) separates the work into two processes, which he defines as 'voice processes' and 'e-mail processes'. The first category indicates customer support over the phone, while the second indicates support via the Internet. Becoming increasingly common is the acronym ITES–BPO, which acknowledges both categories under a broader category of Information Technology Enabled Services – Business Process Outsourcing, used to refer to a variety of non-customer facing, back office clerical and administration work (Ramani 1999; Bain and Taylor 2008).

The development of ITES–BPO work in India has created more employment opportunities in as much as non-voice-to-voice work can be performed during the day when agent seats are vacant due to time differences, making it more profitable for the company and more accessible for women who are unable or unwilling to work night shifts. As the term 'call centre', or BPO, business process outsourcing, is still most widely used in academic studies, media reports and by the employees themselves, I will continue to use it here to refer to all the voice-to-voice, non-voice-to-voice and data entry work done as part of the outsourced service work performed in India for UK businesses.

Profiling the Indian call centre industry

The Indian call centre sector has grown rapidly over the last few years, with revenues for 2008 estimated to be over USD50 billion. Currently, of the total direct employment of about two million in the IT–BPO industry, over 90 per cent is captured by the seven leading locations of Bangalore, Mumbai, NCR, Hyderabad, Pune, Chennai and Kolkata. Within Delhi it is actually located in the larger area of the NCR, which is comprised of New Delhi, Noida, Gurgaon and Faridabad (NASSCOM, www.nasscom.in).[17] In 2004, the NCR had approximately 53 call centres, with an average size of 191 employees; Mumbai had a call centre concentration of 45; and Bangalore and Chennai had 35 sites each (Taylor and Bain 2003a, 2005; Bain and Taylor 2008). Broadly speaking, the NCR hosts two types of call centres: captive call centres,[18] established as subsidiaries for multinationals to run in-house operations (Taylor and Bain 2003a); and third party service providers,[19] predominantly outsourcing firms responsible for handling a number of multinational and transnational clients (Kobayashi-Hilary 2004: 81–85).[20] A recent report suggests, however, that reverse migration of employees from urban centres such as the NCR to smaller cities such as Chandigrah is also on the rise (NASSCOM, www.nasscom.in).

From 1998 to 1999 the IT enabled service industry employed 23,000 people (Mitter 1999: 14). In 2001–02 that number rose to 106,000, in 2002–03 it was 171,000 and in 2003–04 it was 245,000, with current estimates at 1.5–2 million (NASSCOM, www.nasscom.in). Over the last decade, call centre employment grew at a rate of over 25 per cent per year, and even with a conservative estimate of 15 per cent growth rate in employment for the next ten years, the industry will lead direct employment in the sector to about 8 million by 2018, an increase of about 6 million (NASSCOM, www.nasscom.in).[21] Although it is difficult to get a precise figure for the ages of call centre employees, it is accepted that many of them are recent graduates and between the ages of 20 and 25 (Mirchandani 2004a; Taylor and Bain 2003a; McMillin 2006).

Indian call centre analyses have, thus far, been predicated on call centre studies from Europe, North America and Australia, and as such they are grounded in issues and concerns that may prove to be unsuitable as empirical referents. To illustrate this, two descriptions of popular perceptions of call centre work are included. Ian, a soft skills consultant developing workers' soft skills in Delhi, offers the following insight:[22]

> The first thing they hear is that in the West it's a really crap job and only losers are doing this. So here, the opposite is indoctrinated right from the start. They are told that it is a career and not a crap job. So most people may espouse the belief that it is a career, but one day, after thinking this is a crap job, this is a crap job, their bodies can't take it. So they do it for a year, max. two years. If their skills are good, then they may move on to managerial positions, but that's 1 in 15. Most people will probably move out and say, 'Thank you very much. I've got my experience and I can

move on to other things, where I can get my daytime job and get my life back in order.' You can't do night jobs indefinitely.

(Ian, Soft Skills Consultant)

A second perspective is that of Gayatri, a call centre consultant who is currently employed as the country head of a call centre dealing with a medical billing process:[23]

> I have had some people say to me that they think these call centres are just full of prostitutes and all the girls are prostitutes. What prostitutes? The vans pull in; they check into their office, the team leader is shouting, you are sitting on that desk with a phone attached to your ear, they say, 'Today you will take a break from 10 a.m. to 10.15.' If you start at 10.05 you realise you will be in trouble – what prostitution?! The average time on the floor in our office is ten hours. The minimum travel time is two hours. They are spending twelve hours working. When are these kids going to be prostitutes? It is a hard job. People underestimate it.

(Gayatri, Call Centre Consultant)

Ian's comments demonstrate that, in line with other call centre studies from outside India, health issues are paramount, be they night shifts, job dissatisfaction or lack of opportunity for advancement. Call centre work is essentially a difficult job to do wherever you might be, in which case drawing on earlier studies is necessary as they provide substantiated, quantifiable evidence that may not emerge in all of the interviews because the call centre workers in India are focussed on other issues as well. One such issue is aptly demonstrated by Gayatri's comments, as her frustration with people's perceptions of the labour process demonstrates the naïveté and ignorance of the wider Indian community. Both comments make quite clear that there are corresponding similar concerns and a host of other complexities when dealing with Indian call centres. It is necessary therefore to both draw upon the earlier studies and remain open to the inclusion of other concerns. What follows is a discussion of some of the areas for consideration that emerged during my stay in India. Whilst some fit neatly into the literature of call centres, others do not, and they include: facilities, recruitment, retention, training, labour processes, emotional labour, surveillance, resistance and health and safety.

Facilities

Call centre facilities provide possibly the best incentive for prospective employees. Perhaps more significantly than elsewhere, a clean, secure environment in an open-plan office, with gates and security guards surrounding the building, creates a comfortable atmosphere where women feel safe. With many of the call centres built in the last five years, most provide twenty-four-hour access to the Internet at work stations in an air-conditioned environment where employees can chat via e-mail, read international newspapers or look for courses and other educational opportunities. Call centres also provide on-site catering services, some of which operate twenty-four hours a day, that offer free or subsidized breakfast, lunch and dinner depending on employee shift timings. Gayatri describes typical catering services:[24]

> We give them a full course meal: breakfast, lunch and dinner and two snacks, at 11.00 and at 6.00, and we have a mid-morning, mid-evening and a midnight snack served. Feeding people is a huge issue because you're not doing it for one or a hundred you're doing it for thousands and you're doing it daily, seven days a week because they have to operate seven days a week, twenty-four hours a day. You may only have a shift on Saturday, but there are people working all the time. You have to worry about all of these things, because if you get food poisoning you'll have a whole shift go down. And if you have a whole shift go down, your client is going to leave. Some call centres even have gyms, they have 'rec' rooms, sleep rooms. I've seen one facility in Bombay which had a meditation room. In fact, not one, it had two meditation rooms. It was amazing that facility. This is the kind of stuff that they do for their people to keep them happy and keep them coming to work because you are working against your body clock.
>
> (Gayatri, Call Centre Consultant)

Keeping healthy and well is something that call centres have worked hard to emphasize, as much of the media scrutinizes the adverse effects that working at night has on employees. Meal provision is almost mandatory in call centres due to their locations outside city centres and away from eating establishments. The night-time shift timings also mean that it can be difficult to find meals outside daytime hours. The focus on healthy living can be found in most call centres, despite the fact that many employees choose to relax by sleeping, drinking, smoking or going out to socialize.

Recruitment, retention and training

As well as using recruitment agencies, newspaper advertisements, college recruitment fairs and employee incentives for introducing friends and family to the companies (Remesh 2004), many call centres hold walk-in interviews. The recruitment process itself involves several rounds – interviewees indicated six or seven rounds – of tests and interviews, including: written tests to assess English-language skills; listening and analytical skills tests; attitudinal tests; group discussions to assess team playing or leadership qualities; and personal interviews.[25] Similar to findings from other studies, Indian call centres have also geared recruitment material towards young graduates who demonstrate a 'cultural fit' (Taylor and Bain 2003a), with recruiters asking solely for applicants who are graduates and between the ages of 20 and 30, showing explicit discrimination towards older or more experienced people. Many applicants are rejected in early interview and test rounds on the basis of their accents being too thick, or if they do not demonstrate the right 'fit' with the process.[26]

As well as recruiting individuals who are outgoing or sociable, call centres also actively targeted women as traditional perceptions exist that women are 'naturally' better than men at being conversational, and so are able to perform call centre labour more easily. Some studies found that recruitment materials targeting housewives and stating that 'running a house and raising children requires many of these skills we are looking for' (Thompson et al. 2004: 135) were disingenuous in displaying such sensitivity to gender links. The higher percentage of women working in call centres looks to continue, correlating with studies from the UK that point towards a 'ghettoization of female labour'.[27]

Although some have written that retention rates in Indian call centres are close to 80–85 per cent (Budhwar et al. 2006), people interviewed for this research indicated that attrition rates were higher, at 30–35 per cent, as was the incentive to leave and take up work at other call centres for higher salaries.[28] Massive growth in the industry has given rise to call centres in small clusters and areas, making it easier for employees to move horizontally across the sector (Taylor and Bain 2003a: 117). Gayatri points to future changes in call centre recruitment, trends which were beginning to show in 2003:

> Burnout is very high. Normally, after three or four years they can't stay longer. The average at the agent level is one to two years. They leave really fast. The profile of the agent will change, though. Currently we are recruiting college grads, but I see us moving towards housewives, towards the elderly, the able elderly because you have a good English-speaking pool there. They are people who are dedicated, people who enjoy working, retired people – they have excellent English communication skills.
>
> (Gayatri, Call Centre Consultant)

Highlighting good English and communication skills as key factors in recruitment, Gayatri's comments underscore the fact that if workers are already highly skilled in customer services, then the company will require less time and money to train them, and as call centres spend 25–30 per cent of the annual budget on training, retention is of some importance. Gayatri discussed the incentivizing of call centre work as companies try to hold on to employees by offering bonuses, vouchers, trips and prizes for good performances. Many call centres used the 'fun factor', a manufactured sociability in keeping with the absence of a long-term commitment from employers and one which celebrates the impermanence of call centre work (Russell 2002).[29]

Time spent training for new jobs, or new processes when employees transfer within the same company, can range from three days to six weeks. Approximately one-fifth of the training time will be spent on customer service techniques, oral and written communication, and handling difficult customers.

Ian, a soft skills consultant in Delhi, gives a brief overview of the training he provides in his soft skills courses:

> The first would be in communication, face-to-face and listening skills, picking up regional accents, listening for regional comprehension skills, empathetic skills. For example, when someone says, 'I'm in a difficult financial situation at the moment,' you can say, 'I'm sorry to hear that' rather than just saying, 'Okay, how much?' How to relate to customers, things like that. The other is customer service skills, how to sell, persuasion skills, team building, trainer skills, if they want to run in-house training programmes by their own staff. And then coming down to cross-cultural communication, which is more knowledge based, so giving them an overview to the US or the UK, on, say, education, how they think, work choice, slang, etc. And finally, we would have voice and accent training, and the difference here is that in the North American market you want to change the accent – first of all you want to neutralize it, you want to change it to an American accent. In the UK's case, what you want to do is de-Americanize, because most of these guys have been through an American programme, because with call centres America came [to India] first before Britain.
>
> (Ian, Soft Skills Consultant)

Soft skills training, along with voice, accent and culture, forms a significant yet very small part of an agent's training. It is also one area of transnational call centre work that garners much interest from the media, particularly with regard to the adoption of pseudonyms. Along with accent neutralization or the reduction of an Indian accent, Mirchandani (2004b) also found that agents were assigned Western names as their 'work names'.

Labour process and management

High ratios of agents to supervisors in call centres statistically demonstrate the constraints on career advancement and promotion opportunities. These high ratios contribute considerably to two significant dimensions of call centre analysis: first, in terms of agent/management relationships and, second, in terms of the supervisory process. Many of the call centres in India used flat hierarchical structures based on models similar to those in the UK (Bain and Taylor 2008; Taylor and Bain 2008; Remesh 2004). This structure begins with agents employed for the front line or voice-to-voice service work. Gayatri provides insight into the managerial structure:

> Most call centres structures are very flat. You have agents, team leaders, depending on the call centre, an assistant manager, or a manager, a vice-president (VP), or an assistant vice-president (AVP), then you have directors. These designations are changeable across call centres, they tend

to benchmark your designation by the number of people you handle, and the number goes up by the hundreds. Normally, the benchmark is if you handle 400 people and above you are either a director or a vice-president or a senior operations manager, but then you are very, very senior at that level because you are managing huge teams and a manager will handle, say, 100 or less, so usually that's four to six teams. A team leader will handle a team of fifteen. If it is a data process they can go up to twenty [employees] and voice would be about fourteen to fifteen people max. And the manager will handle around a hundred so usually that's four to six teams.

(Gayatri, Call Centre Consultant)

Although the specific titles for positions above that of the manager may vary from company to company, the organizational structure of the labour process remains the same in many of the Indian call centres. In addition to this, there are a number of people employed in human resources, finance, logistics, transport, IT, internal and external communications.

Surveillance, control, resistance

Call centres, as well as other office workplaces, particularly white collar offices, create structures of control similar to Foucault's 'Panopticon' (Baldry et al. 1998).[30] The physical layout of the office plan is instrumental in gaining and maintaining control over the workforce. First, and in a very pragmatic way, the 'Panopticon' is visible in most call centre set-ups. A key way in which surveillance and control are maintained in call centres is through the agent's constant connection to the computer and telephone, accounting for 80 per cent of their work time. The ACD system forms a central part of this surveillance as it is used to track the number of calls taken, time spent on each call, time off the phones and time away on breaks. Calls can also be listened to live or recorded for quality measuring purposes.[31] Furthermore, the ACD is able to record staff attendance to the minute (Richardson and Marshall 1996: 310; Lankshear et al. 2001: 598).

The structure of space and the organization of labour in call centres prompted Fernie and Metcalf (1998) to write that call centres are characterized by the operation of the 'electronic panopticon', in which supervisory power has been 'rendered perfect'. This statement sparked debate amongst call centre analysts, as the immediate implication was that workers had no space for resistance. Bain and Taylor (2000) argue that Fernie and Metcalf's (1998) use of the 'Panopticon' is opportunistic and that they seem 'blissfully unaware' of the debate regarding its usefulness as an heuristic device. However, as the literature on call centre studies grows it would seem that Bain and Taylor are a bit too quick to dismiss Fernie and Metcalf's approach to call centre analysis.

Bain and Taylor (2000) deliberately take an explicitly polemical approach in examining Fernie and Metcalf's (1998) evidence suggesting that the call centre resembles an 'electronic panopticon'. They accuse Fernie and Metcalf of capitalizing on this negative image of the 'new sweatshop' in journal articles and press releases and assign partial responsibility to them for the development of two sharply contrasting images of call centre work. On the one hand, we are presented with images of the 'electronic panopticon' and 'human battery farm' put forward by Fernie and Metcalf (1998), and on the other we have 'optimistic descriptions cultivated by the sector's publicists, who present exciting images of centres, staffed by co-operative team working employees "smiling down the phone" and talking to customers in a relaxed and professional manner in comforting regional accents' (Bain and Taylor 2000: 3). Bain and Taylor argue that Foucault's metaphor is so seductive it gives no account of employee agency expressed as resistance or dissent. Furthermore, resistance is always conceived of as individualistic and fragmented, never as collective. However, in arguing that technology has 'rendered perfect' the supervisor's power, Lankshear et al. (2001: 603) note that some workers internalized company objectives and instilled a self-discipline associated with Foucauldian visions of panoptic surveillance when they *thought* they were being observed.

Bain and Taylor have argued that Fernie and Metcalf's (1998) work has constrained call centre analysis and discussion by 'erecting a simplistic and false model which ignores the complexities of the employment relationship' (Bain and Taylor 2000: 3). However, Bain and Taylor are guilty of similar crimes in that their deliberate debunking of Fernie and Metcalf's work has provided the opposing bookend, which has led to an even more narrow debate. Call centre analysts have fallen into a dualistic exchange, which, whilst flagging the apparent Foucauldian similarities in various call centre analyses, simultaneously maintains the limitations of such an analysis.

Bain and Taylor's (2000) harsh objections to utilizing the 'Panopticon' metaphor in an analysis of call centres is somewhat reactionary and 'opportunistic', as they once themselves accused Fernie and Metcalf of being, in that their analyses of Indian call centres (Taylor and Bain 2005; Bain and Taylor, 2008) are predicated upon British call centre studies, with little consideration for the historical, social and cultural differences between British and Indian call centre workers.

On the one hand, Bain and Taylor have a valid point in that accounts of monitoring in UK call centres included some extreme examples[32] and had reached a fevered pitch, obscuring all other concerns. On the other hand, however, outside the UK agents do not necessarily interpret such surveillance as negative. Freeman's (2000) study of employees in the data processing industries of the Caribbean showed that the women preferred the high level of surveillance as it mitigated the possibility of nepotism and ensured that employees were rewarded on the basis of their performance.

Monitoring of employee output and behaviour is conducted in very much the same way that it is in UK call centres. However, a more complicated issue was the way in which call centres assured employees' families of surveillance and control. Many of the parents of the employees believed that call centres were corrupting their children and introducing Western values that they believed to be contradictory to Indian values. One of the strategies used to mitigate this and assuage parents' suspicions about call centre work was to invite friends and family to the site to see where and how work is performed.[33] In some cases a private smoking area would be available to employees; the reasons for this were two-fold: first, to provide them with a space that was within the safe confines of the company site in which they could smoke or relax in the open air; and, second, to discourage them from leaving the premises, thereby exercising greater levels of surveillance and control.

The Indian call centre context requires a Foucauldian approach given the patriarchal constraints for women present in India, a discussion that will be fleshed out later in this book. For now, it is clear that cultural and social norms found in India, as well as the colonial legacy and historical links to the UK, demonstrate that tools of analysis should not so easily be consigned to the dustbin and that Bain and Taylor missed an opportunity when presenting their analyses of Indian call centres.

Of significance in this discussion of surveillance is the power of resistance, as Foucault (1979) once so eloquently wrote. Of abundance in call centres are the individual acts of resistance that help to alleviate the pressure, stress and monotonous nature of the work.[34] Some have argued that the 'juggling act' (Bolton 2000) of emotional labour and knowing which face to put on can be described as 'dramaturgical improvisational choreography' and as such can be regarded as 'artful' and likened to 'craftsmanship' (Whelan et al. 2002), with employees acting as 'multi-skilled emotion managers' (Bolton 2000).

In performing emotional labour, emotional exhaustion and burnout are inevitable (Kinnie et al. 2000a; Mulholland 2002; Deery et al. 2002; Lewig and Dollard 2003), leading to an emergence of 'communities of coping' (Korczynski 2003) which provide validation as employees deal with job related stress and attempt to assert agency over supervisory constraints and the 'electronic panopticon' (Callaghan and Thompson 2001). Moreover, they have implications for how far the social relations of the workplace were open to managerial controls. Furthermore, employees found ways to relieve pressure by simple forms of misbehaviour such as making fun of the customer (Thompson et al. 2004) as pressures, stress and work conditions often lead to health issues for many of the employees.

Health and safety

Not surprisingly, problems for employees associated with disruption to sleep patterns due to working night shifts were also reported, including stress, psychological effects, emotional and physical burnout, withdrawal and ill health. Odd shift timings and lack of entitlement to religious or national holidays also left employees disconnected from family and friends, resulting in nervousness, chronic fatigue, body ache, insomnia, nausea, anxiety and depression

(Remesh 2004). Other problems reported included gastrointestinal problems such as constipation, ulcer, abdominal pain and heartburn, as well as the development of poor eating habits, and excessive smoking and drinking to cope with the stress and pressure (ibid.). Sachin, an HR manager at an American call centre in Gurgaon, discusses one of the ways in which call centres deal with health issues:[35]

> Because a lot of people would not be from Delhi, not staying with their families, it was more like an attending physician coming in [to the call centre], twice a week or thrice a week. Also, the doctor might not always be there, but you can always get medicine and shots at work, and they had an emergency vehicle outside.
>
> (Sachin, HR Manager)

Gayatri, a call centre consultant and manager, outlines the precautions taken with call centre transport in getting women to and from work:

> Security is very tight in call centres, if you are women alone in a cab there are rules and regulations. If there are girls, the girls get dropped first even if the guy's place is closer because they have to make sure the girls are safe. If there is a group of women, and no guy in the cab, they also get a security guard. There are five to seven [people] in a cab and the cabs know they are on the radio, so if there is an issue they call up immediately.
>
> (Gayatri, Call Centre Consultant)

Safety is paramount and, as I will discuss later in this book, experience of the transport systems significantly shapes women's experiences.

Moving on from these preliminary findings, what follows is an in-depth look at NCall, where data was gathered for the research project. Comparisons made with UK call centres are based on my own experiences working in a UK call centre and on studies based upon UK call centres.

A call centre case study: NCall[36]

Much of the data collected for this book in the form of interviews and questionnaires was obtained from a case study of a call centre in Noida, Uttar Pradesh.[37] Noida is part of the NCR, which in 2003 included Delhi and Gurgaon, but now also includes Faridabad; both Noida and Gurgaon house a high percentage of the area's call centres. This case study draws upon ethnographic observation, participant observation and a short survey questionnaire administered to 113 employees at NCall.[38] The objective of the survey questionnaires was to gather quantifiable data on factors such as age, education, gender, religious and cultural background, as well as many other aspects, in order to present a profile of the call centre labour force in Delhi. The data for this study were collected between November 2002 and August 2003; however, observation at NCall lasted for twelve weeks between June 2003 and August 2003.

NCall is an Indian owned call centre or BPO sub-contracted to perform outsourced work for transnational corporations and domestic companies. Beginning in the 1970s, NCall established itself as a small computer and software development company and as of 2004 employed over 9,000 transnational workers worldwide (1,700 in Noida) for inbound and outbound calls as well as data entry services. It maintains call related and data entry business processes for both Indian and internationally outsourced operations. NCall administers a number of services, including customer service, sales and technical help, for some of the largest global corporations. NCall's offices are located throughout Europe and Asia; however, the head office remains in Noida. One of NCall's biggest assets is its brand name, as it has one of the strongest identities in the Indian call centre industry, cultivating an image that presents the company as cutting edge and energetic, and, as such, NCall is likely to hire and retain a young, university-educated, English-speaking workforce that will reflect this brand name. Thus, graduates are keen to work for NCall due to its reputation, wages and location, which is close to Delhi.

NCall itself is situated outside the centre of Noida and is based on three sites, all within walking distance of each other. The main site houses most of the company's in-house departments such as administration, transport and human resources. The second and third sites were new, purpose built call centres, dedicated to newly acquired tenders for outsourcing processes. The labour process, which provided the main focus for observation, was for a British corporation that had outsourced some of its customer services to NCall. NCall bids competitively for such tenders and in this case had secured the contract for a period of five years, from 2003 to 2008. Immediate observation of the first site suggested strong similarities with UK call centres with regard to the physical set-up and layout. However, upon closer inspection of the two newer buildings it seemed that furniture and equipment had not arrived, as whole rooms were still empty. When asked about this, the management informed me that delays in Indian Customs for equipment were common and had prevented them from starting the new contracts on time.

Each of NCall's three sites had a reception desk and was equipped with office furniture similar to that found in UK call centres. Each desk had a computer, telephone and headset for every employee. NCall had separate training rooms and the call centre 'floor' was set up with rows of desks facing one another, separated by partitions on all sides, with a desk on the end of every second row for the team leader. Each of the sites housed a cafeteria on the top floor, which provided breakfast, lunch and dinner, and several kitchen areas were found on each floor providing coffee and tea, all without cost for the employees (see Figure 2.1). NCall provided one meal per eight-hour shift, despite the fact that many employees were encouraged to work unpaid overtime, and company transport was arranged to keep employees on site for nine to ten hours. NCall managed the free meals on a ticket basis, with each

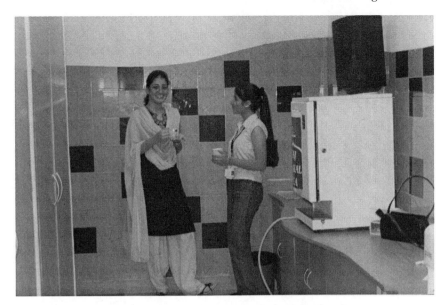

Figure 2.1 Two women on their coffee break in the call centre.

employee given thirty meal tickets at the start of each month. This differs from some other call centres that provided continuous hot and cold food throughout the day to any employee regardless of their shift timings and how many times they had eaten. This posed a problem for some of the employees working longer shifts and one of the ways in which they overcame it was to share meals, ensuring that they received at least half a meal twice a day. One NCall manager explained the company's wish to respect the religious sensitivity of strict Hindus, so that non-vegetarian food was only served once a week and was not beef. However, when pressed, the manager confessed that similar considerations were not taken into account for Sikhs or Muslims, as neither Muslim halal practices nor other religious and dietary factors were observed.

Transport to NCall was provided for every employee through either a private bus service or a shared vehicle, transporting up to six employees at one time. Although employees were grouped or 'clubbed' together according to where they lived, some commutes took up two hours each way. The transport office managed a fleet of vehicles and drivers were given printed assignment sheets with names, addresses and pick-up times at the start of the shift. As employees were on rotating twenty-four-hour shifts, drivers and vehicles were always on site.

The particular process observed at NCall was an outbound call process for a British company where agents contacted customers to ask if they were satisfied with the company's service (see Figure 2.2). The process manager explained that this first stage with the client was like a warm-up act and that

Figure 2.2 Call centre floor.

over the five-year contract agents would be upgraded slowly to take on more complicated processes, eventually involving inbound calls for technical support. The process employed over 300 agents reporting to 16 assistant team leaders (ATL), who in return reported to 8 team leaders (TL), reporting to one manager. The manager was responsible for the entire process and reported to the company's Vice-President of Operations. Many of NCall's employees frequently commented on the transparency of the management structure, stating that they felt comfortable speaking to anyone, from their ATL to the vice-president, about complaints or issues.

The salaries at NCall ranged widely, from a starting wage of approximately Rs7,000 per month to Rs15,000 per month[39] for employees who had been with the company for approximately one year or for those who had come to NCall with considerable experience working for other call centres. Employees were given the option of taking an extra Rs1000 per month and providing their own transport to work as opposed to using company transport, which many of them did as company transport was sometimes unreliable. Employees on this particular labour process were given fixed shift times Monday to Friday from 2.00 p.m. until 10.00 p.m., although this was due to change as the company expanded its responsibilities. Elsewhere in the company, employees were on rotating shifts for both UK and US processes.

Overall the respondents were satisfied with NCall as an employer and mainly indicated dissatisfaction solely with transport issues. Few saw a future career at NCall and they indicated that working in call centres was simply 'time pass'.[40] Many directly spoke of working at NCall long enough to fund further education, plan for weddings or gain skills that would lead to better employment opportunities; almost half of the employees expected to leave after two years. Those wishing to further their careers at NCall spoke of a desire to move away from call handling to other areas such as HR, training or managerial positions. In keeping with the majority of call centre studies, approximately two-thirds of the agents on this process were female, less than half of the team leaders were female, and the manager and the Vice-President of Operations were both male. The age profile of the workforce ranged from the age of 17 to some employees in their late forties, however approximately half of the respondents were between the ages of 22 and 25. All of the respondents spoke good English, most possessed undergraduate degrees and half were in the process of pursuing further graduate studies, mainly by correspondence and mostly in the area of a Master's in Business Administration. The ratio of single people to those with partners was 6.5:3.5, with over half of all respondents living at home with their parents. Over half of the respondents were from the NCR, and in the other half the women came from a total of fifteen different states and the men came from a total of nine different states, showing that women were travelling further to find employment.

Over half of the respondents had previous call centre experience before coming to NCall and approximately 47 per cent intended to leave before the end of two years; 37 per cent intended to stay at NCall for longer than two years. Just under half of all respondents indicated that they thought call centres did not provide good career opportunities and the same number suggested that they hoped call centre work would lead to opportunities in other areas. Approximately 58 per cent of the total sample group noted that they would like to continue working in India, while 77 per cent indicated that they would welcome the opportunity to work abroad. When questioned further about this the respondents indicated the UK, the US, Australia and Canada as their top choices for relocation.

This chapter sets up the backdrop to the chapters that follow in charting the rise of the globalized, transnational call centre industry. The NCall case study and data shown here are in no way exhaustive but are merely offered as a baseline for a general understanding of some of the more customer service oriented call centres. The chapters that follow present more detailed discussions with the women interviewed, exploring their fears, concerns, hopes and ambitions as they take part in what promises to be a significant shift for women living and working in India.

3 Pinking and rethinking professional identities

The construction of women's work identities

The first time we meet is at the call centre language training session. A fast-talking, wise-cracking mother of one, Smita grew up in East Africa and India, and has recently come back from working in France. Her mother a Bengali, her father from Uttar Pradesh, Smita married a Bengali from Orissa: 'It's all a mish mash with us so Delhi is the perfect place to live.' She smiles. At 33, Smita is one of the older women working in the call centre, a distinction she makes throughout our many conversations together. Smita is careful to point out that her experiences of living abroad and being raised by a career-driven mother have meant that her choices in life tend to focus on balancing career and family:

> A few years back I worked in advertising, 1994–2000. That's like being a doctor; you don't know where you are going to go next and there was never any responsibility taken for women who had to work late. They never offered to pay your cab fare if it was after eight o'clock, or pay your auto fare if it was before eight o'clock. How you went or who you went with was never their problem. It was like, 'Just go get the job done. Is it done?' They didn't care what time it was in the night. I was always my husband's responsibility. Which is why I left. No one took any responsibility. It was too vague. It was non-sexist to an extreme. The only difference was the ladies' loo and the guy's loo. At that point, I would have said call centres are rubbish, before I had our baby. Now I don't say that any more. My mother always said you should be a teacher. I agree. If I could be a teacher for three years, and then get back to being a highflying laptop person, I would do it, but right now I have to be there for my baby. It's a very temporary part of life, only for about five to six years then, so a woman should have a career. The career which does not require her to work at night because it is unsafe, and which does not need her to commute either alone or on public transport, because the world is not safe. So if a call centre job can give a woman that kind of security, then it's good.
>
> (Smita, 33, NCall)

Far from the perception that call centres are electronic sweatshops and that the work is exploitative, Smita describes how call centre work has transformed women's work experiences from an atmosphere of neglect to one of measured consideration. Before call centres, women's ambitions to succeed in the workplace, or at the very least to work amongst their male colleagues, is described here as a punishable offence. The wider context of travelling to work or negotiating public transport, as a job requirement, is understood as a woman's individual responsibility or the responsibility of her male relatives, and certainly not one that her employer's may be held accountable for.

Smita's experiences are certainly not unique, as women deal with the daily barrage of assaults, gropes and harassment on their way to and from work. Often termed 'eve-teasing', a euphemism to describe sexual harassment, women's concerns and complaints over the lack of safety or women-only transport options fall on deaf ears. But transport is far from being the only concern for working women in Delhi. This chapter explores the work sites and labour processes of the Indian call centre industry and the changing attitudes of women employed within them, by examining their motives to find employment in call centres and the way in which these attitudes are influenced by varying social, cultural and biological factors. Moving away from the popular analyses examining the name changes and the 'contemporary residue of imperialism' (Said 1993), what follows is a presentation of the discussions concerning the 'pinking' of call centre work, emotional labour and some of the negative implications of call centre work for women.

Women's participation in the Indian labour market

Historically grounded in the agricultural and manufacturing sector, women's participation on the world of work has undergone a sexual revolution characterized by the delinking of marriage and family (Castells 1997: 294), with women working independently and outside familial contexts and an increasing number migrating within India to urban centres for employment (Dyson and Visaria 2004: 127). The liberalization of the Indian economy has created investment opportunities for NRIs and the in-flow of NRIs themselves has had a profound effect on India's population with respect to family and personal life, with the introduction of a 'so-called Western lifestyle' (ibid.). The continuing decline in fertility rates and increased numbers of women entering the labour market (McNay et al. 2004: 170) suggest Sanskritization[1] and the 'marriage squeeze' (Banerjee 1999), the mandatory provision of a dowry in the marriage of daughters making it necessary for women to earn part of their own dowry:

> Most of the women that are working in call centres, well they basically come for a short time to enjoy themselves and also earn some money for their shaadi [wedding]. Of course, there are those who are also looking on it as a career, but I can tell you that majority will be married within a

year. This is like a small break before that time when they are somebody's wife and daughter-in-law, so they want to have fun.

(Rashi, 25, GCall)

Rashi, herself engaged to be married within a year's time, understands the expectations that are placed on women once they leave their parental homes for those of their in-laws. Although Rashi had been working for a few years now and had been promoted to team leader, she spoke as though her time would soon be up, and once the wedding had taken place, she told me that she planned to leave Delhi for Dehradun, where both her own and her fiancé's families were from. Rashi had originally left Dehradun because she did not want to work with her father in his business, wishing to experience greater independence by living on her own in Delhi and working in a new challenging sector. Rashi tells me that her family were relaxed about her working in Delhi at a call centre, largely because her sister had taken up a job as an airline hostess, and although family and friends were disapproving of her sister's career choice, she had forged a path that Rashi was able to follow. Having said this, Rashi also understood that such careers were short lived:

After marriage, it's really up to the guy. I mean, if I am working in the call centre and he is working nine to five, it will be a problem. That is something that we'll have to work out, but it depends on when I get married, who I marry.

(Rashi, 25, GCall)

Rashi suggests here that both partners would take such a decision; however, her fiancé has already told her that he doesn't like her working in a call centre. He has made complaints about her time management, her health, and she tells me, 'He is jealous of the men I work with because he doesn't understand what we do. He doesn't want to really get to know them because he finds all call centre workers really loud. He hates it.'

Like Rashi, it is unlikely that many of the women will carry on with career ambitions as most of them worked out of economic necessity and still conformed to an accepted image of womanhood. Their ambitions regarding work were brought into harmony with the family structure and expectations in making sure that educational qualifications, work experience or confidence gained from economic independence did not outstrip those of their future husbands.[2] Of the women interviewed, over half saw themselves getting married within a year, most often with prospective husbands already sought out by parents. It was difficult for them to be sure if in-laws would permit them to work after marriage, and although many of them said that they would like to continue earning money and contributing to the family coffers, they reluctantly accepted that someone else would ultimately make that decision for them.

Women's employment opportunities have been changing in India for some time now, as women access educational institutions with less difficulty. Most of these jobs are found in the burgeoning area of IT related services, although many still exist in traditional sectors as well, such as teaching, nursing and domestic work, to name a few.

Sneha

I first met Sneha when she was working at a hotel; she was, at the time, 18. Sneha's family, from a working-class background, were unable to pay for her to go to college or university, so Sneha had taken up a full-time job at a five-star hotel in Delhi to fund her education. She worked seven days a week, earning Rs3,500 per month, approximately £50. Sneha worked seven days a week and was obliged to work compulsory overtime as and when it was required by the hotel. The hotel provided meals at work but only provided transportation if Sneha was leaving at night. Sneha specifically chose work in the hospitality industry because of the added benefits of having meals and transport covered, but there were many downsides to the work as she told me that the female staff at hotels, hers included, were obligated to stay after their shifts had ended and entertain guests, as part of their compulsory overtime, by way of sitting and talking with them in the hotel bar. Sneha's only way of returning home at night was with one of the hotel's drivers and cars. If guests were still in the hotel bar when her shift ended, she was not given the transport until they retired. Sneha made clear to me that she was able to leave as soon as her shift ended; however, she would have had to flag a riksha or taxi herself and pay for it out of her earnings.

After six months, Sneha decided to leave the hotel and work at a call centre, where she is earning Rs6,500 per month (approximately £87), with Saturday and Sunday off, as well as having both transport and meals provided for her, with no issues concerning compulsory overtime. With her extra time and money, Sneha is pursuing a correspondence course for a degree in Business Studies, which she hoped, together with her experience at NCall, would lead to better employment prospects.

Sneha's experiences are quite common as women work to gain funds for education and participate in the newly formed Indian middle class, seeking upward mobility (Varma, 1998, 2004). However, the growing Indian middle class, around 350 million, is becoming increasingly stratified, with other middle-class identities emerging, circumscribed by religion, ethnicity and class. Increasing evidence points towards a 'high income workforce' characterized as: 'distinct from the upper class; unlikely to be seen as important investors; in possession of a disposable income that is a function of their lifestyle i.e. spending rather than saving, postponing having children, and setting up two career households' (Sassen 2001b: 285–86). Sassen's definition cannot be stretched comfortably to include many of the call centre workers – yet. They are largely, at this stage, learning to contend with family expectations, so the notion that India will soon see a rise of homes with 'double income, no kids' is slightly premature; however, her argument holds in that a disposable income and the trend to spend rather than save are rife amongst call centre workers.

Preetika, 24, part of the 'high income workforce', living at home and working in Gurgaon, is the daughter of two doctors. She took up employment at American Express so that she would have something to occupy her time outside the family home. Although she is in possession of a master's degree, she has never really had any intentions of working and it has come as a great surprise to Preetika that she is employed and enjoying the work. She has been working for nearly three years in the industry and her fiancé is a former colleague of her brothers. Preetika had become quite fond of him but it was actually her mother who invited him to be a member of the family. Preetika's fiancé has made quite clear to her that he is not interested in being married to a woman that is dependent on him, though he is not suggesting she make a financial contribution. Her plans are to get married to him in the upcoming year, but as both her parents are doctors with thriving practices, this is not an expense that Preetika needs to contribute towards. Her earnings then are simply for her to use as she pleases. She tells me that a large part of her wages goes towards shopping and every month she spends most of her earnings on clothing. 'You need to look smart when working so I usually spend Rs2,500 for a pair of trousers,' she tells me.

In comparing Sneha and Preetika's motives for working in the call centre and their explanations of how they spend or save their money, it is quite clear that there is a need for an analytical framework that is perhaps more flexible and comprehensive than ones that simply account for the quantitative measuring of women's earning and bargaining power. Women like Sneha and Preetika experience unequal power relations amongst themselves. Although many of the experiences of women call centre workers are likely to be similar or related in some way, analyzing their accounts with reference to differences in caste, class or religion is likely to provide a better understanding of women call centre workers and women's participation in the Indian labour market. These differences, although not central to the aims of this research, are indicated throughout this book in a number of ways and present a more detailed understanding of how women exercise agency over the labour process.

'Pinking' the Indian call centre profession

In her study of data entry and informatics workers in the Caribbean, Freeman (2000) significantly developed the concept of 'pink collar work' (Howe 1977) as she highlighted the significance of clothing in the production of a work identity. In the Caribbean, Freeman writes, the pink collar worker signifies a new category of feminine worker with her professional appearance and computer based job, 'a far cry from the cane fields and kitchens in which her mother and grandmothers toiled' (Freeman 2000: 4–5).

The connections made by Freeman between clothing and the construction of women's work identities will be taken up again later when looking at sartorial strategies, cultural consumption and the growing class of professional women workers. However, 'pinking', as originally fashioned by Howe (1977), was used to signify a feminization of certain professions growing out of the pre-existing categories of 'blue collar' and 'white collar'. The 'pinking' of professions indicates an increasing number of professionals needed to perform labour that is deemed unskilled or 'natural' (Elson and Pearson 1981b), such as the ability to 'smile down the phone' (Richardson and Marshall 1996), contributing to a gender divide which sees women employed on the 'front lines' (Kinnie et al. 2000a, 2000b) and men in more managerial positions.

When asked about the higher proportion of women employed on call processes, some of the interviewees at NCall replied that it was due to women's 'natural' ability to remain calm and diplomatic during a heated conversation with a customer, echoing earlier arguments made by feminists regarding differences in men and women's verbal interaction (Poynton 1993). Amrit, Sonali and Monica suggested it was actually advantageous to be a woman for these same reasons:

> People react easily to women. They are really patient to listen to a girl or a lady than to a male, I think; it's easier to build a conversation. They always have a soft corner for women, I think. So it's good to be that. You don't face such problems that males face while calling or building up a rapport.
>
> (Amrit, 23, NCall)

> I think nowadays that people basically think that call centres are meant for women. In marketing, everybody wants to buy what a woman is selling. They think that women are better to convince a person to buy products. The general thinking of people is that call centres are meant for women. Because they are more calm, patient. For example, maybe they are ready to talk to a customer for half an hour, maybe more than that, and they don't get annoyed, don't get finicky about it, don't get angry if the customer is asking you a hundred questions. Whereas with men, they are not that patient compared to women.
>
> (Sonali, 22, NCall)

> Maybe there are more women because call centres are not that great paymasters. It's like your monthly expenditure you can earn but you can't save much from it. A man is expected to do better work where you can earn more and save more.
>
> (Monica, 22, NCall)

All three of these women work on the same process of outbound calls at NCall. They are all in their early twenties. Sonali spoke of short-term career plans that would allow her to earn good money in a short period so that she could contribute financially to her wedding plans. Amrit is one of four daughters who contributes to her family's income, as her father is ill, and is expected to contribute to her dowry, as she told me they had no brothers to support them. Sonali had not informed her parents that she had left her old job at a family friend's business to work in the call centre and Monica had missed out on a job with an airline due to being overweight. Like many of the middle-class women working in call centres, Monica is from a civil service background and her parents worked in steady, government related positions with an average income. As a result of her upbringing, Monica and her sister had a great desire for more exciting lifestyles with a higher income. Monica's parents have encouraged her to lose weight and work for an airline as her sister has done, but her intention is to stay at the call centre, working her way towards becoming a manager. Their observations, though shared individually during interviews, tell an interesting story as they formed their analyses. Initially, they surmised that women were good at pacifying customers and selling products, but having probed more deeply they looked at the gender imbalance from another angle. They suspected, as Elson and Pearson (1981a) once argued, that women do not enter the labour market as bearers of inferior labour; they enter as predetermined inferior bearers of labour (Phillips and Taylor 1980).

This is an important observation as it highlights the understanding that call centre work is viewed as a short-term career move for women and that promotions are mainly for men. Patriarchal understandings of women and work in India place women's contributions to household incomes second to men's contributions; as such, it is not as necessary for them to pursue long-term career opportunities. Gayatri, a call centre consultant, agrees with this understanding of women and work in India and points out that higher numbers of women are employed on the 'front lines' and few are promoted to managerial positions. However, she points out that this is because women are reluctant to stay in call centre work for longer than a few years:

> See, the moment they start having their babies and stuff, they don't want to be working. They are married, and they want to be home with their husbands at night. The cultural situation means that there may not be enough appropriately qualified women for the [managerial] job and there are social obligations. A husband calls up, and his wife says, 'Sorry, darling, I'm at work.' He says, 'I have a business dinner I need you to attend,' or 'The in-laws are over,' which is one of the reasons I quit working at night. It might be one of the reasons there are not women in top positions. I know GE has a few directors that are women. It is not an issue from an employer's perspective because I get calls all the time. It's an issue from society's perspective.
>
> (Gayatri, Call Centre Consultant and Manager)

Monica and Gayatri point towards two possible explanations for the gendering of Indian call centre work: first, that it is seen as a job with low career potential and, second, that social expectations of women tend to overpower their opportunities for work, that women constrain themselves by adhering to family and cultural expectations. Ritu, an employee at GCall, suggests that short-term career prospects are not as restrictive for women as some might believe, in that call centres readily offer women career breaks and opportunities to return to work after marriage:

> Fewer men want to make their careers in the call centre. They don't see a very bright future because, for them, they have to earn a lot of money, and get married and look after a family and they don't see that happening on a call centre wage. Whereas, for a woman, she can get married and still work in the call centre. That's probably why there is a higher percentage of women in the call centre.
>
> (Ritu, 23, GCall)

The understanding that call centre work is an occupation that women can move into after marriage and children is a rather pervasive one, a notion reflected by recruitment advertisements directed towards housewives. Ritu's commitment to call centre work as a possible career for women is under-scored by the fact that her own education was cut short when she returned home to support her parents. Ritu was completing her degree in Ahemdebad studying Hotel Management when her father was forced into early retirement from military service due the terrorist attacks in the US on 11 September 2001. Although Ritu has one male sibling, she felt that it was her obligation to return to Guragon to support her parents, so she accepted a job in a call centre. She has hopes of getting married and starting a family but is also aware that she will most likely need to continue to work as both she and her brother will need to support their parents during retirement.

A second dimension to discussions of the 'pinking' of the Indian call centre profession is one which echoes early feminist arguments that skill definition is saturated with sexual bias (Phillips and Taylor 1980). As discussed earlier in the book (pp. 39–40), call centres in India offer a range of services, from more simplified customer service operations to technical helplines. As Ian, a soft skills consultant, observed, call centre work in India is viewed by those in the West as a 'crap job', a perception that is produced by media reports based on discussions from the UK. Sunita, a 23-year-old electronics engineer, was initially opposed to working in a call centre, believing that it was performed by 'stupid undergrad jerks who just work there for money'. However, due to financial reasons and lack of employment opportunities in her field, she began working at DelCall. Agreeing with Gayatri that women have good chances for promotion if they choose to prioritize work over family, she states:

> Women actually have more chances to be promoted [at DelCall] because those are the people that stick around; they can take the stress. Many usually get very irritated in the end because they can't handle stress. Both

of my trainers were women, technical, and voice and accent. And the head of operations is a woman. Most of the people in the management team are women. But the number of guys to girls in my training class was quite bad. It's twenty guys for five girls. On average on the floor, you will see 70 per cent boys, 30 per cent girls.

(Sunita, 23, DelCall)

One explanation for the lack of women on the floor and the higher proportion of women in management is that Sunita works in a process for which electronics engineers were specifically recruited, thus a higher percentage of men were qualified for the work. However, the field of engineering has fewer women overall, therefore one could conclude that women were unsuccessful as applicants for more qualified positions and were therefore more likely to succeed in call centres. Moreover, the success of women in moving up the ladder at DelCall may be due to the career orientation of the women initially recruited for agent positions; perhaps women are more likely to succeed in call centres for which a higher degree of education and skill is required because they started out with greater ambitions. Upon finishing her degree, Sunita returned to Delhi from Pune where she was studying and was unsuccessful in finding a job in her field. The tenuous connection to electronics engineering that this particular process has, and the lack of jobs in the field, led to her working in DelCall as an agent dealing with inbound calls for a major computer manufacturer helpline.

This distinction between the types of call centres and call centre work is crucial to an analysis of women's participation in the labour process, in that not all call centres are the same, thus not all women who work in call centres will share the same skill level or opportunity for advancement. Returning to Phillips and Taylor (1980), skill definition is saturated with 'sexual bias' and women's work is defined as 'unskilled' simply because women do it. Although Sunita did not view the work that she was doing as unskilled, she did see call centre work, a profession with rising numbers of women, as unskilled work. The observation that call centre work is increasingly defined as unskilled, short-term work with little or no career potential, particularly for men, holds true even for a call centre with women in top level positions, because those women may have started with higher career ambitions and competition with men for those positions may be low. The knowledge that women can achieve top level positions in some call centres is not testimony enough that call centre work environments support women's long-term career objectives. Thus call centre work in India remains in line with other studies in that it can be seen as becoming downgraded or defined as unskilled.

Labour processes that require greater focus on sales or customer services, such as those at NCall, show a higher proportion of women employees. However, those which are concentrated in more technological areas, such as Sunita's, show a higher percentage of male employees. The classification of call centre work as unskilled work, or work requiring low skill levels, connects to the perception that women are 'naturally' more inclined to perform call centre work. As demand for call centre workers with better soft skills increases, the profile of the call centre worker is changing and, as with patterns in the UK, a belief that women are better suited to call centre work than men is emerging. As Ian, a soft skills trainer, notes:

> I think women initially have better people skills than guys as they grow up. I think they are more comfortable communicating. It may be innate skills such as nurturing, a genetic make-up, so it comes easier. It doesn't mean it's exclusive but it comes easier so that the innate skills come through. A difficult customer comes up and you genetically have different skills to deal with it, as a woman rather than a guy. It's socialized and genetic. It's enhanced by your mother, because she is doing multiple roles, taking care of this, that, the other. You're kind of nurtured and guided into different roles.
>
> (Ian, Soft Skills Consultant)

The belief that women 'naturally' convey certain emotions such as empathy has led to a belittling of the difficulty in performing emotional labour (Hochschild 1983). Moreover, the perception that Indian women naturally juggle various roles and responsibilities has been previously identified by Mies (1979) as a common fixed assumption.

Performing emotional labour

As Elson and Pearson (1981b) have argued, the 'nimble fingers' of women factory workers are not an inheritance from their mothers, but are in fact the result of training from mothers and other female relatives. Some decades ago, Mies (1979), writing about the education of women, observed a certain amount of role juggling and performance in balancing a woman's personal desires with social expectations, and noted that women learned from their mothers how to suppress and exert certain emotions to help 'perform' these various roles. Evidence of women as 'jugglers' (Bolton 2000), 'cultural navigators' (Ballard 1994) or 'cultural commuters' (Das 2000: 13) exists in the variety of roles that women play when performing call centre work. While creating and suppressing their own emotions, women create specific identities for specific tasks, which could include the happy salesperson, the productive employee and the disgruntled co-worker, while still leaving room for others to exist. The simultaneous existence of these 'characters' is, in part, due to the spaces created by the nature of call centre work, or 'time–space distanciation' (Giddens 1991: 192), whereby the spaces between the customer, agent and the remote or electronic observation of the agent by a supervisor create the gaps needed for the 'juggling' (Bolton 2000) of emotional labour.

Ritu, working at GCall and supporting her retired parents, offers her insights on why women are better at emotional labour, arguing that women are better suited to call centre work and thus in high demand by employers:

I feel that women are emotionally stronger than men. So they would listen, and assimilate exactly to what this guy [customer] wants. And it is very difficult to find a man who can put himself in the other person's shoes and find out exactly where that person stands, whereas for a woman it is easier to do that. It's because they have so many roles to play. To begin with, a daughter, then a sister, and then go on to become a mother, a wife and a grandmother, an aunt. Probably men do as well, but for them emotional involvement is not so much as it is for women. Possibly, women are more fit for being an agent. I believe that when they are going to hire, they don't think, 'I'm going to hire this many amount of girls or boys.' They will just see that [women] are more apt for this kind of a job.

(Ritu, 23, GCall)

The belief that women are more empathic and can relate to others in a way that men cannot is commonly held one – more so in this case as Ritu left her college education incomplete to return home and look after her parents. In most Indian contexts, responsibility for the parents falls to the sons. However, in this case, Ritu's brother is also attending university and his education would be considered of greater importance than Ritu's. Although Ritu believes that she will most likely have some type of employment throughout her life, her parents would not rely on her wages to support them and would view this arrangement as temporary as soon enough she will be married and contributing to her in-laws' and husband's home as opposed to that of her parents.

The 'social invisibility' (Elson and Pearson 1981b: 151) of these skills is intentional and part of the patriarchal process that perpetuates women's subordination, and as such it is assumed that women are 'naturally' better at emotional labour than men. However, as Gayatri, a call centre consultant, explains, although women are perceived to be better at call centre work, the need for employees sometimes outweighs the need for 'naturally' skilled people:

GAYATRI: There is really no preference for men or women, because really we just need people who speak English and are computer literate. We can't afford to be that picky. Men tend to be more aggressive and women tend to be more patient. But we have many different processes in the call centre. We have inbound calls, outbound calls, telemarketing, they are not always high-end issues. We just tell the guys to be a little more careful. We wouldn't select women over men for any area of work, though we know women are better. We know it. We cannot afford to do it because the pool is very small. We don't have that option; we just need to fill seats. That takes priority over man versus woman.

INTERVIEWER: Do you see that changing in the future?

GAYATRI: In India? Not really, because of night work. The time factor is important and the call volumes are huge so we cannot afford to differentiate. It's a training issue really; we just tell them if the customer is screaming at you we don't scream back at them. Also, men have more of a gift of the gab and more confidence. So I think telemarketing is split 50:50.

(Gayatri, Call Centre Consultant)

Although she suggests women are better suited to call centre work than men, Gayatri's concluding comments highlight again the different call centres and labour processes found in India, suggesting that women, although possibly better at performing emotional labour, may not necessarily be better at all types of call centre work, particularly those requiring greater confidence or aggressive selling techniques.

In spite of the observations above, some of the interviewees felt that being a woman was disadvantageous in call centre work.[3] Urmila and Upasana, both agents at NCall, demonstrate skill in employing 'dramaturgical improvisational choreography' (Whelan et al. 2002) in acquiring 'emotional dissonance' (Zapf et al. 2003) from customers:

Basically I come across weird customers; they flirt with me on the phone. You have to handle every situation well; you have to be frank enough and bold enough. Those are the kind of ladies that work there. If you were reserved, you couldn't do it. They are very, very complicated customers.

(Urmila, 21, NCall)

Actually we get a lot of proposals from men over the phone from Western countries. They often ask if we are single, give me your phone number, can we contact you, and things like that. So I just tell them I am married.

(Upasana, 28, NCall)

Reena, who had only just joined GCall, had been on the call centre floor for four weeks. She was working on an inbound process with calls from UK customers. Her training had lasted several weeks and was largely focussed on skill in juggling emotions and achieving 'emotional dissonance', suggesting an empathetic approach using 'prescriptive acting', which can be defined as emotional labour as prescribed by the company:

REENA: You have to keep in your mind that he is not talking to you, he is not irate with you, he is irate with the organization that you represent. He or she is not abusing you; they are abusing the company. If you take it personally it becomes very difficult. You have to keep this in mind. Second, you have to think about where this person is coming from. Why is this person so irate? There must be a reason, otherwise this person would not be irate. No one likes to get irate. If you can understand why this person is getting irate, then the abuses will not matter so much to you.

INTERVIEWER: Then what do you do with your own emotions?

REENA: I control them. I am a customer service person over here and I have to please this person. I have to get this guy what he is looking for. But sometimes it gets on your nerves as well. I'm not so cool a person. But I usually keep a cool head.

(Reena, 23, GCall)

Call centre employees are encouraged to consider themselves as representative of the company as opposed to individuals, connecting corporate culture to their own emotions, impacting upon the way in which they can perform emotional labour. As Ian, a soft skills consultant, suggests, employees can either use 'surface acting' or 'deep acting' (Hochschild 1983) to make a call successful:

Well, it comes down to sincerity, and sincerity is very hard to come up with. So you have two options: one is that you're naturally sincere and two is that you have it so drummed into you, you start believing it yourself – and you are sincere through that way. They've done it very well; corporate culture is excellent in terms of doing that.

(Ian, Soft Skills Consultant)

Soft skills and customer call quality are essential elements of call centre work. Call centres spend a range of time from three days to six weeks on quality training, and as Sunita, working on an inbound technical support line for a US computer company, notes, soft skills are as important as technical knowledge:

From seven to twelve we have technical training, and from twelve to three it's voice and accent. If you can't pass the voice and accent, you will be transferred to another process or retrained, so it is equally important.

(Sunita, 23, DelCall)

Discussions with call centre managers and trainers indicated that companies were more likely to hire individuals who were already in possession of many of the soft skills that they were looking for, similar to trends in European call centres (Thompson et al. 2004).

Emotional labour, however, is not restricted to simply managing emotions while taking inbound calls, as it has become increasingly significant in a larger understanding of global customer service. As Ian points out, agents are encouraged to leave their own identities and needs behind to serve the '360 degree customer' (Deery et al. 2002), and performance is directly measured by customer satisfaction, which sharply affects the performance of emotional labour. Customer service is paramount in the increasingly globalized India, as Anyuta points out. An IT technician who had previously worked in the United States, Anyuta returned only after 11 September 2001, when jobs became much more scarce for Indians in the US:

In India the reason why a customer doesn't get due concentration is because there are so many of us. The local guy in a shop would say, 'Fine, if you don't want it, don't take it. Somebody else will come and take it.' But in the States or anywhere else abroad people do respect the client and are insecure about business. I am surprised at the way NCall is so sensitive about the customer. We have big posters everywhere, saying 'Customers, we care about them', 'The customer is always right', be sensitive, be positive, appreciative, be apologetic, listen. The way it's been grilled into us here, it's amazing. So, India is learning a lot, especially about customers. We are coming into the global market now.

(Anyuta, 26, NCall)

The rising visibility of corporate culture and India's engagement with a global market have placed greater importance on the need for good customer service and client satisfaction. An examination of emotional labour, whilst providing an excellent starting point for analyzing women's participation in the call centre labour process in India, also extends to an examination of the importance of good customer service in the liberalized Indian economy, distinguishing Indian call centre studies from those outside India. The increased need for emotional labour, 'emotional dissonance' (Zapf et al. 2003) and the enhanced power of the '360 degree customer' (Deery et al. 2002) represent a gendered element to the labour process but also point to cultural shifts in India. Similarly, the 'Panopticon' metaphor, hotly debated in UK call centre studies, provides a powerful tool for the examination of Indian call centres, but also the way in which these call centres figure in an evolving Indian social context.

The 'Panopticon': surveillance and control

Issues regarding surveillance and control were equally important to employees in India and employees interviewed in UK call centre labour studies. However, a significant difference was found, in that the criticisms Indian employees had were of the managers themselves as opposed to managerial controls. Whereas other studies showed significant dissatisfaction with the way in which employee performance was technologically monitored through the ACD system, over half of the Indian interviewees in the sample group expressed greater concern regarding the way in which managers utilized their authority over agents than regarding the way in which they used the technology. Smita, who is older than the majority of call centre workers as well as being married, worked in advertising for many years before working abroad and returning to India when her baby was born. Smita was one of the fiercer critics of the call centre management style:

I have worked in two other places before this, and I worked all through my student life, and I have never seen a place like the way this place works. I was told all call centres work like this. I think it sucks. I think the way they handle people here, the way they get them to do work, the way they deal with people – it's like being in school again. They say things like, 'Cut your nails, your nails are too long.' You can't get up, you can't sit down, you can't answer your phone, you can't get out of your seat, you can't talk. I mean, there are rules and rules from the management. I think it's a very foolish way of getting work done. I don't agree with it. That's how I feel about the management here. They are getting their work done in a very stupid way. It's like a factory. I agree that most of the people working here are young, so maybe they need to be controlled. But if you take away their cell phones, and lock them in a cupboard and tell them that you will only get to see them for fifteen minutes – that's ridiculous, you can explain, you can reprimand, but you can't tie somebody to their seat and say, 'Work!'

(Smita, 33, NCall)

As her parents are both professors, Smita grew up in many places in India as well as Africa and has a rather independent nature. Moreover, at 33 there is a significant age difference between herself and the majority of agents at NCall. Smita often shared her opinions with those around her in a very frank manner and was not afraid of letting her team leader know that she was unhappy with certain methods of management. Smita's main concern was the way in which other young women were, as she saw it, bullied rather than managed by the team leaders. During the many conversations I had with Smita, it was clear that she was prepared to take a stand against any sort of aggression. She shared stories of her experience of racism in Africa and France, not necessarily directed at her but scenes that she had witnessed, and it did not surprise me that Smita was willing to point out what she considered to be unprofessional muscle-flexing by those in authority. Others made comments similar to Smita's, suggesting that staff were treated like 'babies' in 'school', supporting her arguments that despite the high wages and the sleek work sites, the management staff had much to improve upon.

Nidhi, another employee from NCall, stated that she would prefer managers to use a 'computer gaze' (Ng Choon Sim 1999) for managerial control or a technological method of surveillance and control as opposed to personal subjective methods of employee assessment:

If I have a problem with the transport in the company, then of course my manager can look into the matter. But if I have a problem with my work, if I want to switch my process, then it is up to the manager. He can throw me out of my job. He can keep telling me lies. His motive might be just to keep me in the process because he hates me. He can have his personal reasons. In my last company, my team leader, a woman, was a bit crazy and was jealous of me and any girl in my team. She wouldn't even allow me to chew chewing gum, just to have control over me. When I decided to go to higher management, HR was shown a bad report about me so I was out of a job.

(Nidhi, 22, NCall)

Such comments show that amongst the women call centre workers it did not matter if the team leaders were men or women as both genders exercised degrees of partiality when managing their teams. Nearly every single person connected with this research discussed favouritism, partiality and corruption at some point during conversations or interviews; however, they did not feel that this was limited to call centres and that it was a problem intrinsic to Indian culture. Moreover, they argued that such prejudice was less common in call centres because of the electronic surveillance as well as the pseudo-Western work environment.[4] Again, Smita discusses the hierarchical workplace culture found in so many environments in India, expressing her frustration at the lack of professionalism:

Here, there are three women who are team leaders. They became team leaders within the company. They grew to that position. But I don't know, because I heard that to become a team leader you have to suck up to people and lick ass, and that kind of stuff.

(Smita, 33, NCall)

The importing of 'Western' practices and labour processes has garnered much negative media and academic attention, but when speaking to call centre staff, many were encouraged by the imported labour structure and practices. Over half of the respondents stated that the importing of Euro-American management strategies of creating an informal environment and transparency amongst management and employees provided them with a feeling of trust and confidence:

It was my first job. I liked all the transparency, you know, like American companies, where you call all your bosses by their first name. We would want to address them as Sir or Ma'am, but they would say, 'No, call me by my name.' And if you feel that your team leader is being biased or showing partiality or favouritism, then we have a skip level meeting, where you can skip your immediate leader and go to your boss's boss. It's a very open and transparent environment where you are given the right to speak, and things are done effectively. It's not seen as a female speaking or a male speaking. You are just heard as an employee.

(Preetika, 24, GCallB)

Everybody is pretty comfortable with everyone, professional and friendly. Yeah, the concept here in India is that, whoever is your boss, you should call them Sir or Madam. So when these call centres came, it was quite a Westernized culture, where you don't have to call your boss Sir or Madam.

You use their first names. That was something that made people feel very comfortable, like you were on a par.

(Rashi, 25, GCall)

What we had like in the government office like Sirs and Ma'ams, it's not like that here. You just call them by their first name and it's very nice and friendly. They're very approachable.

(Chanelle, 25, NCall)

In a call centre, everyone is on a first name basis. You can walk into your CEO's office you can call him by his first name.

(Sunita, 23, DelCall)

Preetika, Rashi, Chanelle and Sunita are all recent graduates and it would be fair to say that call centres provided their first real places of employment. Their surprise at such transparent hierarchies arises from the comparison of their experiences with the experiences of their friends and families, demonstrating both a cultural and generational transition in work practices and labour processes.

The levels of informality and transparent hierarchies were some of the reasons that the women gave when asked why call centres were such good places to work. In the first instance, the casual manner with which people relate to one another is seen as somewhat novel, but it is the transparency of hierarchy that the women are most impressed by. Given that most, if not all, of them will have experienced discrimination at work at some point, the opportunity to challenge managerial controls comes as a revelation. However, this informality could also be read differently, in that such a friendly approach to employment can lead to exploitation of the employees, creating a climate for control. A study of garment workers in India found that smaller workplaces promoted familial relations in order to deter employees from seeing the exploitative nature of the work (Banerjee 1991), arguing that the workers felt they did not need a workers' organization because 'auntyji is so good'. An example of this was that after four hours of overtime the workers were rewarded by a cup of tea that cost 1 rupee as opposed to overtime pay, which would cost the company 10 rupees. Similarly, none of the call centre workers were ever paid overtime, a source of frustration for some of them given the knowledge that their UK counterparts or others outside of India were receiving extra pay for extra work:

See, the only thing that I would like to tell you is in the UK, if you are getting overtime you will get paid for it, but here we have been doing overtime since we joined and we have not received a single penny for it. So, would anyone be interested in doing something for nothing? No. So why should I? I will do what I am getting paid for.

(Sangamitra, 25, GCall)

Sangamitra experienced a number of issues at GCall over her first few years. In particular she was put under significant pressure by her mother to return to Calcutta to get married. Her mother had taken to contacting her team leader and, as a consequence, Sangamitra believed that he held a grudge against her and had prevented her from gaining a promotion. She decided to work significant overtime and took on tasks for other team leaders and managers outside her process. Sangamitra would arrive at GCall by 10 a.m. every day regardless of what time her shift actually started, and on some days she would actually be at work from that time until 4 a.m.

Incentives came in the form of vouchers, passes to movies, CDs, sometimes TVs, but more often than not they were cash bonuses, as Indu describes here:

> You get a hell of a lot of perks. We can get a monthly bonus of 3,000 rupees. And we also get all sorts of vouchers. Last year, during the Divali bonanza, you could earn 50,000–60,000 rupees per month for your team. The bonus everybody gets every year in March. The incentives are more like TVs, CDs, – you name it. Perform, and take it home.
>
> (Indu, 26, NCallB)

Bonuses were also given for things like attendance, as Gayatri, a call centre manager, explains: 'if you work for the thirty days a month we will pay you extra'. The informality, transparent management structure, employee incentives and bonuses can all be read as extremely rewarding aspects of call centre work, as well as mechanisms of control.

A second dimension to the discussion of surveillance is that the practice of controlling employees through electronic monitoring was simply not a significant issue for Indian employees, in stark contrast to many of the call centre studies that had been conducted outside India. One explanation for this is that most Indian women's everyday experiences are monitored or under surveillance, and negotiated through patriarchal controls. Call centres, enforcing measures of safety and protection for practical reasons, also reinforce the notions that women are vulnerable and must be secluded, as evidenced by Sunita and Preetika's comments on call centre transport:

> [DelCall] has a guard from nine at night until five in the morning. You are not allowed to board the cab if there is no guard.
>
> (Sunita, 23, DelCall)

> The way these multinats work, is that they order these cabs for you. They organize it in such a way that if there are men and women in the cab, then the guy will get dropped off last, so that there are no women alone in the cab. Men do not require the guards with them. Things like this, safety measures, they show their concern like this.
>
> (Preetika, 24, GCallB)

Sunita and Preetika are both university educated, and from upper-middle-class families. For them, safety issues were paramount and both chose call centres with excellent transport services and daytime or evening shifts as opposed to night shifts. This was also due, in part, to the fact that Sunita had a boyfriend and Preetika was engaged, both to young men from respectable families, and thus needed to consider the opinions of their future in-laws.

Like Sunita and Preetika, nearly 85 per cent of the sample group cited the organized transport, twenty-four-hour guards and secure facilities as major reasons for choosing call centre work. The 'Panopticon'-like controls and the sense that somebody is always watching are not new ideas. First, they are a necessity in urban centres such as Delhi, where the number of violent crimes against women is high; second, they are an accepted element of Indian society – the sheer size of the population ensures that you are never alone and always watched.

Despite the acceptance of surveillance controls by most of the interviewees, there was evidence of resistance in the call centres. Though specifically asked about employee–management relations, call centre employees did not discuss the desire or need for unions, relying more on informal networks and ways of resisting management strategies and work practices.[5] Agents often left their seats for up to half an hour to ask questions of team leaders or various trainers, stating that it was in an effort to provide good customer service when in actuality it would be a way in which they could legitimately log out of the ACD system.[6] Coffee and dinner breaks were staggered, with employees taking their breaks together as a team but at different times to other teams, thereby creating more opportunities for them to leave their seats and meet co-workers on different teams for a coffee or cigarette, generally using the opportunity to chat to one to another. Other forms of resistance to the tight call-timing controls were observed when agents interacted with customers online. Calls were dragged out as conversations about India, the weather or cricket took place. Agents were easily able to place responsibility on the customer for these conversations, citing difficulty in ending the conversation.

Taylor and Bain's (2005) observations showed patterns of resistance where agents were engaged in giving customers a 'talla' or hoax solution to a problem (in the form of asking customers to call back, giving customers the wrong answer or telling customers that they did not know the answer). Although resistance was evident amongst the findings of this research project, there was little to suggest that this came in the form of 'talla' or hoax solutions. One-third of the interviewees did express a desire to prolong conversations and learn as much about other cultures as possible, but during the course of my fieldwork I did not come across any examples of hoaxes.

Also evident were informal networks of resistance, or what Korczynski (2003) has called 'communities of coping', as women 'warned' one another of particular employees or team leaders. These warnings were generally passed amongst women, and were of a social nature or in the form of gossip and were based on incidents occurring at workplace social events, outings and trips organized by the company.[7] Of particular interest was the number of times, both formally and informally, that call centre agents took issue with the growing lack of non-vegetarian food in the dining areas. Collectively they complained to management about the lack of non-vegetarian food, though the commonly held perception was that management would only provide non-vegetarian food on national holidays such as Republic Day or Divali because of costs, whether this was in fact true or not. Employees asking for non-vegetarian or special foods did not do so for religious reasons, and complaints about lack of non-vegetarian food were made by employees of all religious backgrounds. NCall's and GCall's responses to these changes were that many Hindus, who by religion were vegetarian, complained of having non-vegetarian and vegetarian food served side by side and the company's response was to limit or remove the non-vegetarian food.[8] The reasons for scaling back the variety of food on offer were never made clear; however, it is quite likely that as the call centres expanded and hired greater numbers of employees, cost savings needed to be made in other areas. What is of greater interest than the changes to the menu is the meanings and explanations offered by the call centre agents, not the management.

The 'misrecognition' (Bourdieu 1984) of scaling back food costs as respect for Hindu religious beliefs masks the underlying 'soft Hindutva' (Rajgopal 1999) or Hindu Right ideology found in Indian workplaces. From observations at NCall and discussions with research participants, it was clear that halal meat was not provided for religious Muslims and egg or dairy free meal options were not provided for religious Sikhs, exercising a 'violence' upon social agents in which they were complicit, one which maintains a strong Hindu ideology. This misrecognition also provided another example or form of 'Sanskritization', as the overt practice of upward caste mobility includes the forsaking of meat and liquor (Mazumdar 1994: 250). The misrecognition of 'soft Hindutva' conflicts with the perception that India has embraced more liberal, global ideologies, as presented by the image on the cover of *India Today* discussed in Chapter 1 (see Figure 1.1). As the call centre profession is open to anyone with a degree and good English-language skills, regardless of religion or caste, lack of access to university would in itself act as a barrier to employment for many. Thus, those who are engaged in call centre employment are predominantly from a middle-class background, demonstrating no strong religious identities. With the widening middle class and the greater emphasis on socio-economic status, identities based on caste, class and religion are increasingly losing significance in the more metropolitan areas in favour of identities based on socio-economic status (Parker-Talwar 2004). Thus the argument for religious sensitivity put forward by management at NCall and GCall appeared weak in its justification to limit or remove non-vegetarian food.

The use of the 'Panopticon' in examining Indian call centres is markedly different from that of European call centre studies in that managerial controls resembled more of a school-like atmosphere and issues regarding surveillance were seemingly less significant for Indian employees. Interviewees indicated that they would prefer greater use of technological surveillance as opposed to more subjective methods of assessing employee performance, leaving less room for corruption or partiality. In essence, if the women were performing well their call targets and quality measures would be high and, as such, they could not be held back or denied promotion, effectively building more trust in the call centre work environment specifically because of the technological process. However, a second dimension of the surveillance measures is found in the necessity for protective measures and safety controls for women. Safe transport and secure premises may help to dilute the sense of surveillance and control simultaneously, though these measures also reinforce cultural understandings regarding women's needs for seclusion. In response to surveillance, there was little resistance resembling the strategies indicated in British call centre reports, and Indian employees were generally in favour of the transparent Western structures of call centres imported to India. The emergence of informal networks of resistance or 'communities of coping' (Korczynski 2003) to deal with managerial issues, as opposed to building formal networks or forming unions, was in keeping with the perceived informality of management practices and demonstrated an overall trust and confidence in the call centre power structure as a whole.

Attitudes to call centre work

Women's successes with gaining promotions at work were contingent upon their perceived attitudes and motives for working in the call centre. The interviewees represented a range of attitudes, impacted by social and cultural factors and biological reasons, for why women were able to show certain levels of commitment to the job. These ranged from those who viewed call centre work as an extension of college life, through those who viewed it as a career opportunity through which they could gain specific skills or earn quick cash, and those who viewed it as a serious profession, to those who saw it as a way to get out of the house and gain some sense of independence. These views were influenced by social and cultural perceptions of working women, commitments to contribute to household incomes, and biological factors relating to motherhood and other health reasons.

Over half of the interviewees cited high wages as the first reason for working in a call centre and free transport as the second reason. Other interviewees presented a range of reasons for working in call centres, from lack of employment in other sectors (engineering and IT) to lack of suitable job prospects reflecting their education in their home town. Many found work in call centres to be flexible and accommodating:

> No other industry gives you such a good start, I think. It's the best paying industry and, that too, you are getting free transport, you're getting free meals over here. And you are getting your teas and coffees free and I think

no other industry will provide you with such things while working. That's the added advantage we are having. You can save a lot while working.

(Amrit, 23, NCall)

The call centre works out to be quite a good job with these two facilities of food and transport. It makes it a very attractive offer. Being in India, especially in Delhi, transport is the main problem. So that's one main thing which really makes you think that, yes, my transport problem is solved.

(Jennifer, 38, NCall)

As Smita pointed out in the opening quotations of this chapter, transportation issues plague women when making decisions about work. The lack of suitable transport for women travelling on their own, or the high cost of daily taxis and rickshaws, acts as a determining factor in career choices. Amrit and Jennifer both work out of economic necessity as neither is married, and they don't have brothers to support their retired parents, so the opportunity to work in a well paid industry and avoid the daily stress and expense of commuting is a welcome relief and allows them to focus on the job with greater attention. The high wages and free transport factor into the attitudes that many women have towards performing call centre work, in that many had taken up the employment for these reasons without seriously considering a long-term career there. Moreover, all of the women were in education or educated to at least degree level, with 22 per cent of the group educated at master's level, and, as such, many women took up call centre employment as a stepping-stone to other work or saw it as something to do as a short-term career, before or after marriage. The data for this research showed that fewer than one-fifth of the interviewees viewed call centre work as a long-term career, with more than 80 per cent viewing it as either short-term employment or casual employment with good opportunity for career breaks:

For living an independent life, the call centres are paying a pretty good amount to lead a decent life for a woman who is alone. That is basically how the call centres are attracting people because of the package they pay, and the atmos[phere] that you get. You get AC [air-conditioning] and all. You get food and everything. What else do you want?

(Pooja, 28, NCall)

I think it's 50:50 ratio: 50 per cent of women are working because they just want to work, they want to do something, and 50 per cent of women are working maybe because they're married, and they want to help their families financially. They just want to earn some money so that they can spend it on themselves. Just some pocket money. It's better than wasting your time. Instead of asking your parents for 10,000 every month it's better that you earn your own money, and be independent.

(Monica, 22, NCall)

Monica, whose parents are both colonels in the army, originally applied for a position with an airline, as her sister had done before her. Unsuccessful at that, Monica had remade her career plans and had settled into working towards a promotion at NCall. Monica's parents encouraged her and her sister to become career women, as their mother was, hence long-term career plans were always a part of the future, and financial independence from their parents, and possibly their husbands in the future, was not something that they had questioned. Like Monica, Nidhi also worked at NCall to gain some independence from her parents and earn her own 'pocket money':

> After I completed my graduation I didn't want to do a Master's in Computer Science. I wanted to do a Mass Communications degree but my father wouldn't let me and I had to compromise to hold him back from getting me married. So I continued with my master's in computers and since I was pursuing it by correspondence I had a lot of time, so I decided to join the call centre industry. I wanted to get exposure to the global market, the corporate world, and earn a bit of money. It was important to me to get out of the house.
>
> (Nidhi, 22, NCall)

Unlike Monica, Nidhi's parents were less encouraging of a career, viewing her education and work experience as adding to her 'marriageability'. Nidhi saw call centres as a way to get out of the house and justified this by laying claim to experiencing the global labour market. Urmila, a trained yoga instructor from Rishikesh, India's yoga capital, joined call centres exactly for this reason, needing exposure to a market that would educate her about her future clientele, namely toursists:

> I wanted to communicate with the customers globally. Basically, I wanted to know about their thoughts, their etiquette, their way of speaking. I just wanted to know about them. I needed independence from my family and to understand more than what was available back home.
>
> (Urmila, 21, NCall)

The majority of women working in call centres looked at it as a short-term career move to make money, gain specific skills or increase their exposure to the global market. Thus the most pervasive attitude to work was one of casualness, akin to an extension of college life, as Smita's suggests:

> It's cool. It's like college here. Everybody is just having a good time. There is a lot of flirting happening, but then I guess everybody's young so … It's not like any other corporate sector where you would find a little bit of professionalism, along with that. The friendships here are much more shallow because people are not going to hang around for long. Everyone is 'Let's have a coffee together', 'Let's go for a smoke', like

college. You're here for today, don't know about tomorrow. It's like an air-conditioned college, except you're getting paid.

(Smita, 33, NCall)

Smita was not the only interviewee to comment on the sexually liberalized, male–female integrated work environment as an arena to meet men. Many women had hopes of finding a marriage partner, thereby avoiding an arranged marriage. As Nidhi told me, 'most of the women in the call centre are looking for relationships with people they want to marry'.[9] Drawing on her experiences as a manager in varying multinational corporations, Gayatri describes the transient, freewheeling nature of call centre work much in the same way as the popular media reports in British newspapers:

So you are young, your food is paid for, your transport is paid for, and you are earning 20,000 rupees a month, and you throw in some incentives. If you are a halfway decent worker, you can get movie tickets, and maybe a dinner for two – so, fine, life is a party. Plus, you met your boyfriend, plus you have a whole bunch of friends, you all work at night, you are all dead to the world during the day, and the days you have off you go party, get drunk, and have a really good time. They are all the same age at that level, so there is a huge amount of dating happening. At night when you walk in the car park you have to get them apart: 'Get up to the office and you're not supposed to be necking over here.' And they come and go in groups. 'I quit.' 'Why?' 'Because my boyfriend quit' or 'My best friend has left here she is going to another company, so I'm going as well.'

(Gayatri, Call Centre Consultant)

However, unlike the media reports and academic studies that suggest such attitudes are a consequence of the imported Western ideals and values, Gayatri suggests that this casual attitude to work is as much a consequence of the rise in call centre jobs and high demand for employees:

They are all studying for their MBAs or other things, and they now have money to buy pretty clothes and take their friends out for drinks. They know today if they don't come to work and they lose their job, tomorrow there will be a big ad in the paper for another one.

(Gayatri, Call Centre Consultant)

When asked, Gayatri argued against the perception that staff in call centres were exploited, and instead pointed out several times during the interview that the Indian call centre industry had in fact been 'exploited' by the employees. Her reasons for saying this were that employees were offered high wages, free transport and food, incentives and bonuses; moreover, there were plenty of jobs available should they encounter any reason to leave. As a consultant in the industry, she argued that the profile of the employee had changed and that workers who were initially keen to work hard were now lacking in ambition and drive due to the surplus of labour. Pratibha, the mother of two children who work at call centres, indicated that this casual attitude to work is actually a product of Indian mentality, a 'Brahmannical mentality':

> People in India are very laid-back, they are not at all competitive, they are very lazy. So maybe these call centres coming up is a good thing for the younger generation. It really perks them up and makes them go-getters.
>
> (Pratibha, 47)

Call centre work is, quite simply, understood as temporary and casual by many and certainly not as a career, and although 60 per cent of the sample group stated that they would continue working after they were married, only 22 per cent indicated that this would be in the call centre industry. Pooja, who has been married for one year and uses her wages as 'pocket money', said that she would eventually like to work in the IT industry but at present was working at NCall to learn more about call centre culture:

> I basically wanted to look for myself what exactly is a call centre. Like I heard through so many medias, like papers, TV, and everything that call centres, [pause] people in call centres are like this and you really have to work pretty hard, the timings are weird and everything like that. So I wanted experience for myself, my working in a call centre is basically, you know, giving it a try. It's nothing like I wanted or looked for a career in a call centre. No. It's not like that. Soon maybe I'll be going into something different.
>
> (Pooja, 28, NCall)

Pooja was one of the handful of married women working at NCall. She wasn't educated in the field of IT or business but had in fact arrived at call centre work via a different route. Her father had held a government position that had allowed him to travel quite extensively, and when Pooja finished college he encouraged her to take a job working for a German non-governmental organizations (NGO). A year earlier, after marrying her boyfriend of seven years and quitting her job, Pooja found herself bored and lonely. She missed the daily contact with foreigners and decided that call centre work might fill that gap for her.

Pooja's comments help to illustrate another motive for call centre workers and that is to alleviate a sense of boredom. A particular term used by call centre employees to describe this attitude to work or possible lack of ambition or 'career orientation' (Desai 1996) is the term 'time-pass', used to indicate, quite simply, something to pass time with:

> There are some people who think they are going to work hard and save money, and some people think, it's a time-pass, you know … have a good time, make some money for their weddings and then quit.
>
> (Rashi, 25, GCall)

'Time-pass' affliction is not something limited to housewives. It also applies to those with money who do not need to work, thus it is used in a slightly more critical and dismissive sense to suggest that people who are there for 'time-pass' are, in effect, wasting everyone else's time as well.

Aside from viewing work as a short-term career move or 'time-pass', a large number of women working in the call centre did so out of economic necessity. Women such as Nisha and Shvetangana, who were from Bihar, Sangamitra, from Calcutta, and Upasana, from Assam, had come from cities in North East India that were up to two days away by train, as job prospects in their own areas were poor for degree educated women. These women, known as out-stationed candidates, represent approximately one-quarter of all women from the sample group working in call centres and several of them stated that, aside from their living expenses, the majority of their wages were sent home to contribute to the household income. This is the case with Urmila, the trained yoga teacher whose parents are divorced, and Yashica, whose father cannot work and whose family is cared for by other relatives:

> I give more than half to my family. My parents are divorced, so I send my money to my mom. My dad has the orders from the court to financially support my mum, but she doesn't take any money from him. It is my grandpa who is taking care of my family, so I want to help. My mum is the only daughter. I spend the rest on myself. Rent, that kind of thing, mobile phone.
>
> (Urmila, 21, NCall)

> Right, I have to send money because my dad – he received a paralysis five years back so he isn't working now. So although my uncles are very caring and they take care of my brother and my mom, but still I take as a responsibility that when I'm earning at least I should send something home. So if they have some general expenses there, they can take care, they can contribute towards the family expenses also.
>
> (Yashica, 21, NCall)

Others, living at home, worked to contribute their wages to the family's income due to unforeseen circumstances, like Ritu who had given up her plans to study in order to take care of her family and ensure no disruption to her younger brother's study plans.

> You see what happened is that there was this depression going around after 9/11 and my father had to take voluntary retirement. And it was me and my mom who were working. Obviously his pension was coming in as well, but when my brother started studying, and he was out of the house, we had to give his pocket money and his fees. So the responsibilities came on to my shoulders to provide it. Now, my father started doing other things. It's better off now, but at that point in time, my whole salary used to go to the family.
>
> (Ritu, 23, GCall)

I am working because of my family's circumstances. My husband was running a business and we ran into financial crisis. And this is the reason that I am doing a job, to supplement my family's income.

(Gurmeet, 31, NCall)

Urmila and Yashica both stated that they would move out of call centres when they could and pursue other lines of work such as yoga instruction and journalism, respectively. However, Ritu, looking for a career, and Gurmeet, working now that her children were a little older, stated that now they had begun working in a call centre they would prefer to continue there as opposed to beginning somewhere else. Thus their attitudes had changed over time and what was initially regarded as an attractive, short-term career with high wages had evolved into something that they were pursuing more seriously. A noticeable tension also settled amongst those women who had once been dismissive of the work and were now overtly reliant on a paid position, such as those above. When new women joined the call centres, out of curiosity or for 'time-pass' as they once did, those who had decided to build careers or worked because they needed to were distinctly hostile. In this way, women constructed identities to produce typologies and patterns of recognition and it is not difficult to see how a woman like Pooja, who claimed to work because she was bored at home, might clash with someone like Yashica or Ritu, whose fathers could not support their families.

Aside from the varying, and shifting, motives to find work, women's attitudes towards call centre employment were influenced by factors linked to social and cultural perceptions of women and employment, as well as biological concerns for motherhood and other health issues. Along with dominant perceptions of women and employment in contemporary Indian society, social and cultural understandings of women's commitments to family had shaped some of the attitudes that women had towards call centre work. Desai (1996) writes that 'career orientation' conflicts with family obligations due to higher inputs of time and energy; furthermore, women have a 'fragmented attitude to work'. Chanelle, who is unmarried, and Smita, who is married, provide insight into this 'fragmented attitude':[10]

Well, call centre is a little difficult because you have odd shifts to work and once you are married you have a lot of family commitments. Like right now, you know, there are no family commitments for me, but once you get married you have to take care of the whole house. You have kids you have to take care of them. So in a nine-to-five job of course you have the benefits, you're back home in the evening, you can cook, you can spend time with your family. But here you're working 1.30 to 10.30, by the time you reach home it's 11.30, your kids are off to sleep and your husband is like, you know, already tired from his work.

(Chanelle, 25, NCall)

Chanelle's point could be made of women working anywhere; however, as Smita points out, it is often women who reject their own opportunities for better employment because of their conditioned responses to how women in middle-class India should be:

> SMITA: There is a lot of, 'I can't work on this day. I can't work Saturdays, Sunday for this reason.' We come with a lot of baggage. For men, it's easier because they don't bring the baggage of home and household, they can give it 100 per cent. I know some women who give it 100 per cent but most of the women won't. I mean, if I'm told to come and work on my son's birthday, I would not. I don't care. I wouldn't. My husband might, which is why I probably wouldn't get promoted. The guy that comes on his son's birthday will get promoted.
>
> INTERVIEWER: So are you saying that women have cultural obligations in society that they have to prioritize?
>
> SMITA: And that they maintain. They happily maintain it. They won't give it up either. They want to work, and they want their family lives. Chalo teek hai, that's fine.
>
> (Smita, 33, NCall)

Originally in advertising, Smita, a career-driven woman, knows that her commitment to her family is part of the reason that she has had to start over in a new sector. She states here that women are complicit in maintaining their roles within a patriarchal order; however, she also speaks positively of this conflict, indicating that women want both and shouldn't have to choose. Gayatri, a call centre consultant, agrees with this but also indicates that women are not always able to exercise agency over their decisions to continue working; for some women whether they continue is determined by their husband or their husband's family. Gayatri also explains how her role expands to that of a mediator between what the women working in the call centre want and what the family wants, as dictated by social and cultural factors:

> I have parents call me up and tell me, 'Please tell our daughter not to come [to work].' 'How can I? Your daughter has a job.' 'Because we are very unhappy and we don't see our children, and when they are at home, they are sleeping.' I try to talk to them, to explain, what to do? I'm telling you, I am responsible for everything and nothing. You have to take care of the children; if they are depressed, you have to motivate them when they are not doing their work. Then somebody has another problem, they can't come in today. Why? 'Because my mother-in-law is here and I will get into trouble if I come in.' You name it.
>
> (Gayatri, Call Centre Consultant)

In many ways, Gayatri's view that she is responsible for 'everything and nothing' suggests that she does everything that is needed to encourage employees to work but nothing that is recognized by the company in her job description. The work–family imbalance or conflicting views that Gayatri deals with are produced through patriarchal discourses that link women, family and reproduction, not only those of the employees who might leave after getting married but also those of the women managers, who are expected to understand such things better than the men in management. The notion that women should not work after marriage was held by 40 per cent of the sample group, many of them citing biological reasons for women's perceived lack of ambition or casual attitude to work:

> And let's face it, women, there are times in the day when we can't work and times of the month when we can't work. There is a phase in our lives when we are pregnant and can't work.
>
> (Smita, 33, NCall)

> Women who apply for leadership levels will probably be older, in her thirties, married and she will seem ambitious. But maybe she'll want to have a baby and have to take maternity leave so you have to judge how ambitious a person is. So, to a certain extent during hiring that is taken into consideration.
>
> (Rashi, 25, GCall)

In line with earlier arguments regarding women's dual responsibility of work and family (Banerjee 1996; Mies 1979), Smita and Rashi's comments show that women's roles in the call centre are almost always articulated within middle-class social and cultural understandings that marriage and child rearing are more important than work. At NCall, women were encouraged to continue working after marriage and employees were presented with a bonus of Rs5,000 (available to both men and women) when they got married and a bonus of Rs1,000 on the birth of a first child. These acts of reward for heteronormative reproduction, although viewed as a way to gain loyalty from employees, only work to further serve patriarchal controls of women which normalize marriage and motherhood as choices for women, again connecting to a larger discussion on the conflation of women's identities and national identities.

Health and well-being also acted as determining factors in attitudes held towards call centre work. Due to the shift timings, interviewees pointed towards the inevitability of exhaustion and burnout from working at night and performing emotional labour (Hislop and Arbor 2003). As such, call centre work was regarded as something which could not be sustained for much longer than two years, as Gayatri, the call centre manager, pointed out. Parents' and partners' concern for their health and welfare also played a significant role in determining women's attitudes to work, as family members or boyfriends put pressure on women to leave work involving night shifts:

> He doesn't like me working in a call centre. Because I spend long hours here, all these dark circles, and all, he says that's from working here. 'You

need to take care of yourself. Go home. Get some sleep. Why work?' He doesn't hate me working in a call centre. He just thinks I should relax. You know, probably sleep on time. But other than that, he's okay. He says that if I have to go to office at night, just to make sure I'm only doing my eight to nine hours and then be back. With me, I tend to spend twelve to thirteen hours in the office, plus my travel. So it gets pretty hectic, which is something that he doesn't really like.

(Rashi, 25, GCall)

The concern that Rashi's boyfriend feels is partly due to the lack of control he has over her life, given that he travels a lot for work, does not live in Delhi and is jealous of her male colleagues. But his concerns echo many of the earlier arguments regarding the detrimental effects to the health of women working in export processing zones in that they are exposed to 'health-sapping working conditions' (Standing 1989) and may suffer from eye problems, headaches, neck, back, shoulder ache and exhaustion both at and away from work (Ng Choon Sim 1999). However, in this instance, what is of significance is the way in which these issues were discussed as expressions of concerns from male partners or relatives. More often than not, when women expressed these concerns, it was usually female relatives rather than friends and in many ways the comments were linked to opportunities for marriage. Comments were made about poor skin, weight gain, dark circles, all cited as things that might deter potential husbands, demonstrating that women's identities are still predominantly produced through patriarchal discourses (Kakar 1988).

Thus a range of attitudes to work, influenced by social, cultural and biological factors, are presented here which significantly affect women's commitment to work and opportunities for promotion. These examples demonstrate how, although call centres have brought about opportunities for women's employment and economic independence, they have also raised questions about the importance of family life versus employment or further education, questions and concerns that shape some the preconceptions that women working within the call centres have of one another and how they identify and define one another.

Macaulay's Minute: names and aliases

Speaking in 1835, in colonial India, Thomas B. Macaulay, in 'Macaulay's Minute on Education', stated:

> We must at present do our best to form a class who may be interpreters between us and the millions whom we govern; a class of persons, Indian in blood and colour, but English in taste, in opinions, in morals, and in intellect.
>
> (Macaulay 1835)

In presenting a socio-historic analysis of Indian society it is difficult, if not impossible, to ignore the 'contemporary residue of imperialism' (Said 1993), but nearly 200 years later Macaulay's words seem to have even greater resonance in presenting an analysis of call centre workers and contemporary Indian society. Using Bhabha's concept of 'mimicry' – 'constructing a subject of difference that is almost the same, but not quite; a subject that is constructed through ambivalence, an expression of difference that is itself a disavowal' (Bhabha 1994: 122) – we can begin to more closely explore the complexities of the identity question for call centre workers.

The relocation of call centre work has indeed brought a further dimension of postcolonial thought to the forefront in Anglo-Indian relations. The use of aliases in Indian call centres has been described as both 'commodification of one's identity' (Seabrook 2003) and 'locational masking' (Mirchandani 2004a, 2004b). It is perhaps the most popular example of the way in which call centre employees transform or 'translate' (Bhabha 1994) the relocated labour process. Mirchandani (2004a, 2004b) has posited the concept of 'locational masking', whereby agents slip in and out of identities as and when they need to. This argument is flawed in its essentialist understanding that a fixed, unmovable 'real' self exists that Indians either leave behind and come back to or draw upon when necessary. Mirchandani implies an ease and comfort with 'locational masking', suggesting that agents exercise agency over which identities to use. However, this grossly underestimates the very real racism or sexual innuendo they are subjected to by British customers due to their Indian accents. Moreover, it simplifies the labour process and does not account for 'emotional exhaustion' or burnout from the putting on and taking off of various masks.

The *Guardian* journalist Siddartha Deb (2004) who spent time posing as a call centre agent, also asserted that an Indian 'self' lies beneath the British or American mask, manifesting itself in different ways and producing alter egos outside the workplace. Journalists keen to focus on the identity question continue to conceive this process as a dialectic or dichotomy, never as a 'cultural interchange process' (Welsch 1999) that is mutually constituted by and constitutive for Indians. The sample group was evenly divided when asked whether they believed there was a loss of or change to Indian culture, a significant finding given that a crucial argument for journalists, and I would argue academics, has been that call centre relocation is exploiting Indians, partially hinging on the evidence that employees are using English aliases as opposed to their own names (Seabrook 2003).

Deb (2004) demonstrates cross-cultural misconceptions as his voice and accent and UK culture trainer, an Indian who once lived in Belfast, replies to a question about real British culture: 'It begins in the pub and ends in someone else's bed.' Deb writes, 'this was a crudely dismissive comment from someone so Westernized', reflecting a middle-class, low tolerance level for diversity resulting in an insular, limited view of their own country. Deb's brief foray into the world of call centres was revealing indeed, as dope smoking, disappointment with wages, double standards for men and women all hit upon a certain note. But Deb is not British, he is Indian and lives in the US, and had several British people been in the training session they may very well have found it difficult to argue against such an observation about British culture.

Deb's offence to the comment was aimed to demonstrate a clash between British and Indian culture, a suggestion that is not accurate. There are plenty of conservative people in the UK who would object to such drinking and bed-hopping, and evidence abounds of liaisons in the larger cities of India. Of course, there is a certain class dimension to the call centre workers, but to crudely define people's responses as products of their class upbringing is unfair, and irreparable. As I've argued elsewhere in this chapter, call centre workers are involved in transformative processes, challenging their own and others' perceptions of culture and identity. Moreover, and this is something neglected by Deb, there is the continued connection that Indians feel to Britain as a product of colonialism.

Swati, an employee at GCall, does not view British and Indian cultures as necessarily so distinct and expresses a deeper 'transnational and translational' (Bhabha 1994) sense of call centre work:

> Although we are very far away from that country, we feel very close. Perhaps we are more close to that country than we are to India because we are working professionally for them. We might not be knowing so much about India the way we are knowing the UK. I know every county, every part, I know everything. If you describe something to me in the UK I will know it because I have that image on my mind. Okay, we're not in the UK but we know the UK better than anyone else.
>
> (Swati, 26, GCall)

The romanticism with which Swati describes the UK can be found every-where – books, films, art, conversations – all contributing to her connection with British culture and a British identity. The implication that the two cultures exist in a dichotomous fashion is somewhat limited in its analytical scope.

Culture clashes and the discussion of aliases, along with accent changes, dilution or neutralization, have overwhelmed any other facet of Indian call centre work. Indeed one of my early questions in the research process was about this 'imposed' Westernization. As well as imposing a British cultural understanding of the labour process, one in which the use of the English language and aliases is determined as exploitative, such an analytical frame-work does not account for how Indian employees may individually exercise agency over the labour process. This is exemplified by the use of aliases, which academic sources have described negatively as deceptive 'locational masking' (Mirchandani, 2004b); however, interviewees from the sample group described the use of aliases as a much more pragmatic business decision:

> I use Jane Williams. I only use that to make the customer more comfor-table. If I tell him that my name is Indu, he will ask me ten times to repeat

it, so it is so much easier this way. We really only change our first name, and that is given by the company. We keep our last names.

(Indu, 26, NCall B)

See, using an alias is something which is convenient for English people. It's just for convenience. For me it's not two different people. It's just so that they can understand the name.

(Anshu, 24, GCall)

Describing it as a 'legitimizing identity' (Castells 1997), Indu and Anshu discussed aliases as similar to wearing a uniform or a nametag, not as something that is definitive in the presentation of their self-identity. Indu and Anshu's view resonated with most of the women and men I spoke with; however, there were exceptions who spoke of a dual identity conflict, but in all cases anyone not comfortable using another name was free to shorten their own name to use on calls.

Urmila presents an entirely different perspective on the alias discussion, expressing a greater sense of 'resistance identity' (Castells 1997) in using 'emotional dissonance' (Zapf et al. 2003) or 'time–space distanciation' (Giddens 1991) from the caller. Here she states that by using an alias she felt more protected and thus free to perform her job without implicating her sense of self-identity in the process. This is further exemplified by the fact that she uses an Indian alias as opposed to a more Western-sounding name, demonstrating that the practice of using an alias is more important than how that alias sounds:

Priya is my alias. I used to use Urmila but then they couldn't make out my name, so I changed it. When I used to say that my name was Urmila it was a bit personal. But now it feels more objective. Being Priya gives me more distance from the caller. All the customer can hear is my voice. I feel free. When I say it's Urmila speaking, I feel bound, like something is binding me. I don't feel free at all, because there are customers that flirt with you too. But by changing my name, I feel a bit safer.

(Urmila, 21, NCall)

By using an alias, Urmila is able to gain distance or 'emotional dissonance' (Zapf et al. 2003) from the caller, thus gaining a greater sense of agency over the labour process. In this way, the backlash against the use of aliases, largely fuelled, I would argue, by British media reports, has in fact disarmed the call centre workers against racial abuse or sexual harassment from customers. So dominant is the myth that call centre workers are attempting to deceive customers into believing that call centres have not been relocated to India that Indian media reports are also claiming that this was true ('Cyber Coolies or Cyber Sahibs' 2003; 'Call Centres Usher in Lingo Revolution' 2003; 'After Hours Accent' 2003). However, I did not find any evidence to support such claims throughout the research period with any of the call centres or research participants; when asked by callers, employees honestly answered that they were in fact based in India. Moreover, NCall informed all employees by e-mail that no agent was to use an alias, a request that came directly from the client, and that if agents so desired they could use a shortened version of their first name.[11]

A further dimension to the discussion of cultural identity as it functions in the labour process, not yet accounted for by previous studies, is the effect of soft skills, language and accent training for employees. Apart from the neutralization or Americanization narratives, the wider implication of this training is the creation of a 'linguistic apartheid' operating on class difference. For Indians, the nativization or naturalization of the English language has enabled oppressed social groups, such as the dalits or untouchables, to prevent Hindi from becoming the sole official language of the nation. For those who are less experienced with Indian cities, it may come as a surprise that English is predominantly used in business settings, universities and the like, and not limited to hotels and tourist sites. This 'democratizing', however, has simultaneously given rise to a 'native elite' (Annamalai 2004: 151) cutting across regions and caste in the name of modernity and cosmopolitanism, creating a linguistic apartheid. Arguments that technology created an 'indigenous elite' (Banerjee and Linstead 2001) and widened the gulf between social classes are now underscored by the creation of the 'native elite', making class based identities increasingly significant in comparison with caste based identities, demonstrating that the use of English is much more complex than others have suggested in previous Indian call centre studies.

The construction of 'global colonial' identities,[12] ones which mark a transformation to cultures of consumption, can be read as Macaulay intended, as 'Indian in blood and colour, but English in taste, in opinions, in morals, and in intellect'. Or perhaps it can be read as an opportunity – for 'the master's tools will never dismantle the master's house' (Lorde 1984) but perhaps they can act as keys to doorways. In her study of Indian call centres, Poster (2007) found that some agents used their Americanized names, accents and identities to negotiate entrance to exclusive nightclubs and get discounts from shops and restaurants. From my time in Delhi, it was clear that nightclubs and bars were only accessed by the privileged few who could afford to pay the exorbitant drink prices. However, during my stay, a number of other drinking establishments opened to cater to the burgeoning call centre population. These bars were open to tourists, students, artists and musicians, in a way that the more established nightclubs were not. Examining the use of aliases as part of a cosmopolitanizing process brings call centre studies in line with other globalizing effects in India, as opposed to spotlighting the labour process and the people who work in call centres as some kind of cultural betrayers.

Negative aspects of call centre work for women

> It was quite a sobering experience for me to listen to as an American—that is, the steadfast composure and professionalism of Indian employees as American

consumers said things like, 'How do I spell my name? F–U–C–K–Y–O–U!'
Employees reported that this happens in about 1 in 30 calls. In my observations,
it happened at least once an hour.

(Poster, 2007: 283)

As surprising as the above quotation may be, Poster's observations are accurate. When asked whether or not they had experienced racism while working
in a call centre, 44 per cent of the sample group said that they had. However,
many more women in the sample group spoke of customers who were verbally abusive on race grounds or cultural differences, yet they did not classify
these calls as racist. Approximately 60 per cent of the sample group discussed experiences with negative callers, which they suggested occurred with
one out of every five calls. These experiences ranged from anger over outsourcing, confusion with accents, subtle racism in asking where the call was
coming from, to more extreme forms of racism where agents were verbally
abused.

Interviewees indicated that most of the negativity experienced during a call
was expressed simply as a refusal by customers to speak with agents, as Upasana
and Yashica note:

I got one call where someone said, 'I don't want to talk to an "MF"
[motherfucking] Asian,' and then they hung up. And on another call,
they did not want to give their details to an Indian and they just hung up.
It's not just me. A lot of my colleagues get such calls but the percentage is
very low, 80:20.

(Upasana, 28, NCall)

One day a customer tells me, 'I don't want to talk to someone who's an
Indian.' She just had to make a payment. 'But I will not pay to an Indian
because I do not trust you.' 'Can you give me a possible reason?' She
said, 'I don't have a reason, I don't want to pay to you, I don't want to pay
to an Indian.' She wouldn't even talk to my TL about that. [Sometimes]
when people get to know that you are calling from India, 80 per cent of
them get really excited and they would really love to come to India and
20 per cent are very negative. They say, 'I don't want to talk to an Asian.
Why should I talk to an Indian? Why should I give my information to an
Indian?' And they use some F words, and stuff like that.

(Yashica, 21, NCall)

Most of the interviewees in the sample group indicated that this was the type
of aggression that they regularly faced and did not classify it as racist; however, based on discussions with them I would argue that although only 44 per
cent stated that they had experienced racism on a call, it is quite likely that all
of the sample group had experienced some type of racist abuse. Moreover,
during interviews many of the women followed these statements with comments

suggesting it was an accepted part of the job and, as such, they were sympathetic to customers and had in fact become aware of changing perceptions of Indians, as Yashica states:

> It's like they are learning quite a lot about us. Whatever notions that they have about us, I think they are changing. You know, like snake charmers and elephants, they know we are high-tech people and people who know how to speak English, who are intelligent. It's really changing the preconceived notions that were mostly negative.
>
> (Yashica, 21, NCall)

Others offered a more analytical understanding of why customers held such negative perceptions of Indian call centre workers, linking the perceptions to historical and cultural contexts in comparing UK and US customers:

> At times there are customers who ask to be transferred to someone who speaks English. Then you have to tell them that, yes, we are speaking English if you could just listen to us. Sometimes they just simply ask us where they are calling, where they are phoning. As soon as they come to know that it is an Indian, then there goes your call for a toss. With Americans, yeah, it is a little bit less because they can accept it, but with the UK people, it's more of a high nose thing. The same thing comes back to 'We ruled you 500 years back, so you are still our slaves. How come I am talking to you? I don't want to talk to you.'
>
> (Indu, 26, NCallB)

With these insights, Indu offers a critical analysis of why customers may show an unwarranted aggression towards Indian call centre workers. Linking these experiences to historical contexts and Anglo-Indian relations, Indu demonstrates that the experiences of racial abuse affect them on a much deeper level than the simple reading of it being a part of the labour process. What her comments suggest is that call centre workers are unable to deflect the negativity of a caller simply by using emotional labour, as the impact of the call extends beyond the employee's engagement with it and in fact calls into question the larger context of Anglo-Indian relations. As demonstrated by the opening quotations by Monbiot and Seabrook in Chapter 1, call centre relocation has provided a springboard for British journalists to discuss the historical contexts of Anglo-Indian relations. Nisha and Anyuta suggest that the hostility they have faced has been media driven and misdirected as it is in fact anger over outsourcing:

> It may have more to do with the outsourcing anger that people have in mind, than to do with racial prejudice. I think the scandal of [British companies] moving to India may affect their mindset.
>
> (Nisha, 24, NCall)

People are upset about the work being outsourced to India. They say, 'I am a Brit, I live in Britain, I have taken services from British company. I have you, you're in a foreign country, you're calling me up, you're taking information from me, and before you hang up you ask me if I have any issues. You are on a remote site. How do you think sitting there you are going to be able to help me? With all due respect to you and your country, I do not appreciate you coming between me and my company in my country.'

(Anyuta, 26, NCall)

Anyuta, possibly more sympathetic to those outside India, worked in the US for some time before having her visa revoked immediately following 11 September 2001. Anyuta had experienced working in a multinational organization and had experienced the multicultural melting pot of the US and was able to apply those experiences to empathize with the caller in a way that many of her call centre colleagues could not. All of the interviewees in the sample group, and nearly all call centre workers in India, are educated to degree level, and many of them presented a critical analysis of the aggression and hostility they experienced while working. They did not view these incidents as acts of simple 'phone rage' or the result of inconveniencing the customer but as part of a wider set of global, racial prejudices that they had to deal with on a day-to-day basis. Their experiences in the call centre allowed engagement with contemporary global politics and economic relations; as such, they had these comments to offer:

People who are racist in the UK, they have no right to be racist, because they are bloody rich because of our money.

(Smita, 33, NCall)

Sometimes they say why, 'Why you Indians?' One problem I had with a woman, she was Muslim, and she said, 'Why is the call centre not in Pakistan? Why is it in India? And I don't want to talk to you.' And she went.

(Ritu, 23, GCall)

Her whole point was that as a Briton she did not want to give me information because I had taken jobs from her country. I appreciated her outlook and could understand. Maybe tomorrow something like this will happen to my country and I will feel this way if somebody from Pakistan or Nepal is calling me and saying, 'Please give me details about your business.' Who the hell? Why should I give it to you?

(Anyuta, 26, NCall)

Again, Anyuta demonstrates how her experiences working and living outside India have allowed her to understand and empathize with the customers – more than that, she quite easily identifies two countries that India shares an uneasy relationship with, making explicit the power disparity that is demonstrated through these racist comments.

The hostility and aggression experienced by call centre workers as a part of their everyday engagement with the labour process did not remain limited to their work environment or their work lives. These experiences held negative implications for them in a wider context. In addition to the verbal abuse and aggression experienced by call centre workers, interviewees indicated that, physically, call centre work was damaging to women's bodies, largely due to the night shifts:

> After some time, you really see the effect on your health. You see a lot of changes in yourself. Getting up late, sleeping at odd times. The whole body clock goes haywire. Your eating timings, your sleeping timings – working in a call centre doesn't leave you any space or time for anything else. I spend at least two hours coming to work, and at least one going back home, so you really get very tired.
>
> (Jennifer, 38, NCall)

> The one thing about the call centre job is that you cannot concentrate on your studies. It's a twelve-hour job, which tires you totally, so you just go home and then come straight back. It's work, home, work, home, Friday night partying out. It's very difficult for you to look after your family; if you have a family and kids, it's very difficult.
>
> (Nidhi, 22, NCall)

> The whole world works in the day. Your doorbell rings, a man has come to collect something, someone has come for a bill, somebody is selling something, the maid can only come in the day. If you have to go to the bank it is also in the daytime. So there is this whole world that works in the day that you have to find time to be a part of which you cannot be a part of because you need to sleep. You are forcing your whole body to work in a different cycle. I used to be half a zombie most of the time.
>
> (Gayatri, Call Centre Consultant)

Jennifer, Nidhi and Gayatri's comments represent the range of views held by over half of the sample group regarding the negative effects of call centre work on women's health. Nidhi's comments demonstrate that it is not an easy business to carry on with studies whilst working, which is an experience that employees shared as many of them were studying via correspondence. Many of them viewed call centre work as something that they would not continue to do after a few years; those that did suggest that they would like to find a career in the industry indicated that they would like to shift from night work to day work. In spite of these negative aspects of call centre work, all of the interviewees indicated that working in call centres had been a rewarding experience and that they had gained a number of skills and confidence in dealing with a global market, two things they hoped to put to use at other stages in their lives.

4   BTMs in BPOs

Using sartorial strategies to establish patterns of identification and recognition

> Everywhere you go you can see the influence of call centres. Everybody is rushing, thinking they are so important. Girls in strappy tops – never mind the girls, even the women are dressing in jeans, and heels, wearing so much make-up with their hair out. You see all these BTMs wearing sunglasses, huge, huge earrings, on the scooter. Drinking beer out of bottles. I'm sorry to say, but no decent woman would do that.
>
> (Pratibha, 47)

In many ways, Pratibha is right. Everywhere you look in Delhi you will see the influence of call centres. From signs advertising English-language training to advertisements for employment on posters, call centres have been enormously influential on everyday, urban life. Walking through the markets one can easily distinguish the call centre workers from others. They are talking loudly, laughing, unaware of who is watching them, generally living life with a sense of reckless abandon. But, more importantly, they are shopping. Stalls selling inexpensive jeans and shirts, jewellery, bangles and shoes are filled with employees on their days off, hoping to unburden themselves of some of their hard earned cash.

The metropolitan shrines to consumerism and changing patterns of consumption have made pleasure seeking a duty (Lash and Urry 1994) for those who can afford it (see Figure 4.1). As Bourdieu once wrote, consumption is a way of establishing difference, not merely expressing it, and as the call centre workers change the social landscape of the city, so they also change the people who share that social landscape; as is demonstrated by the way the relationship between field and habitus functions to produce agent's bodies. For Pratibha, the mother of three grown children, transnationalism, rebranding Delhi as a global city, has produced the BTM, bhenji turned mod – from 'bhenji', a term of respect meaning older sister, and 'mod', short for modern. The term is widely used amongst the middle class in Delhi to mean an older woman trying too hard to be fashionable, a disparaging term that would never be used whilst the woman in question was present. BTM was never used to describe a non-Indian woman, or someone who did not have children. The women labelled BTMs were not particularly fashionable and often it was

Figure 4.1 Multiplex and shopping centre in Gurgaon.

their lack of fashion sense that earned them the title. It is a term reserved for women trying to dress and act young, Western and liberal, and judged to be too old for the globalizing shifts transforming Delhi.

The use of clothing and dress as ways of identifying women and creating typologies, as well as women using sartorial strategies to achieve success in their careers, can be seen in many parts of the city. Conscious of the changing perceptions of Indian call centre workers outside India, the women interviewed were also distinctly aware of the changing perception of call centre workers, and women in general, in cosmopolitan or urban spaces within Delhi. The influential 'mediascapes' (Appadurai 1996) of 'Bollywood', music videos and Indian television programming, along with changing consumption patterns, all contribute to a cultural cosmopolitanism (Delanty 1999) and liberalism found in many Indian cities.

The idealizing of Indian women's roles lies in Hindu mythology and its pantheon of goddesses, particularly Sita and Drapudi, exemplifying many of the characteristics deplored or desired in women.[1] Contemporary practices of sexual segregation are underlined by the mythological and ideological constructs that women are dangerous and must be controlled as their sexuality poses a threat to the social order and can bring dishonour and shame on themselves and their families (Chanda 2004: 221). One of the ways in which this 'subjugation' (Foucault 1979: 139) of the body is produced is through a series of interventions and regulatory controls, signifying 'proper' behaviour of women and identifying those who belong to a collective and those who do not:

> Women are seen as the 'cultural carriers' of the collectivity and transmit it to the future generation; being properly controlled in terms of marriage and divorce ensures that children born to these women are not only biologically but also symbolically within the boundaries of the collectivity ... at the same time women may participate in ethnic processes in different ways ... and develop their own patriarchal bargains.
>
> (Yuval-Davis 1994: 413)

In addition to cultural and social factors, producing the identity of a middle-class Indian woman, to define an identity for an independent India meant defining her in opposition to a woman from a lower economic stratum – a strategy not dissimilar to the process found in Victorian England which pushed women out of the public sphere and into the private sphere (Sangari and Vaid 1989: 11). This is also seen as a continuing of the colonial consolidation project of a sexualized public and private space (Mohanty, 1991a: 20). The view that women from 'good', middle-class families do not work in the public sphere or common jobs is one that is still widely held, as one mother of a call centre worker discusses here:

> I still feel that good families will not send their daughters, but my circumstances are different because I don't have a husband. I don't know whether this is right or wrong, but I do feel guilty. I keep telling my daughter, 'Beta [child], it's up to you. If you don't want to work, wait for a better job. I don't want you to say tomorrow that I made you work in a call centre.' No one from a good family would allow their daughter to work in call centre.
>
> (Bhubbl, 44)

As Chapter 3 showed, many young women took up work in call centres as a stepping-stone to other things. With competition rife, women found it difficult to find work as engineers, IT or finance professionals and instead took up call centre, BPO or data entry work that might in some way be related to their field. Bhubbl's daughter was unable to find work in her field and since the untimely death of her husband a few years back the family had struggled to manage their finances. When I first met and spoke with Bhubbl, she was absolutely adamant that no self-respecting upper-class, urban family would allow their daughters to work in call centres, but as Bhubbl's need for extra income grew, she eventually changed her mind. However, she did voice her concerns over her daughter's reputation and marriage prospects, and how this might affect the prospects of her sons' marriages as well.

The first time I met Bhubbl was shortly after she had been to an interview at GE's call centre in Gurgaon. She describes the experience thus:

> I wanted to work. I've never worked before in my life. After my husband passed away, I had a lot of free time, and all my kids are grown up and on their own. So I thought I'll do a job, and the GE advertisement came

up in the paper. So I went in for the interview. The process of the interview is that they send you an e-mail to come at a certain time at the GE centre, which is in Gurgaon. There was three rounds. The first round, they just tell you to talk about yourself and then they tell you that so-and-so has got in and so-and-so please leave. The second round is a forty-five-minute exercise for an aptitude test. There is a lot of maths, which was quite tough, and I panicked, but I managed to finish it all, and I passed that round as well. The last round was the HR round, and I was pretty confident because out of about ten people there were only two of us left at the end. So I was sure I'll get it because they were looking for somebody for customer service. When I went in, she asked me questions like, 'Why do you want to work for the call centre.' I said, 'I have a lot of free time.' 'Would you be willing to work the night shifts?' I said, 'No, because I've never worked, and I don't want to work the night shifts.' She said, 'What's your salary expectations?' I said, 'It should be about ten, but I applied for part-time as a housewife so give me five.' She said, 'We only give 3,200.' That's quite low but, anyway, I said, 'Okay, fine.' She said, 'Do you have a valid passport?' I said, 'Yes.' She said, 'Are you willing to travel?' I said, 'No, I'm not willing to travel. I just came back from the UK and I'm not willing to travel again.' She said, 'Okay, we'll let you know.' After five minutes, she said, 'Sorry, you haven't got the job.' I was pretty disappointed. As to why, I don't know. I think the reason is that I was too smart for the job. I'm sure of it. I know I was much smarter than the girl next to me. I didn't talk to her but I know I probably speak better English than her. Her attitude wasn't smart. She wasn't dressed right; she was wearing a salwaar-kameeze.

(Bhubbl, 44)

The rejection that Bhubbl felt after that interview had not entirely put her off of call centre work, as she continued to look for work aimed at housewives. She was eventually successful but her early comments concerning why she didn't get the job were illuminating. Bhubbl had been educated at a private school in London and had married a wealthy businessman based in Delhi. Her upper-class credentials meant that taking up work in a call centre was one of her last options. She was determined to be financially independent, however, even though her son tried to dissuade her:

The middle class, the middle-income group, generally work for call centres. That's what my son meant. He knows that I'm from a good family, and we've led a good life. That I wouldn't fit into that scenario of a middle-income group, the middle class. So maybe that's why he was saying that. I think for the middle-income group, 3,000–4,000 rupees that's a lot of money, so they jump at the prospect of working, even that much money. I think they are paying very, very less compared to other jobs.

(Bhubbl, 44)

It is quite clear that a particular class of people are recruited for call centre work, and to a large extent earlier analyses have focussed on the exclusive ways in which call centres hire. However, Bhubbl's experience is something quite different. She is primarily caught between a desire to protect her daughter's reputation so that she can secure her future and a desire to have her own financial independence from her sons. She discussed the frustration of asking her son for money and being accountable for every rupee she spent, the anxiety she experienced when thinking about what neighbours or friends in her social network might say when they saw her daughter being picked up for work late at night:

> With Indian society being what it is, with boys, anything goes. With girls, tomorrow she has to get married, and everything, all these things, come up then. They will say, 'Oh, your daughter is working in a call centre.' I don't think it's considered a respectable job as such in the marriage market. That's the way I look at it.
>
> (Bhubbl, 44)

Class dimensions and the power dynamics they define produce a specific construct of women working in call centres, and although there were many examples of how these were being disrupted outside the call centre, there was much more going on inside the call centre. Call centres provide opportunities to change, alter, better oneself, and one element of that is to lose, or not intentionally discuss, your background as it becomes implicit. Burying class identities even further is 'gross resurgence' of Hindu nationalism in India (Puri 1999: 2), which has brought about a conflation of a Hindu national identity with Hindu women's identities. Women's bodies, acting as a signifier for both national identity and the preservation of Indian (dominantly Hindu) cultural values (Rao, 1999), have become the sites upon which the conflict between Western and Indian ideologies takes place.[2] The fast-growing Indian middle class is increasingly targeted and represented by the media (Banerjee 2003; Butcher 2003; Cullity 2002; Fernandez 2000; Gillespie and Cheesman 2002; Juluri 1999, 2002), with middle-class women ultimately at the centre of these conflicting ideologies, a conflict most dominantly understood through their choices in clothing and dress.

In India, a nationalizing of the global can be found (Fernandez 2000: 611) as 'myths and identities of belonging' are re-narrated (Wyatt 2005) and

> [the Indian media] obliterate the political project of feminisms and appropriate certain aspects of the women's movement agenda into the re-narration of India and the construction of a new sign system which revolves around the subject position 'woman' ... The result is this sub-ject position of New/Liberated/Modern Woman, commodified as a selling strategy for conspicuous consumption.
>
> (Chanda 2004: 228)

Thus women are pitted against two strategies, local and global images of women's identities that see women used as a sign for economic liberalization, and are simultaneously caught between them at work as neither image affords them the desired liberation (Chanda 2004). It is precisely on these battle lines that Bhubbl finds herself caught between economic liberalization and a lack of liberation.

'Mediascapes': call centres as the second wave

Sociological analysis rooted in a discussion of 'film apparatus' is useful in examining social understandings of surveillance and control (Denzin 1995); the 'cinematic society' (ibid.) is nowhere more prevalent than in 'Bollywood' obsessed India. The Hindi film lies closest to a daydream; its powerful ability to engage viewers in the suspension of disbelief is more in the realm of cultural psychology than the socio-economic (Kakar 1989: 28).[3] Indian film audiences are much more active than Western film audiences (Srinivas, 2002: 171–72), often re-enacting the song and dance sequences outside the cinema and in nightclubs.[4] Film texts have produced national discourses for Indian identities as contestations of Indian culture have been played out in national and diasporic films (Kapur 2000).

However, in recent years film texts have shifted from producing identities out of the modernizing and dichotomous positioning of local/global discourses (Giddens 1991). Media discourses on cosmopolitanism and communalism in South Asia are no longer necessarily oppositional but are increasingly found to be mutually constitutive, as they legitimate as well as contest economic liberalization and globalization (Gillespie and Cheesman 2002: 127). This 'cultural interchange' (Welsch 1999), 'creolization' (Hannerz 1992), hybridization (Pieterse 1995) or hybridity (Bhabha 1994) demonstrates that it is cultural specialists who produce state and national discourses as opposed to the view that 'nation' is a fixed or stable concept (Featherstone 1995). The diaspora has vitally contributed to this development of Indian identity as Indian films increasingly feature scenes and storylines set in Europe and North America, working as batteries to 'charge up' emotional bonds in the production and consumption of India as 'home' (Featherstone 1995). Bollywood films such as *Hum Aapke Hain Koun* (1994) (*Who Am I to You?*) show a trend for using family as a trope for nationality, which, in India, was read as opposition to global hegemony (Juluri 1999).[5]

Implicit within the growing liberalization of the Indian economy and society is the rise of a 'soft Hindutva', right-wing Hindu ideology (Rajgopal 1999), an example of which is an advertisement for Sahil Emporiums, an image found in most magazines and newspapers and on most billboards. The caption for the advertisement reads, 'Women, it's time you came out of the shadows', linking it with modernizing discourses of gender equality and liberation. The woman supposedly in 'the shadows', however, is clearly depicted as a Muslim woman dressed in a burqua. The poses of both women, the woman in the shadows dressed in black in the background and the liberated woman dressed in white in the foreground, intimate a transition from tradition to modernity, as the woman pictured in white appears to be flying or embracing the opportunities ahead of her. However, the use of colour is also significant, as the advertisement is for a bridal emporium, and although the traditional colour for Indian brides to wear is red, the liberated woman in this advertisement is wearing white, the traditional colour that Western brides would wear. The image of the 'New/Liberated/Modern Woman' (Chanda 2004) has been commodified as a selling strategy for conspicuous consumption. Moreover, it has been used to produce a nationalist yet Westernized image with an underlying 'soft Hindutva' ideology (Rajgopal 1999).

This is but one example of the changing 'mediascapes' (Appadurai 1996) that interviewees suggested were tremendously significant; revolutionizing features of television images for women in India meant that most of the sample group regarded call centres as the 'second wave' of social and cultural changes in the country:

> People have become more aware of life abroad. Earlier, the exposure was just through cable TV. That was when the soaps were introduced to India, *Bold and the Beautiful, Santa Barbara*. I think call centres are now the second wave to the whole thing.
>
> (Anyuta, 26, NCall)

> Well, I think the television has been the first one to, you know, creep into our homes to make us more Westernized and definitely the call centre industry has definitely helped us to become more Westernized.
>
> (Chanelle, 25, NCall)

Interviewees argued that whilst call centres had indeed created a greater sense of a Western identity, contrary to British media reports this did not conflict with an Indian identity. The emergence of greater media interest in women's choice to become professionals, accompanying changes in Indian economic policy embracing globalization, has created a shift in advertising, one which shows more corporate, successful ideals (Chadhuri 2001). Although perceptions of identity are nurtured in the heterosexual patriarchal family, young men and women are increasingly grounding their identities in prevailing media images (Thapan 2001). The success of Bollywood films and the relationship between the Indian nation and the 'flexible citizens' (Ong 1999) of the diaspora produce complex economic, social and political expressions at multiple scales (Walton-Roberts 2004), thus changing the 'mediascapes' and 'ethnoscapes' (Appadurai 1996) on many levels in and outside India.[6] Call centres have become like Internet kiosks, and cyber cafés have opened up on every corner, giving Indians access to global communications (Das 2000: 338). The Internet and 'cyberspace' (Gajjala 2004) provide a space, Bhabha's (1994) 'Third Space', within which the 'dialogical self' (Chaudhary and Sriram

2001) can be produced or 'performed' (Butler 1990). The power to transform identity grows increasingly strong as women look at how their lives and the lives of other women have changed, in India and abroad.

The increase in cultural cosmopolitanism[7] (Delanty 1999: 368) in India, through film, television and now call centres, has had a tremendous impact on the production and construction of women's identities. The 'cosmopolitanizing' effects for women working in call centres sometimes conflicted with the expectations of women in traditional roles, constructed in a familial context.

Tradition/modernity in a familial context

An excellent example of the tensions between tradition and modernity, local and global is the way in which Indian women call centre workers are represented in the national and global media and the conflicting image held by a large percentage of the wider Indian society (see Figure 1.1, p. 10). Elson and Pearson (1981b: 159) argued that although a daughter's subordination to her father may be overcome by working in a factory, it is replaced by subordination to a – most often – male superior. As kin relations do not contain the relationship, the workers are regarded as 'not quite respectable' and are subject to sexual exploitation. Elsewhere, Mies has written that women who must work for economic reasons must conform to the image of womanhood in which out-of-home economic activity is considered degrading and immoral (Mies 1979: 164). Similar observations have been made about women call centre employees in India as public opinion suggested that they were 'loose' and immoral.[8] These perceptions were based on the fact that the women worked late into the night in a male–female integrated work environment. Interviewees suggested that the erroneous correlation between 'call centres' and 'call girls' also created a negative stereotype of female call centre employees:

> When people learned I had joined a call centre they have a different kind of mindset. Probably, they think I work on those hotline services and all. They cannot believe that we actually deal with UK customers, recording their account details, and that people inquire about their own accounts. This is the perception they have.
>
> (Sangamitra, 25, GCall)

> Well, we come from a very patriarchal society in India. The common lot is not very liberal towards women working at night. There is a fair amount of scepticism about what kind of job it is that these women are doing. I know people who would say, 'Oh you talk over the phone? What kind of talk is it? What kind of customer care? Is it any kind of friendly calls that you are making or receiving?'
>
> (Nisha, 24, NCall)

Like Sangamitra and Nisha, 75 per cent of the women interviewed in the sample group stated that most people outside the call centre industry had a negative perception of women working there:

> Well it's not looked upon as a good industry because basically, to be true, people think it's like a brothel and there's some prostitutes working out here. They think they can take you for a ride whenever they want. And they think they are easy prey.
>
> (Chanelle, 25, NCall)

> Fifty per cent of the people think that the call centre woman is not good. She has no standards, no manners, she works through the night with men, but that is only 50 per cent of the people.
>
> (Urmila, 21, NCall)

All of these women were in fact employed in other industries before coming to work in call centres. Sharing examples of how they had found other work environments, they discussed their surprise at the stark difference between what was said about women working in call centres and what they had actually experienced for themselves. In essence, the negative perceptions conflicted with the interviewees' own identities, constructed as independent, liberated, modern women, and as working in the call centre provided women with opportunities to exercise agency over their lives, ultimately, for many of them, this clashed with family expectations and responsibilities.

When asked how they made the decision to apply for call centre work, 53 per cent of the sample group stated that although their families may have had initial reservations, after some consideration they were supportive about seeking opportunities in call centres. Of the rest of the sample group, 34 per cent stated that their families were not supportive and 12 per cent stated that their families had no issues with them taking up call centre work. Anshu, an employee at GCall and the eldest daughter in her family, met no objections due to her family's liberal outlook on women's education and employment:

> My parents didn't say anything. Just as long as I'm safe. As in, if I am working a night shift they just need to know I'm safe. They need to know that I will get back home safely. [GCall] provides you with all these cabs [free transport], and you've got guards, so it's quite alright with them. So they're not really worried about that. Generally, they were good. It's not like families who freak: 'Why are you working in a call centre, night shifts and everything?' In that way, at least my family has been quite supportive.
>
> (Anshu, 24, GCall)

Amrit similarly felt support from her family, and was encouraged by her sister to apply for a job at the same company. Like Amrit, 20 per cent of the sample group were encouraged by family members to consider applying for call centre work:

> There's no problem with my family ... my father is quite broadminded and now after retirement he is working as a call centre trainer. We have better job prospects in cosmopolitan cities and we need to be independent now, because we don't have any brothers to support us. We are four sisters and my two younger sisters are continuing with their studies at present. Probably they will also look into this industry.
>
> (Amrit, 23, NCall)

Amrit's choice to work in a call centre is partially due to economic necessity. However, her father's position as a call centre trainer also works to negate some of the negative perceptions that people may have of the work that they are involved with. The legitimatizing of call centre work by male family members was a common theme for those whose families were initially against call centre work – as in the case of Dipti, an out-stationed employee from Himachal Pradesh, who needed her brother to convince their father to allow her to apply for call centre work. When she was offered a job at GCall, a reputable British company, her father allowed her to take the job but forbade her from telling the rest of the family. The cases of Gurmeet and Banita are similar examples:

> This was a proposal from my brother-in-law, because he is running a call centre institute in Chandigarh. So, he had seen the atmosphere in a call centre, and it was neat and clean, and he told me to take up this job. So he convinced my family, but my mother-in-law and my husband are already very supportive. They encouraged me and gave me the signal to go ahead with it.
>
> (Gurmeet, 31, NCall)

> This is my first job, and my brother has also worked in a call centre [NCall] for three years. He is okay with it, he hasn't objected, but he can't because he is doing the same thing, and he sees a lot of girls doing the same thing, so he's okay with it.
>
> (Banita, 23, DelCall)

Whilst Anshu's experience is almost entirely a result of the encouragement that her family gave her to pursue other career options, Amrit's, Dipti's, Gurmeet's and Banita's experiences are direct examples of the way in which patriarchal power controls women's decisions regarding employment, and although Banita did not seek her brother's permission, she had prepared a defence of her decision to look for a job in a call centre by claiming equality with him. Gurmeet was faced with financial difficulties when her husband's business had failed and the family took the decision together that she would work in a call centre to contribute to the family's income. Sonali, however, had used a different tactic in telling her parents about her job. Using her parents' lack of knowledge about the industry, she told them she was working at a BPO firm, which is essentially another name for a call centre:

> To tell you the truth, I did not tell them I was working in a call centre. I told them I was working in [NCall]. I told them I was working at a BPO, which is quite different. But slowly, slowly over time, I told them that I was shifting to a call centre.
>
> (Sonali, 24, NCall)

There is very little difference in the labour processes found in call centres and BPOs, but Sonali's family, who live in a small town outside Delhi, had no knowledge of the work that Sonali was doing. Sonali had originally moved to Delhi to work for her father's friend but had since left that position. Knowing that the term 'call centre' might put her extended family off, Sonali chose to gently educate them on what she did for a living. Her long-term plans were to return to her family to arrange her marriage, so in some ways she was working for 'pocket money', and in other ways she was working to gain some independence and freedom, however long it lasted.

Others experienced the interference of community members who were not only unsupportive and suspicious but actively discouraged them from working in call centres due to the negative stereotyping:

> My aunts and most women just assumed that the call centre means call girl, which is very bad. Our neighbours used to come over to our house and tell my mum that she cannot allow me to go to work – not even leaving it up to her because they don't want me to be a bad influence on their daughters. My dad was away for work and my mum was alone at home, and she used to tell me that she would throw me out of the house if I went to work. I was at such a low point. I felt so alone, I couldn't relate to my mom, or my school–going sister.
>
> (Nidhi, 22, NCall)

Although Nidhi had received permission from her father to work in the call centre, whilst he was away for work her mother would be subjected to the scrutiny and criticisms of the neighbours in their colony. Nidhi encountered a number of obstacles dealing with her mother and resorted to lying to her mother to overcome them. Eventually, when Nidhi's father returned after a few weeks, he resolved the matter to some extent by allowing her to work but restricting her work related social activities.

The most distinctive pattern found amongst these reactions was in the geographical origins of the interviewees. Those who were out-stationed employees, 38 per cent of the total sample group, expressed greater reservation in telling their parents or extended family about working in a call centre. It was argued that outside urban centres such as Delhi fewer people actually knew what a call centre was, thus there was more room for misinterpretation.

The greatest conflict with family members that interviewees expressed was over the assumption that they were 'too' Western and 'too' independent. The interviewees stated that they did not see themselves as Western and in fact identified more with Indian culture after working in the call centre. Lim argues that the belief that Third World women are introduced to concepts of Western femininity by multinational employers reveals a feminist ethnocentrism. These concepts of femininity include dress, beauty, fashion consciousness and dating amongst co-workers (Lim 1990: 117). Lim argues that these concepts of femininity are already common elsewhere. This is also true for the fashionable campuses of most universities in India. Although call centres enhance a perceived Westernization of Indian culture, European and American cultural influences can be found in many urban centres in places such as shopping malls, cinemas, cafés, bars, nightclubs and universities (see Figure 4.1).

The conception that women call centre workers were becoming Westernized often emerged in discussions regarding future marriage prospects. Over half of the women in the sample group were single and many claimed that working as an unmarried woman was not something that could last for an extended period of time (longer than two to four years). Pressure from families to get married was not rare as Sangamitra's comments demonstrate:

> My mum used to call up on my manager's cell [phone], and she used to talk over the phone, going ga-ga for marriage: 'You are not taking your responsibilities. You are not doing what you are supposed to do.' I used to get pressure from both the sides. See, we are not supposed to receive phone calls [at work] … out of twenty-four hours in the day my cell is switched off twenty of those hours. But managers can have their phones only on vibrate, so if somebody wants to call up that is the only possible way. So I gave the number to my mum in case there is some kind of emergency, if the need to talk to me, or pass on some information to me. I really didn't know that my mum was going to call like that. I could never concentrate on my work.
>
> (Sangamitra, 25, GCall)

Sangamitra faced a great deal of pressure from her mother as the calls became more persistent, but she was finally able to tell her father that marriage was something she would focus on after she had established a career. Similarly, Preetika, who is engaged to a former call centre colleague, faced pressure to get married. Here she shares her mother's views on working after marriage:

> My mum firmly believes that when you get married, you should be there for your husband. I don't know how working nights would be accepted by my in-laws so my mum was always worried about that. She would try

to find somebody who would accept my working these late hours but, if not, she expected me to leave my job. That's what she expected, and I think she does still.

(Preetika, 24, GCallB)

Sangamitra and Preetika's examples illustrate the difficulty women have in trying to establish professional careers, and Sangamitra's mother's continued interruptions further emphasize Gayatri's comments from Chapter 3 that managers often end up taking on the role of family counsellors in balancing personal goals with family and social expectations, an argument made by Mies (1979) three decades ago. But Sangamitra and Preetika's responses to these expectations are quite different, in that Sangamitra, from a middle-class background, suffered from health issues while trying to work and deal with family pressures, finding no support and help at work. Despite an understanding and awareness of such things, Sangamitra felt powerless to change things. Knowing that Preetika enjoyed her financial independence, Preetika's mum, from an upper-class background and a doctor herself, chose a marriage partner who worked in a call centre, secure in the knowledge that he would be sensitive to her desire to continue to work. This was an option not so readily available to Sangamitra as her parents lived in Calcutta, a two-day train ride from Delhi, leaving them much more removed from her life. These two experiences show clear examples of the way in which class intersects with career ambition and shapes the women's work experiences and the ways in which they relate to one another.

Women such as Chanelle and Dipti, both of whom have boyfriends in the call centre industry, suggested that their future in-laws may hold negative views of call centre workers marrying their sons:

Like, suppose if I had to get married tomorrow and I say that, you know, I'm working with a call centre. I don't think a family would want their would-be daughter-in-law working with a call centre.

(Chanelle, 25, NCall)

My friend said that if you want to look for girls in call centres you will find amazing girls, lots of girls to go out with, but you won't find a wife.

(Dipti, 25, NCall)

Although they offered criticisms of such views and argued that women had the right to work, Chanelle and Dipti did not believe that they could subvert patriarchal norms. Both indicated that although they could exercise agency over decisions regarding how to spend their leisure time and what clothes to wear to work, this agency was not something they could exercise over other areas in their lives, in particular decisions related to family and marriage. Both women were from working-class backgrounds and had boyfriends who were approved by the family, thus they felt disempowered to challenge their boyfriends' beliefs. Dipti shared a few examples of clashes she had with her boyfriend over clothing choices, but ultimately she did what she was asked, precisely because she was aware of the damage that would be caused to her reputation should he break off the relationship. Anyuta's comments below present a stronger example of how patriarchal perceptions of women and employment affected women's decisions about work and family:

> One of my friends, he was a colleague in the IT industry, his reaction to my joining a call centre was very negative. We were really more than friends, changing the relationship to make it more serious. But the whole thing came to a standstill, stopped and broke the day I joined the call centre. I wasn't expecting the reaction I got. Even his parents were not very happy with the idea. They even told me over the phone, 'We do not appreciate you going out and working in the night.' I said, 'It's not something I do during the night. I get home before the night.' But they said, 'No, girls in our family don't do that.' I got a big answer about my future.
>
> (Anyuta, 26, NCall)

Despite the implication that call centres had contributed to a Westernizing of their identities, not all women agreed that this was the case, as some expressed a pressure to conform to the idealized, Western standard assumed by outsiders to be found in the call centre, the process of 'institutionalized cosmopolitanism' (Beck 2004).

Institutionalized cosmopolitanism

The increased interdependence of social actors across national boundaries that have no normative cosmopolitan intent can lead to the emergence of 'institutionalized cosmopolitanism' (Beck 2004: 132), which can be understood on one level as overlapping, layering or hybridizing (Pieterse, 1995) and on another as a cultural clash. Upasana, an employee of NCall, originally from Assam in North East India, shares her views on these cultural dynamics:

> We are just doing a job and I think people are becoming more broad-minded because we are learning a lot about different cultures, and there is a lot of interaction between the West and the East through telephone calls. I don't think we are losing any of our culture; at heart, we are always Indians and we love India. We still listen to our parents, we still follow the rules. Just because we are working at night, does not make us less Indian. We are learning to neutralize our accents, that's it.
>
> (Upasana, 28, NCall)

Upasana expresses an underlying sense of Indianness, a transnational and translational (Bhabha 1994) sense of Indian identity contributing to her 'dialogical self' (Chaudhary and Sriram 2001), developed through the ongoing dialogue in which she participates between the West and the East. Although this appears to further Mirchandani's (2004a, 2004b) claims of 'locational masking', Upasana is arguing for an interactive, mutually constitutive process of identity construction rather than an inherent, fixed, essential Indianness. It is through the process of conversation and dialogue that Upasana feels and becomes more Indian, laying claims to identities when they are challenged. Echoing Lim's (1990) argument that Western values are not just introduced by multinationals and can be found elsewhere in society, Smita's comments below indicate the pervasiveness of Western culture, suggesting that call centres are not responsible for the erosion or 'rubbing' (Griffin 2000) of 'concrete' local cultural processes (Sassen 1998):

> No, there isn't a loss, from my point of view. I don't think I've lost anything; I'm just learning something new. It doesn't mean that I'm letting go of something. It just means that, probably, I might forget. Probably. Or that my child might not learn it. My child might not learn what my mother showed me or taught me. I can't say, 'No, don't watch TV, because I'm losing my Indian culture.' I can't. I can't stop reading the newspapers. I can't stop watching English movies. I can't help it. There is nothing you can do about it. We're not losing anything. Just learning something else.
>
> (Smita, 33, NCall)

Smita has travelled and lived in a number of different places. Her experiences, shared elsewhere in this book, have taught her to embrace global culture and difference. Smita's perspective on changes to Indian culture concurs with what Robertson (1995) and Welsch (1999) have argued, in that culture is part of an 'interchange process', that it is contingent as well as differentiating, much like Bhabha's discussion of mimicry, which in itself is a process of disavowal (Bhabha 1994: 122). Indian culture is not something that is concrete or unmoveable, but rather, as Smita indicates, it is contingent upon global culture, influenced by television, newspapers and movies. Moreover, her use of terms such as 'probably' and 'might' in discussing the loss of Indian culture points to her lack of conviction that globalizing cultural flows will irrevocably affect Indian culture.

Upasana and Smita quite clearly point to call centres as *part* of a shift in India and certainly not wholly responsible for changes to contemporary Indian culture. However, others, who argued that call centres were directly contributing to massive transformation in India and as a consequence their lives had changed in ways that they were not prepared for, did not share these thoughts:

> Whenever [my boyfriend] saw girls pass by in jeans he used to say, 'Come on, what's happening with girls today?' And I used to say, 'I don't wear it so why do you have to comment,' and he would say, 'I know you wouldn't but you would let your daughter wear it.' And we fought a lot about it.
>
> (Dipti, 25, NCall)

Dipti spent time discussing her boyfriend's concern that working in a call centre would change her and establish a trajectory of modernity and liberalism that she would apply to raising their children. Although a greater discussion of clothing is presented later in this chapter (p. 116), Dipti's 'institutionalized cosmopolitanism' (Beck 2004), as perceived by her boyfriend, found her caught between desiring change and unable to experience what that change might offer her, as she was hemmed in by how her boyfriend chose to see her. Clothing in India functions as a way in which to code the body in terms of sexuality and modesty. Dipti expresses a pressure to conform to the norms of call centre culture and a pressure to remain a modest woman in her boyfriend's eyes:

> I used to always wear [Punjabi] suits all the time. It happened that we had a [work] party at night and [my boyfriend] was to accompany me and I was feeling very uncomfortable because I didn't want to go to a disc [disco] in a [Punjabi] suit. And I had to go because I was stamped with being unsocial. And that was a party that I could take him along. I wanted to go but I didn't want to wear a [Punjabi] suit. And he said no. We had a long, long fight.

> (Dipti, 25, NCall)

From a social perspective Punjabi suits, a signifier of traditional female roles, are not acceptable as clothing to wear to discos as they are not considered modern. Moreover, the pressure to conform to the norms of call centre culture, which require her to go to discos or else be labelled as unsocial, is felt in Dipti's comments. The tension between tradition and modernity and the sense of 'institutionalized cosmopolitanism' as it is played out on women's bodies, a contested site for meaning and cultural signification (Jaywardena 1986; Mohanty et al. 1991), go some way towards explaining the patriarchal structures that Dipti must exercise agency through. Caught between the traditional, mythic image of Mother India[9] and the image of New/Liberated/Modern Woman (Chanda 2004: 228), Dipti articulates the difficulty in producing a sense of agency through patriarchal discourses. Her efforts to negotiate with him and, as she later discusses, their shopping trip together serve to further reinforce the argument that Indian women's identities are produced through patriarchal norms and discourses.

A second example of this tension is the way in which call centre culture, arising out of sexually integrated work sites, produced spaces of sexual liberalism, simultaneously increasing pressure on men and women to have a boyfriend or girlfriend. Banita, who was initially opposed to the idea of working in a call centre, was using her job as a stepping-stone to secure employment in the engineering profession. Although Banita had a boyfriend outside the call centre industry, in her first few weeks of training at DelCall she was continually asked questions about her relationship:

> With the guys, a couple of times, you have to tell them, 'Look, I'm seeing someone.' It's always the first question, after the introduction, 'Do you have a boyfriend?'
>
> (Banita, 23, DelCall)

Banita told me that she felt scrutinized by male employees, remarking that the men at her workplace were disrespectful towards their female counterparts, and she offered the following comments as an explanation:

> See, because you spend so much time there, a lot of people have girl-friends and boyfriends, and if you introduce an employee in [DelCall] you get 5,000 extra bucks, so what people have done is got a lot of their friends there. So now it's kind of like a gang culture. People have their girlfriends working. Each and every one has a girlfriend or a friend or someone. So it's like that. After a hard day's work people want to sit around the cafe-teria and talk like that, or probably go out on a Saturday night. It's more of a *requirement* to have [a boyfriend] to freak out with.
>
> (Banita, 23, DelCall)

As part of a strategy to lower attrition rates and to build social bonds between employees, many companies held social gatherings for their employees. Banita stated that DelCall were planning a trip to Goa to celebrate the New Year and they were taking 1,500 people. However, she was not planning to attend as she was not comfortable with the idea that her male and female colleagues would be sharing rooms:

> No, I'm not going to go. I have heard that girls and guys go together, they share rooms. Whatever goes on there, I don't think I'm going to go for it. I mean, it's a nice thing if you have a boyfriend or girlfriend. No one's going to say anything; you can just say you have an office thing. But I'm not going to go.
>
> (Banita, 23, DelCall)

These examples of the perceived 'requirements' and expectations reveal pres-sures on women call centre workers not unlike the pressures felt from family expectations. Like Banita, Nidhi, who was quoted earlier on this chapter, also expressed a tension between the cultural expectations of her family and those of the call centre:

> Because I live in such a conventional area, I have only enjoyed five par-ties. And after that it was no. I promised my father for a lifetime that I would never, never go. I had to lie. Five parties that I went to, five times I had to lie. I said it was an office meeting because it's a call centre, odd hours. They always catch on, especially my mum, looking at me thinking, 'Why is she wearing such nice clothes?' They would wonder why only on

Friday I would wear such nice clothes, sparkling clothes with metallic bits. I never told them I was going to a party. Then they said, 'Even if there is a meeting, there is no need to go out.'

(Nidhi, 22, NCall)

Previously Nidhi had discussed her neighbours' interference in her decision to work and she had promised her father that she would only go to work for her scheduled shifts. She had already bargained with him in trading a subject of his choice to study for a master's in exchange for allowing her to work in the call centre. However, she was unaware at that time how much she would love the social life that the call centres offered. Nidhi was not only banned from attending out of hours office meetings and social events, she was also forced by her father to take on further educational training. She expressed her frustration and sadness, sharing that her only opportunities to socialize with her co-workers were on the journey to and from work. However, she was grateful that her father allowed her to continue working at NCall. This is at least one example of the way in which women make patriarchal bargains to exercise agency over the localized, patriarchal norms that shape their family lives and the globalized, cultural norms that shape their work lives, thus returning the discussion to earlier arguments regarding the use of women as a sign for India's economic liberalization, a sign which does not necessarily afford women liberation (Chanda, 2004).

Dipti's, Banita's and Nidhi's accounts present examples of some of the tensions experienced in negotiating traditional and modern identities; however, all of the sample group indicated that to some extent they felt more Westernized or modern after working in a call centre. A reading that presents this simply as a positive or negative experience would be something of an oversimplification, as many interviewees indicated that although they felt positive about changes to their self-identities, they were uncomfortable with the way in which the changes were brought about. Moreover, they argued that, rather than the expectation that they should conform to call centre culture, they were most frustrated by the perception that Westernization was inevitable: Dipti and her boyfriend argued over what clothing she should wear; Banita struggled with the sexually liberalized atmosphere of the call centre; and Nidhi fought with her parents to fully embrace call centre work life. These accounts of a 'cosmopolitanizing' of their identities were also reflective of how they saw wider changes in society, most notably with regard to sexual relationships and the way women dressed. The following two sections will expand on these wider shifts in society by examining, first, sexuality and relationships with men and, second, the much larger issue of what to wear.

Sexuality and relationships with men

Recent economic liberalization policies have boosted sexual liberalism in India, bringing about new dimensions of sexuality; the marketing and consumption of new cultural and material products invested with modern sexual value and meaning also act as 'crucial markers' of identity (Abraham 2004: 211). Emerging as a signifier of both traditional and modern social norms, the body has become a site for the expression and realization of modernity, as is increasingly reflected in changing 'mediascapes' (Appadurai 1996). Simultaneously, women's sexuality is regarded with ambivalence as they have been constructed as both goddesses and as destroyers.[10]

Sexual liberalism is male oriented as the centrality of marriage is still strong for women due to reasons such as social security; thus liberal sexual attitudes preserve traditional notions of male and female sexuality, perpetuating notions of women's shame and honour (Abraham 2004: 231). Abraham argues that the forces of globalization are inadequate as a challenge to the dominant ideologies that confine women's sexuality, since these ideologies do not protect women, and transgressing them does not liberate women (Abraham 2004: 241). They are caught between the liberalization that is offered and the lack of liberty experienced. Jennifer shares her views on women's growing independence:

> Yes, I think women are becoming more independent now, but because they are entering the industry at a very young age, they are not mature enough and they are getting into a lot of wrong things. They make a lot of mistakes and get into wrong associations and relationships. It [call centres] has made a big difference on the girls' values and principles than it did in olden times. It is a good opportunity for women, but it is making them more vulnerable.
>
> (Jennifer, 38, NCall)

Whilst call centres have increased women's opportunities for independence, the sexually liberated, and I would say sexually charged, atmosphere means that questions regarding women's respectability were raised, reiterating earlier arguments regarding family attitudes to call centres. Of the women interviewed in the sample group, 56 per cent were single, 25 per cent had a boyfriend, 9 per cent were engaged to be married and 9 per cent were married.[11] Of the women who were with partners (43 per cent of the entire sample group), 57 per cent had met their current partner whilst working in a call centre, as Indu explains:

> Yes, we met in [GCall] itself. We were on different processes and different shift timings but we used to see each other every day. Weekends we were always together. Since we both finished by 1.30 on Friday and weekends we had off, we used to both stay in the office until seven to eight o'clock in the morning on Friday nights. Then he used to drop me off at home and on Saturday nights we would go out and freak out. We would go to a restaurant or a disc [disco], or just hang out at the office. The place where I was putting up, my landlady was too strict about guys coming round.

You know the psychology that Indian people have. So sometimes we would simply go to the office and sit for hours and hours and just chat.

(Indu, 26, DelCallB)

In effort to avoid the criticisms of conservative Indians, Indu and her boy-friend found the only way to continue their courtship was in a clandestine fashion, and in such a way call centres offered romantic, private spaces for couples to meet and form relationships. The view commonly held by the interviewees was that call centres provided ideal spaces to meet men, free from familial objections and public scrutiny, spaces where women and men could interact with one another in a safe environment. When asked about men and women's relationships, Nidhi offered these comments:

Well, it depends, 70 per cent of the women are into one relationship. Maybe 2 per cent are into one night stands. Then I think it's about 20 per cent who have very frequent multiple relationships. But I think most of the time people are looking for long-term relationships which will take them to marriage. Most of the women in the call centre are looking for relationships with people they want to marry.

(Nidhi, 22, NCall)

Women did not necessarily enter the call centres specifically to find marriage partners; however, the sexually liberated, charged atmosphere produced conditions in which it was almost a requirement to have a partner, as Banita points out. Given the suspicion concerning women's sexuality and questions regarding their respectability, women were largely seeking out men they wanted to marry rather than date. However, the sample group was evenly divided on the issue of how men viewed women working in call centres with respect to marriageability, often using the phrase 'time-pass' to indicate a transitory sexual relationship (Abraham 2004: 231):

There are very few men who respect women as colleagues, or as their friends. What I would say is that 80 per cent of the men do not respect the women out here.

(Indu, 26, DelCallB)

[Men] probably prefer not to marry a girl who works for a call centre, who dresses up like that, who parties so much. [They] may have a girl-friend who is like that because she's good company but then for him to settle down with a wife, it would be a very different image that he would have. You know he would still be very Indian about that. He'd prefer the girl to be ... Okay, party with him, but not as in call centres and partying with different people. Just party with him, if it's required [for] work, but at the same time be really sober.

(Anshu, 24, GCall)

Ironically, Indu and Anshu were both seeing men who worked in call centres. Indu's comments suggest that her own boyfriend falls into the 20 per cent who treat working women with the respect that they deserve, whilst Anshu chose not to reveal her relationship with a colleague to me. Whether this demonstrates Anshu's commitment to the relationship or her anxiety about being too public with it is uncertain. However, it is clear that both women were struggling with how the 'rules' of the call centre, in which women needed to have relationships to fit in and possibly thwart the attentions of other men, affected their lives outside of the call centre.

Informal interviews and discussions with groups of men and women supported the views put forward by Indu and Anshu; however, a large majority of the sample group indicated that the views of their male colleagues were changing. Here Anshu explains her thoughts:

> Men are kind of changing. We work here about fourteen to sixteen hours … so when you are with people for such a long time and you have parties, and you have these outings with the team, you get to know people, you get to know the girls. So the men also get to know that maybe they party [but] that they are normal nice girls.
>
> (Anshu, 24, GCall)

> They're more sensitive and they have got an idea what women go through while they're working and while they are managing their homes and their studies. They're getting assimilated, into women's issues, basically. Earlier there was not so much awareness about women. They have come to know about what women can do and how they can manage both ends.
>
> (Amrit, 23, NCall)

> Because my process is during the day, they respect women here. They respect the fact that they are working together with women. Most of the men are married here, and a couple of them have women sitting at home, so they respect that we are intelligent and we are working. A couple of them have said, 'I look at you, and I look at the other women, and I go back home and I tell my wife that she should get a job here.'
>
> (Preetika, 24, GCallB)

Preetika's experiences are somewhat limited given the fact that she works on a daytime process and her motivation to work in the call centre is for extra money and to keep busy. Anshu and Amrit are both looking for opportunities to further their careers and have more invested in changing the negative perceptions of working women. The integrated work environment has largely created opportunities for men and women to learn more about each other, particularly in the case of men.

In many ways the views of their male colleagues impacted upon the wider perception of women in call centres, as discussed earlier, but also upon those women who were already in relationships. Banita's boyfriend, although unhappy with her taking a job she was overqualified for, supported her decision:

> He was pretty all right with it. As long as he thought, you know, you can handle yourself. He didn't approve of it initially because he thought that I was overqualified for the job but he's all right with it now. He says, 'It is upon you, if you want to invite trouble, it's there, but if you do your own thing I don't think there is any harm in working anywhere.'
>
> (Banita, 23, DelCall)

Of the women in relationships, 38 per cent stated that their decision to work in a call centre was met with reservations from their partners. The following three excerpts from interviews with Dipti, Gurmeet and Urmila relate some of the views that men expressed to them regarding their partners working in call centres:

> [My boyfriend] didn't like what he heard went on in the office. He was always insecure about me. He used to think I was drinking and smoking all the time. He sees the changes in me. When we first met there is no way I would have a male smoking next to me but now when a female is smoking next to me I am perfectly fine. So he has seen the change in me. And that makes him uncomfortable with me. He doesn't want me to be comfortable with people smoking. When I first started we used to have these night outs and the girls would all go. It was absolutely not Indian, absolutely not Indian. He wasn't happy with that. And he knew I wasn't that kind of girl but he was always scared.
>
> (Dipti, 25, NCall)

> To some extent [my husband] is bothered. The girls out here go to lots of parties and go out but I am not allowed to go because I have to take my husband's permission first, even if I go to a movie with my friends. I do have to take his permission, and let him know who all are going with me. So I'm not that kind of free to move around. I don't think that I will get the chance to go to any of the parties. My husband is not like that.
>
> (Gurmeet, 31, NCall)

> Once I invited him to [NCall], you know. Here we greet each other as friends by hugging, and he saw everything and he was like pissed off like anything. And he said, 'What is all this, that is going on? Do you come here to work or do all this stuff?' I said that this is our way. It's very cool. It's very normal here. So he was pissed off, but now I've quit all this kind of stuff. I don't hug my friends now. I just greet them. I just shake their hands.
>
> (Urmila, 21, NCall)

The subtle differences in the way in which patriarchal power was exercised provides, first, insight into the range of experiences women had working in call centres given the differences in their backgrounds and, second, the ways in which women negotiated with their partners to continue working at the call centre. Although their partners could see changes in them, and in Dipti's case were threatened by them, the women struck 'patriarchal bargains' (Kandiyoti 1988), strategizing within sets of restraints. All three women conceded to their partner's wishes; however, each of them continued to exercise agency within the patriarchal framework, either through direct acts of agency or through more subtle shifts in continuing to work at the call centre and changing family and social perceptions slowly over time.

The remainder of this chapter is devoted to a discussion of clothing and the way in which sartorial strategies are used in a political way and in a pragmatic way, beginning with the significance of dress and the historical context of Indian clothing, and ending with a discussion of patterns of identification and recognition.

Significance of dress and clothing[12]

Clothing provides a means through which we can examine the expression of personal and collective identity as well as being a marker of social identity throughout periods of social change; as clothing is worn in a public space, we dress for others and not for ourselves (Crane 2000: 237).[13] Academic work on fashion has been criticized for its limited analysis of cultural signification and its assumption that non-Western clothing is non-changing and infused with deeper cultural meanings. It has been argued that 'elements from different dress codes are strategically played off against one another in the process of forming other dress codes and body techniques' (Craik 1994: 30).[14] Whilst allowing for spaces to challenge social norms and experiment with identity, fashion also 'opens up possibilities for framing the self, at least momentarily, since fashion is always moving, never stable' (Entwistle 2000: 74).

Freeman (1993) noted that employees in the Caribbean data entry corporations were asked to dress 'smartly' and 'professionally' for work and that if their clothing did not meet certain standards they would be subject to disciplinary action.[15] However, drawing upon Foucault's work concerning the 'Panopticon' and power, Freeman pointed out that the use of a strict dress code presented one way in which the corporations exercised control over the bodies of the employees.[16] The 'institutionalized cosmopolitanism' of call centres is another example of this, as the women interviewed expressed an implicit expectation that they wear 'smart' clothing, marking them as modern, fashionable, cosmopolitan women:

> From Monday to Thursday, you can wear smart casual clothes. That means you can wear trousers, you cannot wear jeans. You can't wear all these round neck tee-shirts and stuff, otherwise you can wear anything feminine. I generally wear trousers and shirts to work. I'll tell you, most of the women working here all wear Western clothes. It's much easier from me to wear Western because all the salwaar-kameeze [trousers] and dupattas

[headscarves] and everything is too much. I've seen other friends who are working really hard on what they wear to the office, 'Because I have a meeting I'm going to wear this.'

(Anshu, 24, GCall)

Anshu, is a self-confessed tomboy and during our conversations it was quite clear that she associated Indian clothing with being older, married and possibly having children. Quite often, when employees work on days that are national holidays in India but are still considered work days for the UK market, call centres like GCall will put on special menus, offer prizes and bonuses, and invite staff to dress in traditional clothing for the day. On these occasions, Anshu has worn a sari to work and has attracted a lot of attention from men in the call centre. Friends of Anshu mentioned that she had many admirers and it is because of this that she often downplayed her attractiveness, particularly by dressing in casual trousers and shirts, and certainly nothing overtly feminine like Punjabi suits.

The desire to dress in clothing that looked professional and the distinction between wearing Western and Indian clothing presented two strategies that women used to identify and recognize one another as certain types in the call centre. Notions of professionalism and modernity are heavily tied into clothing, a strategy which has roots in the Mughal era, when clothing was often handmade and invested with cultural, regional, economic and religious meaning. Impacted greatly by the industrial revolution and the arrival of colonialism, clothing became an expression of class and colonial identity (Tarlo 1996; de la Haye and Wilson 1999; Crane 2000).

During the colonial period, Indian upper-class men incorporated European fashions into their own dress codes as a way to both align themselves with the ruling British class and to separate themselves from the uneducated Indian majority. This remains the case today as men rarely wear traditional dress in everyday life, keeping it for special occasions only (Raghuram 2003). The move to European fashion did not apply to Indian women as they were 'largely shielded from the British and their clothes' (Tarlo 1996: 320). Thus in a country highly stratified on many levels – including social, sexual, religious, political, economic, cultural and regional levels – the problem of what to wear is complicated further by a desire for upward social mobility.[17]

A significant change for women's clothing and sartorial strategies took place in Delhi as the post-Partition (1947) arrival of Sikh, Muslim and Hindu Punjabi refugees from Pakistan and Punjab introduced distinct cultural practices of eating, socializing and dressing, and in particular the popularization of the Punjabi suit or salwaar-kameeze. The salwaar-kameeze, often referred to simply as a suit, is comprised of three separate pieces: the *kurta* or *kameeze*, the salwaar or pyjama, and a chunni or dupatta, which functions as a scarf or headcover. Indu, who started her career as a teacher, discovered that she was regarded as more of a professional when dressed in Indian clothes as opposed to the Western clothes she was familiar with when studying:

> When I was at college, I was all only Western clothes. My [Indian] suits were only for family functions. When I started working with the school I could not wear Western outfits. When I was teaching, I only wore suits, because being young I had to show the students that I still had a hold on them. But when I came to the call centre, I started switching my wardrobe. Now it's 50:50.
>
> (Indu, 26, NCallB)

The direct link between older women and suits is an association that affords women more respectability because society is able to identify them with a collectivity (Yuval-Davis 1994). However, the wearing of Punjabi suits also serves to control women as, the conflation of women's identities with politically constructed Indian identities leads to a direct link between women and morality, particularly the preservation of morality, enforced through the meanings invested in women's clothing. Women's centrality to the preservation and protection of home and nationality continues to persist in contemporary Indian society and is evoked in the questions concerning what women wear (Bhatia 2003: 337–38).

Based on ethnographic observations and the use of 'constant comparative analysis' (Strauss and Corbin 1994: 273), the research found that women in the call centres wore both Indian clothing and Western clothing, and although some of them chose to wear both, many of them wore one or the other for a large majority of the time. The women were evenly split on wearing Indian and Western clothing in the sense that the call centre floor was evenly divided, with no visible majority of one or the other. There were largely two groupings, which were women who had just left college or university and women who were engaged, married or older. Those who had just finished college tended to wear Western clothing, while those who were in the second group tended to wear Indian clothing, mainly Punjabi suits as opposed to saris. However, at least two-thirds of the sample group indicated that they would wear both, with the other one-third indicating that they would only wear Punjabi suits.

As both casual, Western clothing and Indian suits and saris are acceptable clothing to wear to work, questions were raised as to how the women made their choices and why. Anyuta and Urmila share their thoughts on how differently they feel in certain outfits:

> When you are wearing jeans, you can go jump across fences, you can run around, run up the stairs. But when you were wearing a sari or a suit, the way you walk, the way you carry yourself is a little more feminine, a little more soft. I wouldn't be running across the stairs wearing a suit and sandals.
>
> (Anyuta, 26, NCall)

> I feel myself that I'm very much mature when I wear suits. My way of thinking even changes. When I wear jeans, I speak like I'm in college, using

slang. But when I wear suits and all, I skip all that slang and become somewhat decent. Basically a lady.

(Urmila, 21 NCall)

Both women articulate the pervasive notion that femininity, morality and women's clothing are linked, serving to reinforce notions of women's centrality to the preservation of Indian culture. For north Indians, the Punjabi suit or kurta pyjama signifies decency, honour and marriageability, preserving a woman's 'izzat'.[18] This is more so in northern rural communities; however, with the rise in numbers of women professionals, women are increasingly dressing in suits as opposed to saris, contributing to a societal shift which views wearing a suit as power dressing (Reddy 2003). Women use 'power dressing' to 'manage' or limit the potential sexuality of their bodies in order to assert their professionalism (Craik 1994; Entwistle 2000: 32). Furthermore, growing numbers of women are abandoning the sari in favour of the salwaar-kameeze for the sake of convenience and ease when travelling as it is more practical for mobility. For those not wearing a salwaar-kameeze, what was once considered a dignified way of dressing has now been abandoned by the younger generation, who increasingly wear jeans and Western clothes, leaving the salwaar-kameeze for formal occasions and implying that saris and the salwaar-kameeze are for the 'dull, dumb, and unsuccessful' (Reddy 2003):

I wear Western a lot now. Earlier I used to wear suits as well but ... Quite long back I used to wear suits, about three years back. But I have left it now ... Totally ... Occasionally, if you're going for a wedding or if you are going for any puja [prayer], then ... if the occasion demands ... But I am quite comfortable with jeans and trousers because you don't need to carry your dupatta [headscarf], it's going here and there [laughing]. You need to be very concerned about such things while wearing suits.

(Amrit, 23, NCall)

I don't feel very comfortable in suits. I feel better when I'm wearing a skirt. I feel more comfortable and it's easy to walk in. Suits with dupattas all the time, and this is the rainy season, so it gets very messy. And because I drive I need to be free, not with my dupatta flying somewhere, and my hair going somewhere. And when you think of a call centre you somehow think of women wearing Western clothes because it is not a very Indian concept. Call centres are not an Indian concept at all. When you walk in a call centre, you don't expect a woman wearing saris or suits with bangles – you think, 'What is this?' In fact, you would rather see a girl dressed in a skirt or shorts, something Western.

(Monica, 22, NCall)

Both women's comments here underscore the need for mobility. Not only do suits signify maturity and notions of cultural preservation, they also function as items that limit the actions of the body, oppressing them and making mobility difficult. Amrit's and Monica's comments also highlight the growing transformation of urban centres in India, where women imitate the glamorous images of Bollywood stars and 'Miss Indias', aspiring to become a part of the 'mobile elite' (Bauman 1998). The images of stars, constructed to show India's ability to 'impress, conquer, or tame the West', simultaneously intensify the patriarchal insecurities of the new middle class (Sangari 2003: 7). Moreover, the images of independent Indian women participating in a liberalized economy directly conflict with the BJP-constructed images of self-sacrificing Hindu women, a conflict acutely felt by women call centre workers, as Reena's comments show:

> The call centre industry is not governed by Indians. You don't have to wear a suit, you can wear trousers. But there are girls who dress quite skimpily. They are wearing spaghetti straps and very short minis. But you have to wear clothes, even if it is an American culture. You must cover yourself. We are becoming more and more Americanized, especially the call centre industry. Whatever they are leaving, we are picking them up. The general trends, I mean. We are becoming more Americanized in the way of our dressing, the way of our talking. There are girls that dress this way and come to the office and people think everyone in the call centre must also dress that way ... because of that one or two females, the guys are taking every other girl for granted.
>
> (Reena, 26, NCallB)

Reena's own way of dressing was a mix of Indian and Western and it was clear from her conversations with me that she felt pressure to dress in fashionable Western clothes. Whilst the majority of women wore jeans at college, there was a clear understanding that now they had left college and were earning salaries, such outfits were inviting attention from men. Reena, like many of the other women, also discussed wearing suits when she felt the need to be comfortable and wear loose garments, indicating that jeans and tight clothes were revealing and required confidence, hence the jeans took on other meanings concerning power dynamics amongst the women.

Moving beyond a challenge to social norms, politicized use of clothing and an expression of self-identity, fashion and clothing are always in process and never fixed (Entwistle 2000: 74), thus meanings are contingently produced through social, political and cultural contexts. From the comments above, it could quite easily be read that modern, cosmopolitan women were largely rejecting an Indian style of dress in favour of Western clothing, but such a reading would be simplistic as much more was happening with the women's clothing and fashion sense. As I have argued elsewhere in this book, the local and the global do not exist in opposition to one another but are mutually constitutive of one another, as seen through the cut-and-mix style of fashion.

Ethnic fusion

Fashion can also allow for the appropriation or rejection of cultural hegemony or social norms, resulting in globalized or hybridized identities (Bhachu 2004; Crane 2000; Tarlo 1996; Tulloch 1999). Whilst Western clothing previously signified modernity and the modernizing process (Craik 1994), it would seem that now the fusion of non-Western and Western clothing could be interpreted as a signifier of modernity. Mani proposes using a Butlerian framework (Butler 1990) in substituting race for gender, in which 'ethnic identity becomes a series of temporally bounded performative acts that are enacted in synchrony with (though not congruently to)' hegemonic social norms (Mani 2003: 122), demonstrating how dress can act as a form of re-territorialization.

Objects such as clothing can be emptied of their original meaning and reconstituted as signs or signifiers, erasing traces of territorialization (Lash and Urry 1994: 14–15), thereby investing clothing choices with distinct, political meaning that disturbs the 'assumed coherence between categories of race, nation, and culture' (Mani 2003: 119). Arguing that articulations of hybridity can be taken to mean that Western culture is not pure, the origin or the destination of everything, Grewal and Kaplan (1994: 7) suggest that hybridity can be read as a challenging of hegemonic codes (Bhachu 2004). This resonates with what both Hansen (1999) and Milgram (2005) have identified in the second-hand clothes trade in Zambia and the Philippines (respectively). Although on the one hand understood as a 'dumping' of unwanted secondhand clothes from developed nations, this can also be reanalysed to discern a 'personalized logic' through which these clothes are received and marketed. This 'hybridization' or 'creolization' 'emphasizes the inflow of goods, their reception, and domestication thus shifting attention from a focus on the outflow of goods from the West and the intent of Western producers' (Milgram 2005: 135). This highlights the creativity and agency of consumers and re-contextualizes the goods within local practices and values. Milgram also suggests that it questions the extent to which the goods retain their original value or power. The transfers of new meanings privilege the subjects' local and cultural political agenda rather than assuming a powerlessness or naïveté (Milgram 2005: 136), similar to Freeman's (2000) work as she argues that the pink collar informatics operator represents a new category of worker empowered by her professional appearance and far removed from the field and kitchen work of her mother. Again, this employment was not viewed as merely back office work, but as a professional, modern form of employment.

'Asian chic', 'self-orientalization' (Leshkowich and Jones 2003; Nagrath 2003), 'kitsch cool', 'classic chic' (Gahlaut 2005), 'ethnic chic' and 'desi' (Tarlo 1996: 311) are just some of the many terms used to describe the fusion of Indian and Western clothing and styles.[19] Recent trends in India linking identity politics with consumption show Indians turning the Orientalist gaze back on themselves, engaging in 'ersatz Orientalism' or, more aggressively, 'cultural cannibalism' (Toor 2000), as seen in the Lakme Fashion Week held in Mumbai.

Traditional-style dresses and ornaments are increasingly marketed in contemporary urban India as 'ethnic fashions'. Some have argued that when an ethnic group begins to sell itself as an ethnic attraction the group members begin to view themselves as living representatives of an authentic way of life (Bhattacharyya 1997). However, in South Africa 'Africanization' of clothing is understood as a link to the strategy for constructing a post-apartheid national identity (Klopper 2000). 'Ethnic chic' or 'ersatz Orientalism' forms part of a strategy designed to produce a nationalized global identity, where cultural specialists have reinvented tradition and reshaped ethnicity.

By destabilizing the space of performance, the limits in reproducing national narratives can be interrogated (Mani 2003: 123). Evidence of this destabilizing can be found in the popularization of the kurti, signifying an upward mobility[20] and a distinction from the assumed Americanization of call centre workers. The release of the film *Chalte Chalte* (2003), starring Shah Rukh Khan and Rani Mukherjee, created a fever pitch for 'ethnic fusion', as one of the film's defining elements was the use of kurtas and kurtis paired with jeans for its two lead actors, a look that was already popular on college and university campuses. The ethnically fused look reached a wider market and the design of kurtis went from simple cotton ones to detailed silk and brocade ones for the upper class. Ethnic fashion in India is a strategy used by upper-class educated Indians to distinguish themselves from the uneducated Indian majority but also a way in which they can differentiate themselves from the West (Tarlo 1996: 324–28), leading back to observations that the first world is increasingly found in the third and the Third World is found in the first (Hardt and Negri 2000). The Indian upper classes, and increasingly the middle class, use sartorial strategies to maintain their identities as members of the 'indigenous elite' (Banerjee and Linstead 2001), a strategy used to tighten particular social circles whilst excluding others. Banerjee and Linstead draw upon Howes' use of the term 'creolization' to denote

> the process of recontextualization whereby foreign goods are assigned meanings and uses by the culture of reception ... Although Third World people may *seem* to be manipulated into buying consumer goods which are alien to, and destructive of, their cultures, in fact, they are actively employing consumer goods to express and forge their own unique identities.
>
> (Banerjee and Linstead 2001: 699)

The pairing of jeans and kurtis demonstrates both the recontexualization of foreign clothes and 'Ersatz Orientalism', constructed to signify an identity that is both Indian and Western, local and global.

The association of jeans with college life, and modernity, is a common one, with the many college and university students fusing kurtas and kameeze with jeans, as Smita comments:

> Oh! [In jeans] you feel younger, sexier, tighter, sharper and jumpier. You could probably jump off of a gate. In a suit, you have to get into the car

quietly and get out of the car nicely. And normally you wouldn't end up talking in a loud voice. It's two different people. That's jeans versus suits; it's like jeans versus an evening dress. In suits, I become more feminine. In jeans, I'm back in college.

(Smita, 33, NCall)

These consumption patterns were particularly evident with call centre workers, of whom many had some disposable income and spent weekends and days off shopping in markets.[21] Dressing in fashionable clothing distinguished them from other professions and shopping was a favourite pastime on days off with other co-workers. An important question that must be raised here is why the issue of clothing has been made so significant for a customer service labour process in which the employee does not actually see the customer. Returning to the notion of emotional labour and Bourdieu's (1984) arguments on investments in appearance, the consumption patterns of call centre workers took an interesting turn in concentrating on clothing, appearance and the 'aestheticization of labour' (Witz et al. 2003).

Aestheticization of work identities

Just as the deep acting of emotional labour (Hochschild 1983) can lead to transformations of the self, aesthetic labour (Witz et al. 2003) can lead to transformations of the 'flesh'. Embodiment is implicit in the manipulation of presentation and performance, 'which must be maintained in order to become and remain an employee of a particular organization and to "embody" that organization' (Tyler and Hancock 2001: 25).

An increased feminization of the labour process has transposed the feminine 'habitus' into the economy. This feminization is understood to be constitutive of a reflexive attitude in relation to gender in the work environment (Adkins 2002: 74–75). Dress codes are about more than looking nice or professional; they reinforce feminine qualities and foster competition amongst workers (Gottfried 1992: 452–53). The nature of call centre work, however, as a voice-to-voice labour process rather than a face-to-face labour process, means that customers never actually see the call centre agent that they are speaking with. In this way, I would argue that the investment call centre workers put into their clothing and appearance is related to their chances of material or symbolic profit, and is in fact very closely linked to their position occupied in social space (Bourdieu 1984).

Interviewees expressed a range of perspectives on how much preparation they put into getting ready for work:

It depends on my mood. If I'm feeling quite lousy and sleepy, then I prefer my trousers because I feel they are the most comfortable, and if I'm feeling like I'm in a good mood, then I'll wear a suit and all my jewellery and then come to the office. It depends particularly on my mood. If I'm dressed up properly and I feel, yeah, I'm looking good, I feel more confident in coming in to work and I feel peppy the whole day … with me if I'm dressed up properly I feel confident. I feel like working, you know, everything is peppy and the whole day goes good.

(Yashica, 21, NCall)

Wearing Indian clothing often requires greater preparation than wearing trousers and shirt as there are bangles and bindis to coordinate on top of the usual shoes, bags and jewellery.[22] Yashica feels a stronger sense of professionalism when wearing Indian clothing primarily due to the effort that she has put into deciding on her outfit. Many of the interviewees indicated ease with wearing both Western and Indian clothing, stressing that although a professional attitude and smart, feminine clothing were required, management were very relaxed about appearance:

It's like you can wear anything you like to as far as you're comfortable in it. So there's nothing like you have to wear formal clothing. It's up to the person. I feel comfortable in trousers and jeans, less [with] suits, so I wear more of these. So the people who feel comfortable in suits they wear suits. Anybody can wear anything.

(Pooja, 28, NCall)

Recalling Amrit and Monica's comments earlier about feeling more professional and mobile, interviewees indicated greater concern for posture and movement when wearing Indian clothes, stating that they felt restricted by the dupatta when wearing Indian suits. Urmila adds:

According to my personal experience, when I wear jeans I feel more energetic and active and when I wear suits I feel like a married lady. I feel very mature. I don't feel like running or going here and there. In my suits, I just feel like sitting and concentrating on my work. In my jeans, I feel much more active and energetic.

(Urmila, 21, NCall)

In an environment where freedom of movement is generally restricted due to wearing a headset connected to a computer, it was interesting to hear of concern for movement limited by a dupatta and not movement that was limited by a headset, implying that there was greater meaning invested in wearing a dupatta. Although many of the women implied that jeans or Western clothing were considered sexy, the explicit connection betweens jeans and sex appeal was never made. Punjabi suits and dupattas are about restrained femininity, both in and outside the call centre. Jeans and Western clothes, on the other hand, suggest a disregard for such norms.

However, Punjabi suits also functioned in more pragmatic ways, with the dupatta acting as a shawl or scarf. Although intended as a headcover, the dupatta, when worn correctly, should cover a woman's chest and shoulders, thereby preserving her modesty and decency. Traditionally, the dupatta works to preserve a woman's respectability and izzat, thereby making suits more restrictive of movement and requiring more maintenance. Moreover, the notion of women as bearers of traditional and cultural meaning is implicit in their comments, in that they equate jeans with girls and suits with women, suggesting that a lack of husband and children indicates a lack of responsibility in preserving cultural values. Entwistle (2000: 34) notes that in the West women often removed their suit jackets while in their own offices but were careful about wearing their jackets when walking around the workplace, thereby covering their breasts to avoid sexual glances from men. Similarly, the dupatta is used by many women, not necessarily to cover their heads, but instead to cover their chests, thereby mitigating their sexuality. Almost all of the women observed in the call centre carried a dupatta or shawl with them. Furthermore, suits suggest an adult status with 'post pubertal girls' and 'cover the body in a way that is not possible with Western skirts and dresses' (Puri 1999: 66). Many of the interviewees remarked that once married they would wear Western clothing infrequently if at all. Gurmeet, one of the few married women interviewed for the research, wore Punjabi suits exclusively:

> I always wear suits. Since I got married, I have been wearing suits. Especially getting married into a Punjabi family and moving to Punjab, and being in a joint family. I always wear suits, and now it has been so long, about twelve to thirteen years since I got married, so the idea of wearing jeans doesn't come into my mind now. I don't think that, working in a call centre, you need to wear jeans. You don't need to be very hip or to be that kind of person. It's about your work, not your clothes.
>
> (Gurmeet, 31)

Gurmeet's comments touch upon an important point regarding 'organizational bodies', which Tyler and Hancock (2001: 25) define as the process by which an employee embodies the organization. Gurmeet, who is married and wears suits all the time, does not see a need to wear Western clothing to perform well. However, many other interviewees, such as Monica, felt that call centres were not an Indian concept, thus rejected Indian clothing in favour of Western clothing and embodying a call centre identity. Clothing choices are therefore linked to both an embodiment of the organization and notions of women's respectability which in turn produced patterns of identification and recognition for the women employees.

Patterns of identification and recognition

The issue of what to wear is much more complex than simply presenting a professional appearance. Sartorial strategies are used in creating distinctions and identifying with particular social groups (Banerjee and Miller 2003).

Clothing is invested with cultural and social meanings contingent upon 'global cultural flows' (Appadurai 1996), and in this way the women in the call centre produced patterns of identification and recognition. Sartorial strategies were used by women to identify themselves and one another with particular groups. During interviews, the interviewees used dichotomous thinking in defining one another, and although categories were labelled married/unmarried, career oriented/time-pass, homely/freaky, the identities came to bear a greater significance in how the women understood and constructed their own identities and their participation in 'multiple identity projects' (Yegenoglu 2005) as 'skilled jugglers' (Bolton 2000; Whelan et al. 2002).

A survey by the Centre for Women and Development Studies (CWDS) found that 38 per cent of all women working in call centres were from out of town (out-stationed employees) (Bamzai and Doshi 2005). Data gathered for this study would support this, as 38 per cent of all interviewees in the sample group were also out-stationed employees. However, data from the larger survey at NCall showed this number to be much higher, at 54 per cent, suggesting that this number may be on the rise as the process at NCall was new and employees had only been recruited within the four weeks prior to the case study. When asked what kinds of women worked in call centres, many of the interviewees pointed towards out-stationed employees and from this constructed the image of how they perceived these women. Out-stationed employees generally do not live with family members, often choosing to live with other call centre employees in PG (paying guest) accommodation, similar to chummeries;[23] as such, they have fewer restrictions with regard to how they dress and how they spend their leisure time, causing some friction with women who live with their families. Banita, who lives at home with her mother and two brothers, offers this on out-stationed employees:

> Those are the people who don't want to go home. So instead of doing an eight-hour shift, they do twelve hours, fourteen hours. It gives them more money, then they just go home and sleep; they get up in the morning, and go to the call centre. That is their life. They will also work on the Saturday extra, which gives them 500 more. So it's like they are just working, sleeping. So those are the people that hang around and indulge in these kind of stuff ... [they] keep hanging around, they miss one cab, the other cab, most of them make boyfriends at work. You can even see people wearing split skirts, miniskirts. It's very common.
>
> (Banita, 23, DelCall)

Banita deliberately misses a crucial part of this description in that the women who are out-stationed have usually travelled some distance from their parents' homes to find better employment opportunities, many of them working out of financial need. Given that they are new to the area, they won't have the same social circle that a woman who is local, like Banita, might have. Many of the out-stationed workers were responsible for sending money home to families and, possibly to abate the loneliness as well as earn extra money, they worked longer hours and extra shifts.

The overriding concern that the interviewees expressed was the misconception that all call centre women could be described this way; these negative perceptions of call centre workers were pervasive and most interviewees indicated that they felt misrepresented and marginalized:

> Even, you know, the guys that I worked with, they have a perception that a girl who's working in a call centre, she doesn't have any values and ethics, she doesn't care about her family, she can go ahead and do anything and she's just not bothered about anything, the freaky kind, she just comes here to pass her time and if you're an extrovert on top of that then they'll think she's not – you know – a good lady to be with and this is the perception that I have seen around this.
>
> (Yashica, 21, NCall)

Out-stationed employees were often, though not always, the women who visited nightclubs and roadside restaurants and bars, places deemed unsuitable for women of good character or morals. Contributing to a cosmopolitanization of call centres and of Delhi in general, the women constructed 'resistance identities' (Castells 1997), viewing themselves as 'privileged nationals', while others understood them to be outside a national discourse, 'national outsiders' (Kofman 2005). Those constructing 'resistance identities' and rejecting patriarchal norms were sometimes labelled the 'freaky' kind and those constructing 'legitimizing identities' (Castells 1997), the women who were married or lived at home and produced out of state and national discourses, were labelled 'BTMs'.

The word 'freak' is used by call centre workers to indicate a number of things such as relaxing or enjoying time off. It was also used as a euphemism for 'fuck', as women were described as the 'freaky kind' or the type who would 'freak around', as Yashica indicated above. Not all women thought of out-stationed employees as the 'freaky' kind. Harshdeep, who lives with her parents while working at NCall, challenges that perception, arguing that one does not need to live independently to be labelled freaky or to make the most of one's time off work:

> Half of the girls live at home with their parents and are typical Indians. They lie to their parents about having Saturdays off so that they can claim to be at work. They want to keep one day with them to go out at night to do whatever they want, so they say they are going to the office and then go out. They can just freak out.
>
> (Harshdeep, 25, NCall)

For Harshdeep, classifying somebody as the 'freaky kind' did not necessarily depend on whether or not she lived at home, but more on an understanding of how sexually liberated that woman was. This is the case with the second type, the 'BTM', the older, traditional sister embracing modernity in a foolish way:

> I smoke, I drink, and to a certain extent I think I'm very cultural [Indian]. But the person next to me, who doesn't smoke and doesn't drink, might think that I have no [Indian] culture. I think everybody is changing, but very slowly, and at different levels. So for somebody else, I might be a bhenji who is always wearing [Punjabi] suits. But for somebody who doesn't smoke and doesn't drink, and doesn't even want to try a drink – not even a glass of wine – for me, that person is a bhenji.
>
> (Smita, 33, NCall)

Although the 'freaky' and 'BTM' labels described identities that were linked to sexual liberalism and modernity, they were in fact much more representative of how the women experienced independence. Half of the interviewees indicated that women in the call centres did not 'gel' and that they formed separate groups. Although they divided these groups along the lines of those who lived at home or on their own, those who were married or single, those who were traditional or modern, many of their definitions and categories overlapped and were conflated with one another.

However, these labels were significant for the women in identifying and recognizing one another, and sartorial strategies constituted both a manner of identification and a form of resistance characterized by a negotiative aesthetic. Given the negative perceptions of women working in the call centres, the practice of negotiating the presentation of the self was significant in constructing one's own identity but was further complicated by the practices of 'distinction' (Bourdieu 1984), used to enforce the inclusion of some and the exclusion of others.

Kanter (1977: 233–37) introduced the concept of 'tokenism' by identifying four dominant, stereotypical roles in Western corporations developed around token women who made up the minority: the Mother, the Seductress, the Pet and the Iron Maiden. Although such categories did not necessarily exist in Indian call centres, stereotypes were constructed, and I would argue that women are unable to achieve critical mass in overcoming gender inequalities whilst reliant on such stereotypes. Collins has also identified how specific stereotypes were created and maintained to oppress women and that these constructs exist in opposition to each other in a dichotomous pattern:

> As a part of generalized ideology of domination, stereotypical images of Black womanhood take on special meaning. Because the authority to define societal values is a major instrument of power, elite groups, in exercising power, manipulate ideas about Black womanhood. They do so by exploiting already existing symbols, or creating new ones.
>
> (Collins 1990: 69)

Collins' argument leads directly back to the start of this chapter, where the argument was made that Indian women's identities are produced through politicized national discourses and images which serve to enhance a global image of India and India's liberalized economy. However, as the arguments show, these liberalized images do not necessarily afford women liberation; women's bodies continue to embody the struggle between local and global discourses and tradition and modernity. Although they were recognized as independent working women, the identities that these women constructed for themselves deepened the insecurities of their partners, presenting a microcosm of contemporary shifts in India, as demonstrated by Urmila and Dipti:

> My boyfriend has told me that I have to wear suits now. He said no more jeans to the office. He is correct. He says, 'You go there to work. You don't go there to show off the clothes you have.' I'm going to get married to him soon, so it's up to him. It's enough that he lets me work in the call centre, and 'Even after marriage, he said, 'if you want to continue working, that's fine, I have no issues at all.' Basically, it does matter how you dress. It matters a lot.
>
> (Urmila, 21, NCall)

> My boyfriend takes me shopping now but I have to fight with him to wear jeans. He says that it does not suit [an almost] married woman. I have to show him, 'Look how many women are in jeans.' Finally he gave in and bought me some but I have to try and show everything to him first.
>
> (Dipti, 23, NCall)

Although Dipti has her own salary, it was necessary for her to 'take permission' from her boyfriend when buying Western clothing, demonstrating how some women had little control over the patriarchal structures that governed their lives. Moreover, the women recognized that they were complicit in the construction of these identities, noting their responsibility in creating and maintaining such categories:

> SMITA: Working in a call centre has made me younger. I never used to gossip, and I started gossiping. It's cool. It's fun.
> INTERVIEWER: Who are you gossiping about?
> SMITA: Oh! All the other women! It's college once again!
>
> (Smita, 33, NCall)

> The gossip factor is always there. It's the spice of life. We are always talking about who is going around, who is sleeping together.
>
> (Ritu, 23, GCall)

Although they expressed a lack of control over the pervasiveness of some of the dominant, negative stereotypes that were circulated in contemporary society, as Rashi suggests below, it was understood to be a temporary thing:

Maybe, they might have a perception about the call centre women, because earlier the reputation definitely was there for the hotel industry. Hotel, airline ... but now people have gotten over that. So now, I guess the latest being the call centre.

(Rashi, 25, GCall)

Most of the interviewees argued that perceptions of women call centre workers were changing and that with more women working stereotypes would change, increasing the social acceptance of working women and opportunities for gaining greater independence:

I think it's for the women who want to grow independent on their own and are going through a transition phase like they are planning yet to go on to some specific field and this is just a transition phase while they are taking their own time to think about or wonder about some point – about where they need to go ahead in future.

(Amrit, 23, NCall)

Moroever, they argued that, ultimately, the fate of women was in their own hands, that despite the dominant cultural and social understandings of working women, particularly those in the call centre, all of them had greater access to better employment opportunities and further education, affording them greater independence and the ability to exercise greater agency over their lives:

It has given them an identity of their own ... a voice to the women ... in this industry, they treat you like an equal. It's not like they say, 'Okay, you are a woman and you can't do this.' They know that if you are a good performer that you will do well, like anyone else. It has given an individual identity to women.

(Sonali, 24, NCall)

Women from every aspect of life, be it from a middle-class family or a well-to-do family. I have so many friends from Patna and Bihar, which is considered to be backwards parts of India, but still those girls are doing very well out here. So girls from each and every aspect of life are into call centres.

(Gurmeet, 31, NCall)

In this way, the patterns of identification and recognition that the interviewees pointed to functioned in two ways: first, to enable them to identify with other women in the call centre; second, to enable them to better construct their own identities. The labels that they used worked to destabilize the categories built upon dominant Hindu and mythological images of women that categorize them as dangerous. Caught between the glamorous image of the New Liberated woman and the nationalistic Hindu woman, these women were involved in constructing identities that simultaneously rejected and accepted these constructions. By using relative terminology that functioned in such a way that it included all women, the women rejected singular identities, claiming multiple identities contingent upon their social settings.

5 Techs and the city

Challenging patriarchal norms through spatial practice

> Spaces can be real and imagined. Spaces can tell stories and unfold histories. Spaces can be interrupted, appropriated, and transformed through artistic and literary practice ... [and] the appropriation and use of spaces [can be] political acts.
>
> (hooks 1991: 152)

The previous two chapters looked at the work sites and labour processes of call centres and the way in which the experiences of working in these places have impacted upon the construction of women's identities. Contingent upon these processes are the production of socio-spatial relations found in the NCR. If we follow the call centre workers from home to work and explore the way in which spatial relations are reproduced or transgressed at home, en route and at the office it becomes evident that clothing functions as spatial practice (Secor 2002) to negotiate unsafe places. Spaces are increasingly important, particularly in geographies of women's fears, and as Delhi negotiates its status as a global city, the call centre functions as a 'Synopticon' (Bauman 1998), a retreat from the 'Panopticon' of society, offering safety from the many who watch the few. The popularity of dhabas, road-side eateries, and an in-depth look at Zaika, a dhaba in Gurgaon, determine the extent to which socio-spatial relations have been shaped by the workers of transnational call centres and, in particular, how women have transgressed the boundaries of the private/public divide into 'male only' social spaces.

The significance of space

'The everyday is the arena through which patriarchy is (re)created – and contested' (Rose 1993: 17) and cities present fascinating examples of how the social is made 'concrete' (Sassen 1998). Castells argues that space is not a *reflection* of society but an *expression* of society and that 'space is crystallized time' (Castells 1996: 441, my emphasis); thus the social and the spatial must be considered together (Massey 1994). In viewing globalization as a series of 'scapes' and global cultural flows (Appadurai 1996), space must be considered *as process* and *in process* (Crang and Thrift 2000: 3), something that is continuously constituted and reconstituted over time.

The notion of place as fixed is somewhat limiting and it is perhaps better understood as a 'constellation of social relations, meeting and weaving together at a particular locus' (Massey 1994: 154). This is not to undermine the significance of place, as a sense of location or identity (Massey 1994: 154), as Upasana describes how that 'fixedness' is integral to the construction of her self-identity:

> At heart, we are always Indians and we love India. We still listen to our parents, we still follow the rules. Just because we are working at night, does not make us less Indian.
>
> (Upasana, 28, NCall)

In spite of arguments that call centre workers were becoming more Westernized, comments like those above made by Upasana show that the employees actually felt a very strong sense of Indianness, heightened by their experiences of working in the call centre. Upasana, from Assam in the North East of India, was one of the interviewees who had moved 2,000 kilometres to Delhi for work, due to limited work opportunities in her field at home. The process of urbanization and the high numbers of out-stationed employees in call centres has meant that women in call centres increasingly identify themselves regionally; thus, when asked about processes of globalization, they responded with greater emphasis on a national identity, pointing to a need for a 'sense of place' (Massey 1994: 151) or a 'homing desire' (Brah 1996). However, identifying place as a fixed location is problematic in that the identity of place is always in progress, contingent upon its location in multiple sets of social relations stretched over a space over time (Massey 1994).

The role of place is crucial in the process of identity construction. As Said has written, 'just as none of us is outside or beyond geography, none of us is completely free from the struggle over geography' (Said 1993: 7). That struggle is complex and ambitious because it is not only about wars and borders, but also about ideas, about forms, about images and imaginings. Imagination as 'field of social practice' (Appadurai 1996) functions to undo place as a fixed construct, producing that which is 'contingent' (Robertson 1995) upon global 'scapes', such as 'mediascapes' and 'ethnoscapes' (Appadurai 1996). In India, Bollywood shapes the construction 'Indianness' and, as it does so, the film text assigns a place with an Indian identity, which becomes a part of India's landscape in the viewer's imagination.

Differences are constructed through lived geographies of placement: 'axes of identity such as those of race, class, sexuality, age and gender never operate aspatially but are inextricably bound up with the particular spaces and places within which, in relation to which, people live' (Bondi and Rose 2003: 232). These two constructions of place, imagined and lived, are best described as 'power-geometries' (Massey 1994), similar to 'global disjunctures' (Appadurai 1996), in that different groups and different people are placed in distinct ways in relation to the flows and interconnections of space and time. The time–

space compression works in such a way that those who have mobility also have power and control, and that there are those who are more in charge of it than others (Massey 1994). Although Massey places great emphasis on the mobility/power correlation, this is not necessarily a causal relation, in that the perceived 'local' or the immobile continues to maintain some sense of power and, as such, the 'local', like mobility, also works in definitive ways within discussions of globalization and identity formation.

The gendered association of time with masculinity and space with femininity suggests that space is the opposite of history and therefore depoliticized (Massey 1994). A further set of binaries associates space with the universal, the conceptual, the theoretical and also therefore with the global, while place is then associated with the local: 'Thus, the term local is used in a derogatory reference to feminist struggles and in relation to feminist concerns in intellectual work (it is only a local struggle, only a local concern)' (Massey 1994: 10). This gendering of spatial concerns is argued further by Legg, drawing on Rose's interpretation of Irigaray. As she writes, 'while Man builds and constructs, Women are contained and enclosed, so that women may always remain available for men's needs' (Legg 2003: 22).

The identification of Indian women with the domestic sphere has its roots in Hindu mythology. One of the most pervasive myths regarding women in India is the story of Sita, who, by stepping outside the circle drawn around her for protection by her brother-in-law, was kidnapped by Ravana, a demon, which began an epic war. Sita's disobedience and disloyalty to her husband underscore the gendered ordering of public and private space in Indian society. 'Containment stories' rework and retell class and gender relations so that women are continuously inscribed and reinscribed through discourses, cultural representations and everyday practices (Hanson and Pratt 1995: 16–17).[1]

The gendered ordering of public and private space has implications for the way in which women are represented, limiting their contributions to a nationalist agenda or identity. As noted elsewhere in this book (p. 95), idealized roles of women are used to signify an Indian national identity where women are constructed as 'cultural carriers' (Yuval-Davis 1994: 413), though to some extent this was partly shifted during the 'Quit India' (1939–44) campaign when Gandhi crowned women as 'Queens of the household' in a compromise between the need for women's agency and the forceful demands of an emerging 'new patriarchy' (Legg 2003: 13–14).[2]

Male-led social reform movements were preoccupied with selectively encouraging women's entry into the public sphere, by instituting modes of surveillance which in turn controlled women's entry into the labour force and into politics, as well as legislating and regulating the sexuality of middle-class women (Mohanty 1991a: 20). Thus women were not simply confined within the home; rather, the home was reimagined as a site of agency and resistance, a site which, however, was defined by patriarchal power relations. Places outside the home were constructed as spaces that would 'dishonour' women, particularly middle- and upper-class women. In this way spatial confidence became a manifestation of power (Koskela 1997), and danger, as a social construct (Valentine 1989), became one way in which way power was exercised over women.

Some feminists have regarded the home as a space in which patriarchal relations are reproduced and dominant codes of gender segregation are enforced (Walby 1990; McDowell 1999). Theorists such as bell hooks, however, reconceptualized the home as a subversive and feminist space, rejecting the notion that the home is an oppressive place and claiming it as a site for resistance.[3] Whilst men in India dominated the public sphere via patriarchal power relations, excluding women from this space, women in turn claimed the domestic space.

The educating of young women has allowed women not only to move into the public realm but to become visible in it; however, this has not been reciprocated by allowing men into the domestic realm in similar ways.[4] A tradition of female only spaces in the home has created exclusive boundaries that do not grant access to men. Although Persian and Muslim in origin, the 'zenana' is a strict women only space in the home which men are forbidden to enter, and this exclusionary practice can still be found in contemporary Indian society. These spaces can be conceptualized as spaces of empowerment in that they are exclusive to women. Thus the home can be constructed in three ways: as a site of oppression, a site for resistance and, as I will argue below, as a site for leisure.

One of the findings emerging from this study was the conceptualization of home as a site for leisure. For women call centre workers, home was read in two distinctly significant ways: first, as a site for leisure where women sat doing nothing; second, as a site of oppression. Women's motives for working in call centres ranged from boredom at home to economic necessity; as such, their interpretations of private and public spaces varied and in many ways reflected their class status. Women such as Preetika, Pooja and Banita, who all came from upper-middle-class homes where they were not expected to work, viewed home as a place of leisure where servants were responsible for all domestic duties. Thus, not wishing to be viewed as lazy or lacking intelligence or ambition, they took up call centre work as a way in which they could exercise agency over their lives and gain some independence from their families:

> At least I feel I am doing something. I would have been sitting at home having dinner with them [the family] but then the total day I would have been doing nothing. So at least I'm utilizing my time for something. At least by the end of the day when I go back home I don't feel, 'Oh, I have done nothing today.' At least I've done something.
>
> (Pooja, 28 NCall)

> I have seen the difference between an educated lady at home and an educated lady outside the house. The perception is so different. Even if

the lady at home carries a lot of respect, she will not get her full respect, just sitting at home.

(Nisha, 24, NCall)

The 'pinking' of office work and the opportunities that call centres have provided for women to take up part-time employment, along with the growing middle class, have changed popular notions of women and work. Where once it may have seemed vulgar or inappropriate for women to work, and indeed for many people this remains the case, the widely held view amongst women interviewed was that women who stayed at home ordering their servants around were ignorant of world matters and had little to offer by way of conversation, thoughts and opinions.

Women in the call centres did not necessarily view home as a site for resistance as over one-third of them were living away from home and often spoke of their desire to return home more frequently. Faced with doing domestic chores on their own for the first time, these women saw home as a place that provided them with warmth and shelter, as Amrit's comments indicate:

Sometimes you feel homesick, because you need to do all the stuff you don't do at home. You have to wash your clothes. You need to manage your things – like you have to get in the stuff for cooking. You have to do the homely things. Here I have to do each and every thing by myself.

(Amrit, 23, NCall)

A shift in the cultural and social landscape of India, one which sees women move out of the home, initiates the process of constructing home as a place of meaning and identity, fuelled by a 'homing desire' (Brah 1996). For many of the out-stationed employees, arriving to a new job in a new city is a daunting and lonely experience:

When I first came to Delhi, for the first fifteen or twenty days I missed them a lot. Its 300 kilometres or seven hours away, and at that time I didn't even have a cell phone with me. But now it's been two months since I last went to my home town. I [try not to] miss them as much because I know that they can't come here and I can't go there.

(Urmila, 21, NCall)

Associating their parents' home with feelings of warmth and security was not uncommon; however, this wasn't necessarily shared by all the women. For some, home was a site of oppression, as many women talked of how independent they felt once they left home and how things have either changed or remained the same at home since they left. Upasana, from Assam, does not get the opportunity to return home very often; however, for her home is a site of oppression:

I have cousins who are older than me, and they are in the same situation as my mum. I do whatever I want but obviously within my limits. Back at home, if I come home by eight o'clock, this is okay. But my cousins who are five to seven years older than me, they must be home by three or five o'clock. They should be home when it is still day.

(Upasana, 28, NCall)

At the time of the interview, it had been nine months since Upasana had been home and she indicated that it would probably be another six months before she would go back. Upasana felt that her family back home were too traditional and, more importantly, she felt that she had changed from when she had left and the lifestyle back home certainly would not suit her now.

Given the traditional links between women and the home, women's identities are inextricably linked to domesticity and reproduction:

Because of their reproductive capacity, women are seen as the transmitters of group values and traditions as agents of socialization of the young. Their roles as wives and especially mothers are exalted, indeed fetishized. Woman's 'place' in the home and in the family is lauded. It is Woman as Wife and Mother – not women as workers, students, citizens – who is ideologically constructed in the discourse and the program of the movement. This is why women's dress and behaviour become so important ... [these notions are] centred on an implicit or explicit regulation of female sexuality.

(Moghadam 1994: 18–19)

This conceptualization and construction of women's roles are central in understanding the construction of women's identities as they are performed outside the home and how far women must or do go in an effort to maintain these linkages. Clothing and dress are certainly a part of fetishizing women's roles and, as Moghadam writes, they play a part in the regulation of female sexuality. However, there were also examples of women making use of clothing to present alternative images of themselves, thereby manipulating the ideological constructions of women as wives or mothers. Dipti's comments offer up another way of examining the significance of clothing, as perceived notions of deceit or insincerity, as women present themselves in contradictory fashion at work and at home:

I would say that call centre occupation for women is good and bad, if you are okay with this culture. I say it's like foreign culture here and you don't find much Indian culture over here. Women are playing two part roles. In the office it's like a foreign culture and they go back home and they have to act totally Indian. Dressing in formals for work and wearing suits at home.

(Dipti, 26, NCall)

Dipti articulates what many women discussed and what was observed in and outside the call centre. However, her interpretation of this as a disingenuous act of liberation is largely born out of her own frustration at not being allowed by her boyfriend to dress in Western clothes. Although some women might find Punjabi suits more freeing and relaxed than, say, jeans, trousers and collared shirts, Dipti has chosen to interpret the change from work to home as deceitful. Some of her comments elsewhere in this book demonstrate how intensely she felt the contradictions between her personal life with her family and boyfriend and her professional life at the call centre.

However, observation of dress codes could also be read as a subversive way to reject social norms. Dipti interprets the act of changing clothes to mean that women 'revert' to a predetermined role when they 'return home' rather than interpreting it as part of a process with which women can begin to construct new identities. This transition is not unlike the transitions I myself underwent when moving between conducting interviews and returning to the backpacker area in which I was staying. These transitions give credence to the argument that call centre women are juggling 'multiple identity projects' (Yegenoglu 2005) and that this further suggests that identity is contingent upon social contexts; thus, the clothing that is acceptable at work is not acceptable at home and vice versa.

Clothing has already been determined as a significant dimension of the discussion of women call centre worker's identities in that it is strategically used to express identity and establish patterns of recognition. However, it is also used in a pragmatic way, one that affects mobility; thus, what Dipti reads as a disingenuous act of liberation could again be read differently, as a negotiated strategy for mobility and safety.

Migrations and mobility

The prominence of borders, boundaries and demarcations continues to figure heavily in discussions of globalization and identity and lays particular significance on the examination of space and place. Although some could argue that call centre workers never physically leave India and a discussion of migration is inappropriate, this is not true, as call centre workers virtually migrate to work every day. Many of the employees worked six days a week and up to fourteen hours a day, and so in many ways they spent more time 'in' the UK than they did in India. Recalling some of the earlier discussions in this book concerning racism and sexual harassment over the phone, call centre workers experience a sense of migration in which 'difference is confronted, boundaries are crossed, cultures are mingled, identities become blurred' (Robins 1991: 42–43). Thus, migration theories are not entirely inappropriate in an analysis of call centre workers' experiences as they offer up interesting ways of thinking about the cultural shift from India to the UK.

There are two journeys that are undertaken by the call centre worker when going to work. The first is the virtual migration from India to the UK, whilst the second is the corporeal journey through Delhi, or their home neighbourhood or enclave, past shanty towns to the call centre (see Figure 5.1). The virtual migration cannot actually be physically located but instead occupies what Adams and Ghose refer to as the 'bridgespace'. They define this as

> A collection of interconnected virtual places that support people's movement between two regions or countries and the sustenance of cultural ties at a distance ... it is not the Internet or part of the Internet; it is a space built in and through the Internet and other media ... it is an environment and not an actor.
>
> (Adams and Ghose 2003: 419–20)

The 'bridgespace' is a digital or electronic version of Bhabha's (1994) 'third space' within which a 'dialogical self' (Chaudhary and Sriram 2001) or a 'cyber self' can be constructed as part of the 'digital diaspora' (Gajjala 2004) or 'cyber publics' (Ong 2004). However, Adams and Ghose call into question the innocence of the 'bridgespace' in asking who the architect of the 'bridgespace' is and for what purpose the 'bridgespace' has been constructed. They posit that the NRI community are the architects, for the purposes of maintaining and encouraging global cultural flows, Appadurai's (1996) 'mediascapes', 'ideoscapes', 'technoscapes', financescapes' all rolled into one and serving the needs of a particular 'ethnoscape'. Examples of this include the dating and marriage sites BPOShaadi and BPODating, which aim to bring together men and women working in call centres for dating and to find potential marriage partners.

Figure 5.1 Shantytown behind call centre in Gurgaon.

The second journey to work is the corporeal journey through their locality to the call centre itself. One of the reasons for providing transport is to ensure the safety of women as they arrive at or leave work late at night or early in the morning. Women call centre workers faced a good deal of harassment from the local community, both men and women, due to the odd work hours, thus any issues with transportation, either being late or not turning up, were quite serious. Below Smita gives her thoughts on this:

> When I get out of the cab [company transport] at home everyone puts me in the good woman category because I am married and I have a kid, which puts me at different level, which puts me in the not available, good woman category. But, even then, every time I get out of the cab, and pass the security guards, I always think, 'What must these people think of me? What are they thinking? Do they know that I'm working in an office? Where do they think I'm coming from?' You know? I always think that. It always comes into my mind. But I have never faced any hostility, because there has never been any opportunity for it. But, yes, I would imagine it happens. If I was in that situation, single, then yes. Oh my God! And living alone in a flat? Oh my goodness! Half the girls here do that. I don't know how.
>
> (Smita, 33, NCall)

Women are watched almost all the time, if not by their neighbours, then by security guards or other staff working late at night on their street or in their colony. Often the suspicious looks and hostility they face occur when leaving for work. For some this is late in the evening when others are arriving home. Women must factor in waiting for transport and the journey to work in the cab when they get dressed for the office.[5]

As spaces are gendered, women must be cognizant in their efforts to dress for the office and for the journey between home and work (Entwistle 2000: 34). Whilst Western clothing may be appropriate for call centres, that same clothing travelling to work or back home might make women feel vulnerable. Sangamitra and Urmila, who travel to and from work via the company's transport system of vans, jeeps and buses, share their experiences whilst waiting for transport before a shift. 'Eve-teasing', a euphemism for sexual harassment, is a common occurrence and may include 'being whistled at, being subjected to catcalls, comments, lewd behaviours or gestures, being touched or sexually assaulted' (Puri 1999: 75). Everyday routine events such as travelling by bus or train or going to the local store can expose women to sexual harassment (ibid.). The body is appropriated through self-surveillance (Foucault 1979), which is demonstrated here by the use of clothing to avoid sexual harassment:

> They pass such dirty comments on the clothes you wear. You must be knowing the types of outfits you wear to a club? You can't wear those

types of outfits, coming from office or between clubs, so whatever you were wearing even something over, they comment. Even if your hair is open, they pass comments on your hair. And if you have put on make-up, they will comment on your make-up, all dirty stuff. I am not too comfortable with it.

(Sangamitra, 25, GCall)

I used to have shifts that started at 1.30 in the night until 9.30 in the morning, so it was all night. So when I used to wait for my cab, people used to stare at me like anything. They used to ask me, 'Where are you going?' I used to tell them I was going to work.

(Urmila, 21, NCall)

Sangamitra and Urmila are both out-stationed candidates, living with other women call centre workers in rented accommodation. Unlike where Smita lives, where there will be a security guard at the gate to the colony, Sangamitra and Urmila have no such extra measure of security. Sangamitra lives in Gurgaon, not too far from her office, but the street is still somewhat busy and certainly offers no place to wait for a cab late at night. Similarly, Urmila, who lives in Noida, lives in an area with accommodation that caters for call centre workers or other recent arrivals in the city.

Women call centre employees followed social norms and codes governing dress for the streets late at night whilst also ensuring that they followed the call centre's dress codes of wearing 'smart' office clothes, negotiating these inconsistent identities:

I started off wearing [Punjabi] suits, because I was told to, but then I saw that people were very casual, and I went on to jeans. But I don't wear short tops or anything. I'm a little careful about that. You can wear anything as long as it's not too revealing or not too fashionable.

(Banita, 23, DelCall)

Although the virtual migration and transnational nature of call centre work are significant to the discussion of identity construction, the corporeal or embodied journey that women undertake is equally significant. Readings of dress and clothing choices offer ways of examining how women identify with one another, demonstrating how dress is freely chosen and how that choice is bound within particular practices.

In a study of Turkish women, Secor has identified veiling, a form of dress, as a spatial practice that gains its significance through women's urban mobility; marked by a pattern of shifting 'regimes of veiling', the spatialized norms of dress affect the meaning and enactment of women's veiling choices (Secor 2002: 5). She argues that to understand veiling as a situated, embodied practice, it is necessary to view space as relational, as encompassing more than the body, tying to it Massey's (1994) notion that space is produced through a web of power relations. Dress is crucially linked to mobility, and as dress can constrain, so too can it enable women with regard to mobility:

> The study of dress as situated practice requires moving between, on the one hand, the discursive and representational aspects of dress, and the way the body/dress is caught up in relations of power, and on the other, the embodied experience of dress and the use of dress as a means by which individuals orientate themselves to the social world.
>
> (Secor 2002: 39)

Women in the call centres wore shawls, jackets and headcovers to cover their upper bodies and once at work they would remove these garments to reveal the fashionable, trendy office clothes underneath. Building on this, Secor writes that the socio-spatial experience of veiling or not-veiling is best understood if the city is considered as comprised of different regimes of veiling:

> As women travel in and out of different veiling regimes in the city, they are markers and they are marked. They are markers in that it is largely through their own veiling and mobility choices that informal regimes of veiling are created and normatively enforced; at the same time, they are marked in that their choice to veil becomes reinterpreted according to the norms of the particular veiling regime into which they enter. It then becomes a woman's choice whether to modulate her own dress to accommodate these different regimes or to violate them ... In this way women play an important role in both reproducing the boundaries of veiling regimes and, as transgressors, in opening them up for debate.
>
> (Secor 2002: 8)

Women policing their own dress can be read in two ways: first, as unwittingly reproducing power relations and, second, as opposing women's erasure in public and reclaiming urban spaces (Koskela 1997: 309). In this way women call centre workers who choose to wear Western clothing can be read as transgressors, forging new spaces for women who do not wish to be confined or restricted, either literally or figuratively, by Indian clothing. Women in the study chose to cover themselves with dupattas (headcovers) and shawls as they were waiting for their transport vehicle to collect them, thus moving from the home, which uses one regime of veiling, to the street, which uses another regime of veiling, and finally to the office, which requires a third veiling regime. Women efficiently moved through these varying veiling regimes, sometimes complying and other times transgressing, and in this way dress functioned as both constraining and enabling. Veiling functioned as a spatial practice by means of which women could enable themselves to move safely on the streets.

The spatial is an expression of the social, and the constitutive and mutually defining relation between bodies and cities is neither causal nor representational but both, in that the body must be considered active in the production and transformation of the city (Grosz 1995). This is exemplified by the corporeal negotiation of everyday terrains and the way in which the city has become the site for the body's cultural saturation through the takeover and transformation by images, representational systems, mass media and the arts. This cultural saturation, produced in part by the dominance of filmic texts, underscores the Indian cinematic society's perception that the call centre is a site of excitement, drama, intrigue and glamour. Bauman's work on the 'Synopticon' (Bauman 1998) is particularly useful, uncovering how the security measures that keep the call centre off limits to most also work to code it as an exclusion zone for young men and women. Whilst the call centre keeps women safe and secluded, it also makes them inaccessible, thus desirable.

The call centre as a 'Synopticon'

In a comparative analysis of Indian and US management strategies in an Indian based multinational firm, Poster (1998) both exposes and questions the importing of gender ideologies from home countries and argues that a hybrid system of control is created. Poster terms these two systems 'normative controls' (US) and 'confinement controls' (India) and suggests that whether or not these controls are regarded as exploitative and ethnocentric they undoubtedly result in a homogenizing of the labour process.[6]

Confinement control in India is focussed on the separation of women from men, particularly non-familial men, as it is believed that they have a polluting influence on women (Poster 1998: 43). Segregation thereby seeks to protect women by limiting contact with men to those who are considered safe, a very narrow group of men inside the household. Alternatively, normative control, in the US, focusses on restricting women's access to privileged male domains within organizations, and within this women generally regulate their own actions. The key element in confinement control is the segregation of women from men outside the work environment. While normative control governs gender relations within the multinational, confinement control is used to govern gender relations outside the multinational. With the increase of multinational organizations and call centres, this definition of safe men has been broadened to include those working within the workspace as well. This has resulted in a separation of spheres of relations, a Westernized environment confined within the space of the call centres. The separation of spheres supports the notion that particular social relations between men and women are acceptable and in fact encouraged within the call centres but not outside the call centres. Thus the cosmopolitan work identities discussed earlier are either to remain within the call centre or, once outside the call centre, are subjected to scrutiny.

Returning to Dipti's earlier comment that women are playing two roles, one in the office and one at home, it could be argued that the contradiction is unavoidable. As the Westernized professional work environment of the call centre demands that women and men not only work together but also 'play' together, it seems inevitable that the women would, at some point, carry those identities home with them.[7] The choice, it seems, would be either to continue performing contradictory roles in the work and home environment or to seek ways in which to fuse the traditional roles or Indian identities with the new cosmopolitan work identities. Dipti's comment further illustrates Poster's (1998) argument that women are also responsible for the controls placed upon them. Although it discusses the way in which women regulate their actions within normative controls by not pursuing men's jobs, it is evident that women also regulate each other's actions within confinement controls by demanding that the cosmopolitan social relations of the call centre remain within the call centre.

Bauman's (1998) critique of the limitations of Foucault's 'Panopticon' used the term 'Synopticon' to advance the theorization of the way in which space and surveillance are used to gain power and control over people. He argues that in the pre-modern era social elites used public space to demonstrate their power over the populous and that in modern times they retreated and used 'Panopticon'-like surveillance to watch and control them. His concept of the 'Synopticon' accounts for the process by which those 'watchers' became 'the watched' through the increased availability of technology, referring to celebrities or those who live their lives in the media, in the eye of the public and thus always subject to scrutiny by the masses, such as Bollywood stars or cricket players in India.

Call centres attract much attention from the local residents and those working in the area. They are bigger, brighter and newer than most of the buildings around them; moreover, they are surrounded by high fences, with guards positioned at the gate. Formal identification is required to enter and all transport staff must wait outside the call centre to take people home; all of this serves to create a glamorous image of call centre work, particularly to those who are unable to access it, such as the lower classes. Further suspense is added to this image when workers are seen to be going into the call centres at various times throughout the night.

Given the sheer size of the population of India, it is almost a certainty that one is always being observed and as such call centre workers may be less resistant to 'Panopticon'-like surveillance measures due to their exposure to constant supervision in the public realm. Call centre workers are not simply more accepting of being under continuous surveillance but are in fact oblivious to it.

The transport services provided by the call centres consist of signature white vehicles that can be seen moving in large fleets in and out of the call centre lots. Individuals, mostly men, who are generally loitering around the call centres, watch the arrival and departure of call centre workers. These individuals are there for a number of reasons; for instance, they may be tea-sellers, food vendors, women selling crafts, road workers, cleaning staff, beggars or people living in the nearby shanty towns located next to the call centres. Thus, the call centre workers become the watched and through this watching they are subject to surveillance and control. Bauman's 'Synopticon' suggests that the watchers become the watched: the call centre workers, the 'myriad of well-wishing little sisters' (Castells 1997: 342), who are surveying and observing those in the UK, are now the watched, surveyed and observed by the locals in whose communities their work sites are physically located.

Interviewees often described the call centre work sites as spaces within which they could escape the outside world. In a very practical sense, that escape could be from the heat or the monsoon, but on another level it is also an escape from conservative Indian society. Call centres are seen as fun, sexually charged atmospheres that resemble college, where women can smoke or chat with male colleagues and not be judged as they would be in public spaces. This understanding of the call centre sets this study apart from others in that freedom from surveillance was found within the call centre. Employees felt free from the societal 'Panopticon' once they arrived within the confines of the call centre, and so the surveillance within the call centre was not as prevalent.

This multi-layered exercise of watching and being watched is enhanced by prevailing images found in cinema and television wherein the popularity of Bollywood and cricket stars is so overwhelming that every public space is adorned with images of celebrities. In a cinematic society (Denzin 1995) such as India, call centre workers are positioned as actors or objects to be watched and gazed upon by the populous, and so Bauman's metaphor of the 'Synopticon' serves as a heuristic device for analysis of call centre workers' experiences in a way that is more accurate than Foucault's 'Panopticon'. Although problematic in its limited discussion of agency, the 'Synopticon' offers up useful ways of examining the role of surveillance and control in an analysis of Indian call centres.

Call centre sites appear almost monolithic and with more of them materializing all the time the landscape and geography of Delhi and surrounding areas have been transformed. Delhi has become a global city (Sassen 2001b), with processes of cosmopolitanization and transnationalism impacting upon the way in which men and women interact with each other, and the way in which women are transgressing male dominated public spaces and forging sites of resistance.

Delhi as a 'global city'

Sassen's 'global cities' (Sassen 2001b) include New York, London and Tokyo. Her later arguments (Sassen 2003) on globalization and cities have included many other world cities; however, Delhi is not included in this list. Delhi remains somewhat problematic in its placement on a digital 'map of meaning' (Hall 1996a) and though some of the city can be viewed as transnational or cosmopolitan, with its technologically advanced buildings, much of the city remains undeveloped. Thus it is best described as a 'heteropolis' (Dear and Flusty 1999). Despite the slow industrialization and development in public services, Delhi is in many ways a global city, with transnational citizens virtually migrating to work every day.

The rise of the call centre industry in Delhi and the increased interest of multinationals have given way to the creation of shopping centres termed 'entertainment centres', which some see as the apex of globalization (Parker-Talwar 2004). These centres have emerged as spaces where global brands such as McDonalds, Pizza Hut and Benetton are found alongside Indian brands such as Café Coffee Day and Barrista. Moreover, as Gayatri points out,

> Gurgaon is not just for call centres. Most corporations have moved to Gurgaon. If you look at it most multinationals have their corporate head-quarters in Gurgaon. Coca-Cola is here, Nestlé is here, Gillette is here – name a big brand and I guarantee you its office is here. You have great facilities here, great offices, great buildings.
>
> (Gayatri, Call Centre Consultant)

Within these air-conditioned, sanitized, exclusive entertainment centres are cinemas, bars, restaurants, cafés and shops. Sector 18 in Noida, and PVR Priya, Lifestyle and DLF in Gurgaon were places where a large majority of the rising middle class would spend their leisure time.[8] In Delhi, commodity culture has undermined historically constructed social divisions based on religion, caste, class and gender (Parker-Talwar 2004). The use of first names in restaurants, cafés and bars makes it appear that employees have gained upward social mobility, as surnames are often indicators of caste status. The shopping malls themselves are 'p(a)laces of consumption ... [that] soothe tired shoppers, enhance the sense of a natural outdoor setting, create exotic contexts for the commodity, imply freshness and cleanliness, and promote a sense of establishment' (Goss 1997: 275). Such modern consumer sites aim to symbolize democratic values such as a classless culture, gender equality and sexual liberalism, although this is in tension with a rise in religious fundamentalism and its accompanying patriarchal values, and a deepening of class divisions (Parker-Talwar 2004: 8). Furthermore, multinationals aim for extremely high standards of hygiene, while shortages of clean, safe water supplies continue to overwhelm Delhi's social and political landscape.

These new entertainment centres or leisure complexes in India provide a space within which men and women can socialize together without the negative associations of such relations. As these centres are cosmopolitan, modern sites of consumption they carry with them global or Westernized ideologies that legitimate public social relations between men and women. Entertainment centres provide spaces for the performance and expression of identities constructed within the call centres; the call centre agents are viewed as actors moving in and out of the entertainment complexes, eating dinner, going to the cinema, spending money in a modern, high-tech, air-conditioned environment. Many of the call centre workers are engaged in activities that could not be described as particularly Indian, like Pooja, whose husband enjoys the very English activity of going to the pub:

On Saturdays and Sundays my husband and I like to go to some pubs, watch movies – that's my favourite pastime.

(Pooja, 28, NCall)

Gayatri, on the other hand, describes the shopping centre in Gurgaon where she works, sharing the bewilderment some people experience when they go:

You come to these shopping centres on Sunday and it is a disaster. It's such a culture shock; this is something worth seeing. You'll see this girl in her tight little jeans, midriff showing, and she'll get to the escalator and she'll be stuck, she won't know what to do. And you'll find a lot of people, grown-ups riding up and down the escalators, like little kids. It's like a joyride. I still cannot get over it. The other day, my husband had to push one woman on to it because there were ten people behind us. And then you have people just looking and watching. You have to see it, it is true. It's a sightseeing visit. People don't go there to shop; they just go there to see locals, people from Delhi.

(Gayatri, Call Centre Consultant)

Although the shopping centres are regarded by call centre workers as sexually liberalized spaces within which they are free to engage in more Westernized activities, these spaces are full of 'tourists' who are engaged in a process of sightseeing, engaged in the process of watching.

In spite of what they had experienced in the call centre, for some these sites raised concerns in that the long-term effects were unknown:

In the year that I was away things have changed a lot. I've come back and seen Subway, Taco Bell. Teenagers are totally different from when I was one, and you have people who have never been abroad talking in accents. I hope we are not getting into the same set-up back in 1857, where the East India Company happened. I just hope it is not another wave where our culture gets washed out of our roots. We should be proud of being Indian.

(Anyuta, 26)

Anyuta articulates a tension experienced by the call centre workers, in that the labour process has impacted not only upon the construction of their identities, but also upon social spaces. Anyuta, who had only recently returned from working in the US, offers the popular perception of call centre workers' experiences, pointing to loss of Indian culture and identity. Though it is tempting to focus in on these thoughts and what they could mean, they are presented here to show that whilst every call centre worker that I met or interviewed had been to the multiplexes and enjoyed fast food, a large number of them felt an ambivalence, and it is through this disavowal of what was Western that they could decide upon what they thought was Indian.

More significantly, the entertainment complexes offered safe spaces for women to go out with their friends to cafés, bars, restaurants and cinemas.

The control of women's bodies and the regulation of women's sexuality are fundamental to the maintenance of patriarchal power relations within which women are finding ways to forge spaces, both physically and discursively. Women's movements in a physical realm produce a wider discourse in which to discuss women's agency; simultaneously, the discursive spaces produced by these actions name women's participation in the public realm. These discourses and action provide women with a greater sense of agency over patriarchal power relations. In other words, as women move more freely in public spaces with or without men, a discourse is produced that acknowledges women's growing sense of independence, thereby 'naming' these independent women and opening up discursive spaces for other women. In spite of the concern Anyuta felt at the possible repeat of imperialism and having Indian culture 'washed out' of their roots, she argued for the optimistic transformations that they encouraged in women, as did Pooja:

> I was surprised when I joined the company and I saw young girls, fresh graduates, staying away from their families. At their age I couldn't have dreamed of leaving home. They have set up their own rooms, their own lives, are stepping out of the house to earn a living. And it's admirable to watch. I was really amazed, because something like this is really prevalent in the States. It was a lot of change in the one year that I was missing. It's amazing.
>
> (Anyuta, 26, NCall)

> I think it has already changed the way that men and women interact in the public. As you see, if the female is independent, she can lead her own life. No one can predict the future – today she is married, tomorrow she can be separated or whatever, but at least she has something in her hands, she can walk on and she can look for a future. She really doesn't have to be dependent and she really doesn't have to be, you know, with her other half, her partner, she can raise issues. If someone is a quiet person, they worry if in-laws are not good, she'll be chucked out of the home, and what will her parents think about it, she can't go back to her parents. But now the woman can change, she can live alone, she can lead her life alone. So definitely it's a big change.
>
> (Pooja, 28, NCall)

Anyuta, after spending time in the US, draws a positive comparison between India and the US, and she, like Pooja, argues that changes brought about by call centres, though negative in some ways, are ultimately encouraging in that they give women a greater sense of independence.

Despite growing evidence of the globalization and cosmopolitanization of urban spaces, it is difficult to present an argument that simply suggests that this indicates that Delhi is a global city. Although I have argued that in some ways Delhi participates in global and transnational flows of activities, the city itself is located in India and bounded by rural Indian communities. Whilst middle-class, urban Indians participate in new consumerist, modernist life-styles, groups such as Shiv Sena, Hindu right-wing fundamentalists, and Patit Pavan Sanghatana, an organization connected to the Hindu fundamentalist party, and the Bharatiya Paksha, violently oppose such spaces and the modern, liberal values that accompany them. Both groups are particularly active around Western celebratory occasions such as Valentine's Day (Shukla 2003). The groups are known to hold demonstrations, destroy advertising materials and threaten violent action. Claims are made that Hindu culture is under attack by the Western world and that 'Valentine's Day is another feature from the culture of AIDS' (Shukla 2003).[9] Studies have been made showing links between Hindu nationalism and fascism (McDonald 1999) as well as a rise in arguments that economic liberalization has brought about a 'westoxification' or 'bourgeois urbanism' (Baviskar 2003) evidencing a hyper urbanization as Delhi is delinked from a national space and linked to a transnational space.

Tensions between local communities and the rising multinationals that dominate the landscape are increasingly on the rise. Drawing on Kaviraj, Arabindoo writes:

> in the years immediately following [Indian] independence, waves of immigration from the countryside to the city meant that any unoccupied open space could be squatted and settled upon by the incoming communities, creating what Kaviraj has referred to as 'a precedent of a soiled conception of public space.' Any feeble attempt at creating a legible blueprint for the cityscape had to be restricted to the built environment, and this too could only be partially executed, as shanty towns and slum settlements sprang up cheek-by-jowl with the middle and upper class residential areas and colonies to service their needs.
>
> (Arabindoo 2005: 3)

Indu and Sangamitra met when they were working in a call centre and though Indu has changed jobs the women still live together in Gurgaon, a satellite community of Delhi and part of the National Capital Region, located in the state of Haryana, just outside the border of Delhi. Both women have had a number of problems living in the area but, given the proximity to their workplaces, they are reluctant to move:

> I have been in Gurgaon for nearly two years. The first place I lived was the [GCall] guesthouse, which was terrible. It was totally isolated and you couldn't go anywhere. It was only to the office and back home. We couldn't go over to see our friends in other guesthouses, because they were so far away. Transportation itself is a big problem in Gurgaon. I have moved three times since then. My first landlord was fine, because they were a

young couple. They were fine with guys coming during the daytime, they didn't like guys coming in the evening, and they didn't like girls going out at night. But that place was too far from office. The next place was good, we liked it. It was very homely. The landlord was an older man. It was very near to the office, very near to the market and close to our friends, but the landlady was too strict about guys coming, not during the day, not even for a single minute. Outside the gate, we could do anything; inside the gate, no. No guys inside the gate. But the general psychology in Gurgaon is that if you have a guy inside your flat you must have a relationship with him or that you are doing some hanky panky stuff. They do not take it as just a simple friendship. They always assume that if a guy is staying back, then you must be up to something.

(Indu, 26, NCallB)

In the wake of post-independence urbanization, 'bourgeois environmentalism has emerged as an organized force in Delhi and upper-class concerns around aesthetics, leisure, safety, and health have come significantly to shape the disposition of urban spaces' (Baviskar 2003: 90). Delhi's special status and visibility as national capital has made state anxieties around the management of urban spaces all the more acute: 'Delhi matters because very important people live and visit there; its image reflects the image of the nation state' (Baviskar 2003: 90).[10] Yet, despite the wave of transnationalism shaping Delhi into a 'transterritorial centre' (Sassen 2002), Delhi as a locality is continually reconstituted by surrounding rural areas. Local communities in these areas, particularly young men, have expressed unease with the cosmopolitan culture that has entered their communities. Discussions during interviews with both men and women in the call centres detailed experiences ranging from harassment by local men whilst waiting for transport vehicles, through threatening, violent behaviour which eventually involved the police, to territorial clashes between male call centre employees and local men over eating and drinking areas. Sangamitra discusses her thoughts on living in Gurgaon:

Staying alone is a major problem in Gurgaon because they [locals] know you are going out at night, they know you are working in a call centre, and they think that probably you don't belong to a good family. They feel that we are very forward girls. That is the problem that we face with the landlords and landladies, mainly. I have been switching my places quite often. In the span of 2 1/2 years I have changed seven to eight places. Staying in Gurgaon is not safe at all. Guys are like letches. And that too, if you are staying in an apartment with just girls, always you'll find people [men] hanging around there.

(Sangamitra, 25, GCall)

The tension between globalizing and localizing forces exists, with clashes over spaces and the right to occupy them. Chatterjee offers this:

This new metropolis will belong to the managerial and technocratic elites and a new class of very highly paid workers – professionals, middle and lower-level managers, brokers and middlemen of all kinds. The elites will form their own community – a spatially bound interpersonally networked subculture built around business centres, segregated residential areas, exclusive restaurants, country clubs, arts and culture complexes, and easy access to airports ... consumer industries will be driven ... by the new high spending workers ... a globalized cosmopolitan subculture.

(Chatterjee 2003: 82–84)

Though they are a long way from enjoying country clubs, it is not difficult to understand how participation in the globalized cosmopolitan subculture of call centre work in Gurgaon might result in locals carving out areas for themselves that are hostile to the employees.

At the end of the working week, many of the women wanted to use their wages to have fun; however, to engage in this leisure-world is to engage in the negotiation of affection, companionship and perhaps sexual favours in exchange for protection and safety. Notions of women and respectability are constructed as a way to control and confine women, with respectability used as a mechanism operating between identity and space and producing gendered subjectivity, spatial knowledge and ultimately gendered space (Boyer 1998: 267–68).[11] Women in areas that are not deemed respectable can be read as threatening to morality and social order, and are thus subjected to harassment by the local men:

Many of the women have been harassed and followed, because the men in Haryana think that they are easy. Gurgaon is not a very developed area and when the men see women travelling around the night and see them at dhabas and thekas, especially when they see women getting bottles and drinking. Yes, this definitely does exist.

(Preetika, 24, GCallB)

Women working in call centres were encouraged by their companies to participate in the social events and parties and though some engaged in these activities, others did not participate due to the negative association with places such as bars and clubs. Women who did engage in these social activities did so also to bond with other employees, suggesting that they might be ostracized or termed a 'BTM' if they did not participate. One such example is the way in which call centre workers, men and women, frequented roadside taverns and eateries called 'thekas' and 'dhabas', such as Zaika, a dhaba located close to many call centres in Gurgaon.

Zaika and the geographies of women's fear

Danger is a cultural construct (Valentine 1989, 1992; Koskela 1997) and space is constructed into 'safe' and 'dangerous' places (Pain 1997). From an early age girls are socialized into a restricted use of public space through observing both their parents' fears for them and the control of the spatial range of their activities in relation to boys (Valentine 1989: 386). Defensive tactics such as the avoidance of perceived 'dangerous places at dangerous times' pressure women into restricted use and occupation of public spaces (Valentine 1989: 386). Most women do have some form of frightening experience, however, and such incidents become associated with particular environments, reinforcing possible avoidance of 'dangerous places' and developing personal images of fear over time and space (Valentine 1992: 28). Women's inability to enjoy independence and freedom to move safely in public space is therefore one of the pressures which encourages them to seek protection from one man against all others (Valentine 1989: 388). In their study of women's perceptions of fear in Singapore, Yeoh and Yeow (1997: 276) identify four main sources of 'fear' information, namely, personal victimization experience, socialization in the family context, the mass media and informal communication.

Media sources produce the 'rhetoric of danger and threat' (Koskela 1997: 309), evidenced by the Indian film industry, in which violence against women is not only depicted but also eroticized as male heroes use force to win the affection and hearts of their beloved (Derne 1999). By disproportionately publicizing attacks committed in public places as opposed to domestic spaces, the media generates images about the spatial and temporal contexts of crimes against women and places the danger women fear in the public environment (Valentine 1992: 25). Similarly, one can observe the production of the 'rhetoric of danger and threat' in the Indian media, as publications such as *India Today* highlight the growing threat of violence against women (see Figure 5.2). As articles within the news magazine focussed on how unsafe women feel in Indian cities, the focus was on single women as opposed to married women and statistics highlighted issues such as clothing and transportation, thus subtly reinforcing the expectation that married, respectable women were less likely to experience violence in a public space. Highlighted in large text, the following is used as a snapshot of violent incidents against women:

> In May 2005 a call centre worker leaves her home to go across the street with a friend to get a bite to eat. She is abducted by four men, one of whom is a call centre driver, and is gang raped for two hours. Police do no react despite the fact that her friend had reported it to them five minutes after she was abducted.

> (Bamzai and Doshi 2005)

Moreover, photos inside and on the cover draw a substantial link between the sexuality of women and the fear of violence. The front cover maintains a filmic 'male gaze' (Mulvey 1975), with the masculine figure in the foreground appearing more than twice the size of the woman, his victim, who appears in the background. The masculine figure is shadowed, thus maintaining his sense of anonymity, whilst the woman is posed in a way that emphasizes her

Figure 5.2 Cover of *India Today*, 13 June 2005.

breasts, waist, hips and butt. She is dressed in revealing clothing and high heels and is positioned against a brick wall, indicating that she has reached a dead-end or has nowhere to go. Such images, and indeed the articles in the issue, continue to place responsibility for violence against women on the shoulders of women, suggesting that they are provoking such attacks rather than criticizing the misogynist culture found within Indian society.

In 2002, there were 374 reported rapes in Delhi, making it the most unsafe city in India; 80 per cent of women surveyed by newspapers said that sexual harassment existed at work and 70 per cent said that they face inappropriate behaviour at work, of which verbal abuse is the most commonly reported form of abuse ('The Male Gaze' 2002). In 2005, over 50 per cent of women surveyed felt unsafe in the city that they lived in, and in Delhi only 4 per cent of single women and 15 per cent of married women felt that it was safe to go out unescorted after 10.00 p.m. (Bamzai and Doshi 2005).

Violence and threats of violence against women are everyday concerns and present one of the reasons that call centre companies must work hard to set up efficient transport systems. Sangamitra, who lives and works in Gurgaon, not too far from her office, does not use public transport and instead uses the transport that is offered by her employer. On one occasion, Sangamitra's driver was over two hours late collecting her for work. She was advised by her manager to come to work by riksha (cycled transport) and that she would be reimbursed for the fare. She asked the driver to take her to work via a specific route that she was familiar with:

> That guy, first he asked me where to go, and everyone knows that GCall is in Sector G, then he turned about and then I realized, man, shit, I don't know this route at all. It was all very isolated, deserted place and I was not aware. I told him twice, thrice, 'Bhaiya [brother], I don't know this route. Do not take me from this route. If you want more money I have all the willingness to give you more money, but take me from the route which I want to take.' This guy said, 'No, it's okay. You want to reach, no? We'll reach your office, no matter how much time it takes.' That way, he was speaking very reassuringly, all bullshit attitude he was showing me. Then I sensed something wrong was happening. I somehow managed to get down from the rik. He went ahead, he stopped his rik, then he looked back, and the way he was looking, I got scared like hell. I could not stand there on my feet. I just started running. And that's because I was aware I had a police station very nearby. Somehow, I managed. I had my sandals, my bag, everything. I went into the police and the first thing when I told the police exactly what happened with me he said, 'Okay, have you been raped?' 'You wanted me to wait till I got raped, and then I could have come back and then I would have lodged a complaint or something?' He said, 'Yeah, because if you haven't got raped we can't take any action against a person.'
>
> (Sangamitra, 25, GCall)

Sangamitra's experience shows, first, the growing tensions between the local community and the employees of the multinationals but, more importantly, the institutionalized and embedded misogyny rampant in India. The interviewees shared many stories such as this one. Moreover, my own experiences in the field indicated that such examples are the norm rather than the exception.

However, despite the social construction of space as dangerous, by demystifying and routinizing it space can be tamed for women (Koskela 1997: 308–09). The transgressions of women as they move into public spaces or increase their mobility with male companions have had a constitutive effect on socio-spatial forms and relations (Sassen 2001b), one which demonstrates the contribution of transnationalism to the changing morphology of the city (Sassen 1998). Moreover, Koskela found that women who had previous experiences, either abroad or through travelling, of encountering strange places expressed a greater sense of courage than women who did not have those experiences (Koskela 1997: 307). Pooja, who had travelled extensively and had previously worked in a German NGO, had been exposed to places outside Delhi and India, linking confidence with experiences of travelling:

> To be very frank, my life has been – my parents are so open and I've travelled a lot. I've been to Brazil, you know. Because nothing has happened to me it's hard to relate to that woman who has been really disgraced or leading the [disgraced] life because you know my life has been totally – I can't comment on anybody's life. It's like that. I can just say, you know, be independent. That's it.
>
> (Pooja, 28, NCall)

Pooja describes women's independence, and thus a sense of safety, as contingent upon her experiences and although geographies of women's fear are, in part, socially constructed, women's agency and mobility are constrained by patriarchal power relations, confining and controlling their ability to 'demystify', 'routinize' and disrupt 'no go' spaces.

The opening of Massey's (1994) essay 'Space, Place and Gender' describes football pitches as a 'no go' area for girls; Zaika, a dhaba and after hours eatery, is another 'no go' area for girls.[12] Whilst the entertainment centres provide modernist, global spaces for a rising group of a relatively privileged and educated young middle-class people, only two miles down the road from these towering structures are the local 'dhabas' and 'thekas'. Dhabas are largely male only spaces that function as roadside cafés for truck and bus drivers, while thekas are licensed spaces that sell only alcohol. Though it is illegal for thekas to operate at night, many of them do by using a discrete side window or door. There are many categories of dhabas, ranging from family-style dhabas with a grassy area for children to play and several other shops selling sweets or tourist items to dhabas found on Delhi street corners, which are simply a cart with a gas stove and a few boxes as seating. Generally open twenty-four hours a day, dhabas provide good 'sastaa khana', good cheap food, and are known for basic, simple but filling dishes. Although there is a wide range of dhabas, the majority tend to function as social spaces for men in the local areas. Many dhabas can be found in the areas around call centres, but for this discussion I will focus on Zaika, a dhaba which was located across the highway from the GE call centre in Gurgaon.

Zaika is located at the intersection of the two main highways that cut across Gurgaon. The first is the highway which runs from Delhi to Jaipur (north to south) and the second is the highway that cuts across Gurgaon (east to west), thus Zaika's position makes it very visible and very popular. The restaurant, which resembles a take-away food counter, remains quiet and slow throughout the day, with most of its staff waking up only to serve the occasional customer. However, at around 10.00 p.m. every night the workers set up chairs and tables to seat approximately sixty people (see Figure 5.3).[13] All of the people working there are lower-class and lower-caste men and approximately 90 per cent of the customers are Haryana men.[14]

Call centre employees who frequent Zaika tend to go after a shift at work is finished, which can be anywhere between 10.00 p.m. and 2.00 a.m. as shifts finish at various times. This means that Zaika is generally at it's busiest between the hours of 10.00 p.m. and 5.00 a.m. Gayatri, a manager in a call centre, points out that there are very few places for people to go and socialize late at night:

> I have friends who would call me at two or three o'clock in the morning and say, 'Can we come over?' and I say, 'Sure.' People would say, 'Hey, what's going on?' But I also know as a person who works at night, if I don't see them at two in the morning, I won't see them. So you meet your friends at really strange hours. Zaika is always crowded on Sunday night, because most people are planning to work on Monday morning and they

Figure 5.3 Zaika, a dhaba in Gurgaon.

[call centre workers] are planning to work on Monday night. So they are out to party because they can't sleep. Nobody understands that. That these poor people can't sleep any more.

(Gayatri, Call Centre Consultant)

Women from the call centres do not ever go to Zaika alone or with other women only; they are always accompanied by men. Some of the women interviewed discussed the fact that they were not always comfortable with sitting in Zaika and preferred to wait in the car while the men they were with ordered food, and when they did move to the seating area it was generally to the outer edges of it:

I would go with my friends, but I would stay in the car, because it's good food and it's close to work but it's a very scary place.

(Preetika, 24, GCallB)

As argued earlier, women in the city can be seen to present a threat or a danger to men (see also Bondi 1990; Massey 1994). First, in the metropolis women are free to escape the patriarchal social controls dominant in smaller communities and, second, cities represent a realm of uncontrolled and chaotic sexual licence and women must therefore be rigidly controlled to avert this danger. In this way, the women of the nearby call centres were interpreted as posing a threat of sexual chaos or disorder to Gurgaon, particularly by transgressing the space of the 'dhaba'. Women being accompanied by male companions was one way in which this threat could be mitigated and accepted by the local men.

Rashi, a team leader at GCall, discusses why places like Zaika, though unfriendly and intimidating for women, are still popular places to go. Her comments also demonstrate a class dimension to the use of dhabas, claiming a space for women that attends to their needs as working-class women:

RASHI: You see, we don't have anything that is twenty-four hours. If you want to go drinking or even for a coffee, generally you have to go to a five-star [hotel] because that is the only thing that is open all night. But then, for a person who is working in the call centre, not everyone can actually afford to go to a five-star. I mean, I'll talk about myself. I would love to go to a five-star every day but I can't afford it. But if I want to go for a coffee or I want to eat or go for a drink what am I supposed to do? Do I just go home? I have to go to a place like this, and it's become really casual now, especially with the call centres. It's not like you are going out of your house at that hour. You are already out. You are coming back from your shift, and you are just stopping for a moment.

INTERVIEWER: So how do you think that the men who go to these dhabas and thekas respond to all the women there?

RASHI: They are not very comfortable with it. In fact, the other day I had gone, not that I'm very comfortable going there, but then when you see that there are no other options, you don't mind going there. You think, okay, I'll ignore the rest of the people sitting around, I'm with my friends. But when you see someone who is sitting at the next table, abusing [swearing] left, right and centre – all the abuses, or is looking at you kind of funny: who are you, why are you here? Like that. But I think even that has reduced a lot, because they are pretty used to seeing the women coming in. So they probably would stay busy on their own. So we can still go ahead and have our nice time.

(Rashi, 26, GCall)

Although her presence at Zaika is not appreciated, Rashi still feels that she, someone who cannot afford the luxury of five-star hotels, has a legitimate right to be there. In line with Rashi's description of it as the only place to go at night for inexpensive food, others commented that Zaika is 'similar to Barrista [a coffee shop] but with booze'.

In this way, dhabas operate in a similar way to local pubs in the UK, with call centre employees frequenting dhabas close to their work premises, forming bonds with co-workers. Thus when they change jobs they move to another 'local' dhaba, widening their social networks as they go, as Preetika indicates:

I have also seen a lot of call centre hopping, going from one to the other. You're not growing, you are not moving. For those people who have no ambition, they love this kind of life. It is an extended version of college. They just come in their torn jeans and stand and smoke, and when another set of [job] interviews comes along they just move to another job. Hopping, hopping.

(Preetika, 24, GCallB)

This description of Zaika places it alongside the liberalized, cosmopolitan spaces of the shopping complexes, restaurants, cafés and bars, thus transforming it and demystifying it through routinization. Zaika, and other dhabas similar to it, has been reconstituted as a space for both genders, demonstrating the way in which the call centre industry has impacted upon the changing morphology of the city. Moreover, it presents an example of how the social and the spatial are constitutive of one another, in that the spatial is produced out of social relations. With the dhaba acting as a 'local', social relations are produced out of these spatial contexts, meaning that women's identities are contingent upon the spaces they inhabit.

6 Conclusion

Agency and identity

What began as a research project on the experiences of women working in Delhi's transnational call centre industry developed into a wider narrative of what happens outside those call centres as well. It wasn't until the project was well under way that the significance of space and the social relations produced out of spatial contexts emerged. The mutual influences and determinations of home, work and public spaces were acute reminders of what little agency the women possessed, regardless of how independent they were or felt they were.

As a brief caveat, this book finds itself articulating a moment; it is temporally and spatially bound and can only speak to social transformations occurring in Delhi, Gurgaon and Noida from 2002 to 2003. Linking the call centre labour process, the ways in which women construct identities and the impact of working women on socio-spatial contexts, this book finds itself in the midst of an ever-evolving narrative, full of partial and incomplete truths.

In endeavouring to privilege women's voices and contribute to transnational feminist research, the concepts of agency and identity were used to examine the ways in which women construct both work identities and consumer identities. The call centre labour process, with its virtual migration, allows for the construction of 'the dialogical self' (Chaudhary and Sriram 2001: 380), performed in the 'third space' (Butler 1990; Bhabha 1994), the space between utterance and interpretation. The significance of this space is not to be underestimated as employees in transnational call centres transform their work sites into 'cyber cafés', with individuals using the Internet at work to connect to people all over the world. The interpretation of their Indian identities in these global contexts is not necessarily reflective of their experiences in everyday life, as they are grounded in an Indian locality; however, they do contribute to the reflexive processes of identity construction. These spaces are constructed over and over again throughout the labour process, in an exchange with every new customer. Each customer brings his or her own understanding of what it means to be 'Indian' to the exchange and, through a dialogic process with the call centre worker, constructs a new identity for the employee, similarly to the way the interviewees constructed varying identities for me. In this way, for example, British customers express cultural knowledge of British Asians and thus through the dialogic process construct an 'Indian' identity for the call centre worker that is rooted in a British and British Asian discourse.

'Dialogical' exchanges widen the discursive practice of identity construction, as individuals acquire new ways of articulating self-identity. Numerous examples of online marriage services and websites catering for the needs of the global Indian community, such as Shaadi.com, are increasingly found, indicating a reflexive dialectic contributing to a 'dialogical self' living in the 'digital diaspora' (Gajjala 2004). Websites such as BPOShaadi and BPODating, aimed exclusively at arranging relationships and marriages for call centre and BPO workers, are in the process of being re-framed, turning away from the global Indian towards the Indian living in India, in essence localizing a globalizing process.

The dialogical self profoundly shapes the process of constructing self-identity, of narrating a biography and a trajectory from the past to the anticipated future. But it is in the physical world, grounded in the local, that identities take on stronger social meanings.

Globalization is not a homogenizing process and there is a lack of evidence to suggest the universalizing of identity or the emergence of a supranational or 'global colonial' identity (Banerjee and Linstead 2001).[1] Of greater significance is the knowledge that local and global social processes enable and constrain, so that women are complicit in patriarchal paradigms whilst resisting them.

In some ways this book has given women an opportunity to speak for themselves and discuss the ways in which they negotiate social, cultural and familial expectations in exercising agency and becoming independent. Many voices are included here to demonstrate the conflicts that the women experienced amongst themselves. There is no true image of women call centre workers; rather, there are stories that collude and contradict, and as much as women may be exploited or disempowered by the dominant forces of globalization, so too are they able to see out the spaces within which to articulate their self-identities, ambitions and futures.

This book began with the pairing of two quotations from *Guardian* journalists, and although Monbiot and Seabrook seem singled out for criticism, this is not the case. These quotations were used to demonstrate the indelible and virile nature of such analyses, so influential that five years on Indian call centre studies continue to focus largely on the exploitative nature of the labour process as opposed to the wider impact that call centres have had on the cities of India. This begs the question as to why the issue is continuously raised by journalists and academics alike.

Spivak (1988: 27) has made an excellent argument regarding the troping of 'white men saving brown women from brown men', taking issue with claims that place benevolent colonialists alongside the intellectuals who claim to speak for the disempowered. Women call centre workers may speak, but they are misheard and ignored, their actions interpreted through frames of reference that privilege the relationship between India and the UK.

A number of call centre studies have emerged since this research was completed in 2003, but few resist the alias and accent discussion. Cohen and El-Sawad's study is one such study, disagreeing with popular perceptions that call centres foist new, Western identities on employees. In fact, they found that rather than focusing on any contradictions or cultural conflicts, employees discussed subtle aspects to do with the historical relationship between India and the UK. They also noted a strong sense of East and West; however, they argued that these are not necessarily offered as windows into respondents' feelings about cultural identity but as rhetorical devices used to justify certain patterns of thought and behaviour.

It is difficult, if not impossible, to ignore the postcolonial, global colonial relationship that India and the UK share. It is certainly on the minds of the call centre workers dealing with UK clients and customers, and rather than assessing this on the basis of relocated call centre work or economical disparity between the two countries, perhaps it would be more reasonable to use the frames of reference offered by the workers themselves.

Responding to questions about globalization, the women call centre workers argued that the focus on aliases was directly linked to how they understood the British to perceive India with regard to colonial histories and discourses. Questions that I posed regarding accents and names were dismissed relatively quickly as they used their time to discuss what they understood the real concerns to be.

The consideration of a British dimension to these globalizing discourses was not an explicit focus of the research from the outset simply because the questions regarding globalization and identity were conceived of as relating to the global–local dynamic. In other words, discussions of globalization and globalizing discourses were understood as global and not necessarily as having any origin or context. The women call centre workers pointed towards the differences in callers from the UK and US, demonstrating that UK customers had a distinct perception of Indian call centre workers, rooted in and expressed through colonial discourses, not global discourses. In this way, postcolonial relations were felt and understood as oppressive and global relations were felt and understood as liberating, though some might argue they are one and the same (Banerjee and Linstead 2001).

Migration theories and discourses on transnationalism helped to articulate the call centre workers' experiences. However, the workers themselves did not physically leave India; moreover, the construction of their online identities was contingent upon their individual discussions with customers. These interactions did not necessarily mean that the women call centre workers were losing their Indian identities. They discussed a Westernization that was enhanced by the call centre and the labour process, but they still identified as Indian, particularly through the use of clothing, wearing ethnic chic and the practice of veiling to increase their mobility in public spaces. In this way they could be read as becoming more Indian.

Culture and identity are mutually constitutive of one another and contingent upon social processes, global and local. In this way, women's identities are socially produced through local, global, national, patriarchal, traditional and modernizing discourses, all of which come together in the 'third space' where meaning is constructed; however, as this space is continually shifting, so too are the meanings produced from it. Thus social processes, all social processes, influence the processes of identity construction to a large extent. However, this does not suggest that agency cannot function within these discourses; as the research has shown, many women found ways to exercise agency.

The research is bound in two significant ways: theoretically, the concept of power remains somewhat problematic; empirically, the parameters are established by a specific focus on women workers in the National Capital Region of Delhi, Gurgaon and Noida. The women all possessed varying degrees of power in relation to one another, though this did not mean that they were powerless, for 'where there is power, there is also resistance' (Foucault 1979). They were afforded agency in different ways. Those who were living away from parents argued they could make choices independently of other's expectations. These choices could involve where to go that evening, how to spend their money, where to live, or whether or not to apply for a new employment position. Women who lived with families or husbands argued that they were given a certain respectability which protected them from some of the more dangerous aspects of call centre work.

A second consideration of power was introduced by my identity and position as the researcher conducting feminist research, problematized by the 'outsider/insider' relation in conducting research on one's 'own' community. The research participants identified me in various ways: an NRI, an employee of NCall, a friend, a British PhD student, amongst others. These roles impacted upon the research in that they created certain power relations. For example, women who knew me to be an 'outsider' presented more socio-historical narratives of their lives during the interview. Others who knew me only as an NCall language trainer sought help in writing CVs or asked if I knew how to apply for domestic work in the UK. As a consequence, the knowledge was produced as a social construct, born out the relationships that were constructed with the women.

With regard to empirical considerations, the parameters were established by Delhi's geographical boundaries. Call centre workers were recruited from many regions throughout India, and despite bringing specific regional and cultural knowledge to their experiences in Delhi, some of the issues of concern to them are markedly different to issues concerning them in their home communities. Women in Delhi experienced acts of aggression and violence directed towards them, and although this was not directly linked to their employment in the call centre, their Western dress sense did increase their visibility in public spaces. This is significantly different in cities such as Mumbai and Bangalore, where the call centre or ITES–BPO industry is almost as prevalent as in Delhi and attitudes towards working women are perceived to be liberal. Moreover, some of the issues regarding clothing could be read differently in places such as Bangalore, a more cosmopolitan city in South India, or Chandigarh, a more rural city in North India.

Second, call centres in Delhi are of a range of types and provide many different services and, as such, the six call centres used in this research do not necessarily represent all types of call centre work found in India. The industry showed signs of increased diversification, moving beyond basic customer services into more technical areas. Although some of the call centres in this study, such as DelCall, recruited employees with engineering degrees, much of the labour performed by employees in this study was customer service oriented. Moreover, the snowballing strategies used to generate the sample group might suggest some homogeneity in the responses to research questions. However, this is not necessarily the case as all but one of the women had worked in more than one call centre, making it possible for them to draw upon a range of experiences during the interviews.

The lack of discussion of caste and class presented a minor limitation. As interviews were semi-structured, a brief interview guide looking at key themes was used. However, interviewees were encouraged to present narratives of their identities and, as such, some of the interviewees chose to discuss caste and class while others did not. Although there is diversity amongst the interviewees with respect to socio-economic positioning and class origins, a university education and experience working in the call centre suggested a similar class destination. Moreover, call centres provide employment opportunities for almost anyone with good English-language skills and a university degree and in this way afforded each of the interviewees a degree of anonymity. Call centres are not necessarily secular; however, issues of caste and class are less and less significant in cosmopolitan centres and such a discussion may have affected the overall interview in a negative way.

The main arguments of this book link three distinct areas of interest: the call centres, the women who work in them and the lives they live outside them. These three areas are the sites anchoring the women's narratives. Their personal stories wove through the analysis of globalization and identity; however, the call centre and the labour process acted as a gateway to further investigations. The women were curious, judgemental and altogether sympathetic about how the women working alongside them came to be there. Whilst their motives for working, the labour process and their ambitions shaped their relations with one another, it was what happened outside the call centre and after work that most women wanted to discuss.

The 'pinking' of the Indian call centre industry continues with a workforce comprised of predominantly English-speaking graduates between the ages of 23 and 25. Their 'nimble fingers' (Elson and Pearson 1981b) and 'natural' ability to perform 'emotional labour' (Hochschild 1983) ensure that skill remains 'saturated with sex' (Phillips and Taylor 1980). However, the technocratic nature and controls of call centre work were welcomed against the discrimination many of them had faced in other areas of employment, as was the sexually liberalized, college-like atmosphere.

Whilst the call centres have decreased the economic gender divide they have also deepened some of the negative stereotypes of working women. Caught between images of traditional Indian women and the new liberated woman, call centre workers found that whilst such symbols enhance the image of Indian economic liberalization, they do not necessarily afford women liberation from patriarchal discourses. Moreover, they carry the baggage of an 'institutionalized cosmopolitanism' (Beck 2004) with regard to social activities and sexual relationships. The resulting 'aestheticization' of work identities (Witz et al. 2003) gave rise to 'ethnic fusion', signifying modernity and upward mobility, whilst also claiming a globalized Indian national identity.

Whilst 'aestheticization' of work identities can be enabling inside the workplace, it is constraining outside it, starkly setting apart the virtual migration from the corporeal journey to work. Call centre workers are acutely aware of moving from the 'Synopticon' (Bauman 1998), where they are observed moving in and out of glamorous, high-tech work sites, to the 'Panopticon' of the labour process itself. Greater levels of control exist outside the call centre, where issues of danger and violence are paramount and mitigated only by further surveillance.

As the discussion concerning call centres in India unfolds, greater attention may be given to agency, as scholars move away from the superimposed framework of analysis born out of call centre studies outside India. A culturally specific framework for analyzing the effects of globalization is emerging, providing better opportunity to investigate the ITES–BPO culture of Indian cities, demonstrating how the global and the local are mutually constitutive and always in process.

The women call centre workers in Delhi are aware of the 'power of identity' and that the sites of this power are in people's minds. 'Cultural battles are the power battles of the Information Age, they are fought in and by the media to impose behaviour' (Castells 1998). Cultural specialists reinvent tradition, producing cultural identities increasingly drawn together in a tighter configuration of competition with one another.

Indian call centres invite curiosity and interest; they also provide exciting departure points for discussions of globalization and postcolonial subjectivity. They remind us that globalization is not homogenizing, nor should we be concerned with its purported homogenizing effects; rather, we should seek answers to questions concerning how the debate has been shaped, whose voices are privileged and whose truths are complete.

Epilogue

Every Friday for one hour in the afternoon we meet with Mrs R, who happens to be the wife of Mr R, the head of the company in England. She was working in a government organization in the UK before she came, so she's on a long-term leave. Now she indulges in charity work, and she meets people, she promotes handicrafts, she's into those kinds of organizations.

The whole point of our discussion revolves around the UK, and if we have any questions to put forward to his wife, then we can ask her. It's an exchange of thoughts and ideas, views, and if we have any questions regarding the country and how women are in the country. How the work environment is, how women take care of family, how the government helps women when they are pregnant. Young mothers, teenage pregnancies, how it is handled. Various issues and various topics, like dressing, shopping, marriage, extramarital affairs, the royal family, how gay and lesbian relationships are handled in the UK, examples from her life, about her family, day-to-day living. Basically we've had an exchange of thoughts. So how it goes is that she selects certain topics every Friday, every class, every meeting that we have – I wouldn't call it a class.

What I have comprehended out of visiting two of these sessions is for women here to be able to relate to people over there. Somebody who comes straight out of the culture, who belongs there, who is white, so you can put to her all your questions and queries, and you can understand the culture better. I think that's what the idea is behind it. But I'm not sure why it's called a women's forum. A forum is to address problems faced by women basically, to be able to help them so that people, so that you can reach out to somebody influential, so they can help you out with your problems. But I'm not sure why this is called a women's forum meeting because we are not addressing any issues as such. Nor are we finding any solutions. It's just an exchange of thoughts, knowledge or culture. We never discuss Indians in the UK, only the UK as a whole. It's like an information exchange between UK and India, except we only really talk about the UK.

In India, the outlook is different. You are a woman, you will get married and you will have kids. With all the setbacks I've had, with my marriage plans, education plans and the economy, I have to look ahead. I am a career-oriented girl. The world is changing, we have gone into the next century, countries are globalizing and women are coming out. The concept of women's revolution seems like history right now and there is nothing like men versus women. We are here, we work together for a better future. You need a woman, you need a man. So if I meet somebody who sounds like he is one hundred years behind, am I looking for that kind of family?

I've seen women around me doing well and it has given me confidence. One girl I know was put on fast track. I'm sure that the management is not discriminating between the sexes. However, they might think that a woman has more commitments to home than a man does. My last boss and I had a one-to-one and he said, 'You're a girl and tomorrow you'll get married. A career is not that important to you, it's just pocket money.' I looked at him and said, 'You cannot decide on my behalf why I am here.'

I'm passionate about my country. I know my country has many things to overcome. But talking in terms of industry, I think India is *the* place to be. It's the place where companies from all over the world are investing. We are emerging big. There is so much scope for us to earn money, to learn more, to make a place for ourselves. I saw Americans coming here for a little while, but now I see Malaysia, Singapore, Hong Kong, Germany, Thailand, UK, Europe – everyone is rushing in to India, because we have such a wide market.

Now I see more respect for women in India. I see more responsibility. I see more appreciation. India has made a breakthrough.

Glossary

bhenji	older sister
chunni	headcover or scarf, same as dupatta
coolie	an unskilled labourer from India
dhaba	roadside eatery, generally for men
dupatta	headcover or scarf, same as chunni
khadi	home spun or hand woven cloth; a term used by Gandhi to encourage Indians to make their own cloth during the Quit India campaign
kurta(s)	loose garment like a shirt or tunic with long sleeves
kurti(s)	variation of the kurta, only smaller and shorter in length
multinats	multinational corporations
pyjama	tight trousers taken in at the ankle to gather the fabric
salwaar-kameeze	a two-piece outfit consisting of loose trousers with wide cuffs (salwaar) and a knee-length top (kameeze)
sati	widow sacrifice ritual from the nineteenth century (also spelled 'suttee')
sahib	respectful term for a white European in colonial India
theka	roadside licensed spaces selling alcohol

Notes

1 Introduction: 'a myriad of well-wishing "little sisters"'

1 The US and the UK are but two of the many countries that now export back office work to India and other countries in Asia.

2 A postcolonial, or post-independence, context indicates a discussion historically and temporally situated after India's independence in 1947. Theoretically, discussions of India and modernity are expressed through a 'postcolonial discourse', 'postcolonial context' or 'postcolonial condition' (Bhabha 1994; Said 1978, 1993; Spivak 1986, 1988, 1999), by which institutional conditions in former colonial societies and a continued discursive and power imbalance are indicated. Although they are varied in their character, McWilliams notes that postcolonial theorists share an attempt to 'unweave the complex structures put in place by colonialist rule ... revealing the complex interactions of colonizer and colonized ... to discuss how subjects are constituted now that the colonial powers no longer have overt political control' (McWilliams 1991).

3 Said (1993: 22–24) points to the loss of Vietnam and Iran to radical nationalisms and the Salman Rushdie affair, during which a 'fatwa' was declared on Rushdie's life for writing *The Satanic Verses*.

4 Here Said (1993: 405) refers to the work of Toni Morrison and Salman Rushdie.

5 Websites such as www.nojobsforindia.com (accessed September 2008) have focussed on the continued increase in the outsourcing of call centre and data entry work to India and more specifically on job losses for US employees. The tone of the site can be read as aggressively blaming Indians for American job losses and includes statements such as: 'And to someone indian [sic] who wants to say your [sic] better. Don't bother, your [sic] not better, just cheaper. You say we weren't competive [sic] enough, we are but we all can't cut our salarys [sic] to 1/10th or we won't be able to survive here in America'.

6 See Treanor (2002). The *Guardian Weekend* published a feature on 3 April 2004 examining call centres in India, with journalist Siddhartha Deb posing as a potential call centre agent. Deb attended the training and, focussing primarily on his personal perspective, extensively discussed the issues regarding name and identity changes. There was little engagement with other call centre employees in this piece.

7 Newspaper articles collected from the *Times of India*, the *Hindustan Times* and *India Today* from 1999 to 2002 reveal a bias towards the positive economic effects of outsourcing work to India. From 2002 to 2005 articles were biased towards the social effects, focussing on positive and negative changes to Delhi's middle class as well as health and safety issues, particularly for women.

8 During 2002–03, this research was conducted in the National Capital Region (NCR), comprised of Delhi, Gurgaon and Noida, which, at the time, presented itself as a

logical research site as it housed up to 50 per cent of India's call centre industry. However, the industry's remarkable growth has seen the NCR expand to include Faridabad (NASSCOM, 2008). Throughout this book Delhi is used to indicate the NCR.

9 In this book, postcolonialism functions in three ways: first, as a challenge to the intersecting histories of modernity, colonialism, capitalism and nationalism; second, as a critique of the hegemonic discourses and inequalities that cut across national societies; and, third, as a term that positions cultural production in the fields of identity construction and transnational economic relations (Grewal and Kaplan 1994: 15–16; Puri 1999: 15–16).

10 Feminist research argues, amongst many things, for the importance of focussing on women's experience, emphasizing 'the aphorism "the personal is political"' (Roseneil 1993: 178), with feminist practice providing a checkpoint for feminist theory (Karam 2000: 182–84). Wolf writes that feminists raise more questions about the ethics of research because they are moved by a commitment to the women's movement rather than simply pursuing their own careers (Wolf 1996: 2).

11 Spivak (1988); see Jagger (2000: 5).

12 Drawing upon accounts of benevolent colonialists who saved Hindu women from immolation in the practice of nineteenth-century widow sacrifices known as sati, Spivak (1988) takes issue with claims that place the colonialists alongside intellectuals who claim to speak for the disempowered. Arguing that the basis of a truth claim is no more than a trope (an embellishment) and that woman or the racial Other is a kind of troping of that truth of man as the norm for universal humanity (Spivak 1986), Spivak claims that the interlocutors have silenced the subordinated subalterns and established a trope understood as 'white men saving brown women from brown men' (Spivak 1988: 27). In this way, 'the subaltern may speak, but she is misheard, ignored or her words and actions are misinterpreted by a dominant culture whose terms of meaning, truth and understanding exclude subalterns by positioning them and interpreting their actions through dominant frames of reference' (Hubbard et al. 2004: 276–77).

13 For a discussion of Western feminist theory and Indian feminist theory, see Chaudhuri (2004) and Gedalof (1999).

14 Natarajan (1994) argues that woman functions as a signifier in many ways in the imagining of India, not least as a pan-Indian identity, relinquishing caste based hierarchies in favour of modernity. She looks at woman in three moments of nationalism: the movement from regional to national in the modernizing process; the threat of communal or civil rupture within the body politic; and the rise of fundamentalism. Woman's body is a site for testing out in the first moment; in the second, as Mother India, a site for mythic unity in the face of fragmentation; and in the third, as 'daughter of the nation, a site for countering the challenge posed by Westernization' (Natarajan 1994: 79).

15 It has been argued that the breakdown of the patriarchal family is the principal cause for fundamentalist and communalist movements, particularly for the Hindu Right (Mies 1979; Moghadam 1994). Women's traditional identities are produced through patriarchal discourses (Kakar 1988) and constructed around female goddesses or icons, such as Sita, Ram's long suffering and virtuous consort, or Durga, warrior goddess, and Rani of Jhansi, which allows women to be strong and angry whilst remaining virtuous (R.S. Rajan 1999; Shurmer-Smith 2000: 126–28).

16 The term 'gharbzadegi', or 'westoxication', is the title of a 1952 publication by Ahmad Jalal al-ed, an Iranian writer and social critic, and refers to the loss of Iranian cultural identity through the adoption of Western values. Those most perceived to be vulnerable to this threat are upper-middle-class, educated women, viewed as agents of imperialist culture; in response to which the practice of 'hijab' (veiling) or sexual segregation is encouraged and enforced (Moghadam 1994: 13).

17 With specific regard to call centre studies, studies from the 1980s and early 1990s indicated that telework was closely linked to gender and home based work (Armstrong 1999), and many of the definitions of telework were based on this correlation (Huws et al. 1990; BT Martlesham Reports 1992; ILO 1990; Houdart-Blazy 1996); given the representation of women as home based workers, a gendered dimension to the discussion of telework emerged. It was argued that the 'electronic cottage' produced by teleworking was ideal for all women as they could work the hours that suited them and their needs (Toffler 1980); furthermore, they would be free from the patriarchal constraints of traditional work environments (Stanworth 2000). This over-optimistic image of telework providing autonomy and flexibility, particularly for women, was criticized as studies showed how ICTs were used both to intensify the labour process and to measure and monitor employee work output (Phizacklea and Wolkowitz 1995). Despite these criticisms, the glamorization of telework as knowledge work continued and the diversity of mundane tasks that existed in the office was largely ignored (Stanworth 1998). Initial reports and investigations attracted by this glamorization tended to focus solely on the knowledge work aspect, excluding consideration of tasks such as data entry, telesales and word processing – tasks usually performed by women. With an increase in call centres and data entry operations, the ignorance regarding call centres and the call centre labour process was challenged and a number of academic articles investigating the industry began to emerge. A shift in academic interest from telework to call centres was paralleled by the industry's recognition that call centres were not only cost controlling but profit generating (Bagnara 2000). (See Armstrong 1999; Baldry et al. 1998; Bain and Taylor 2000; Greenbaum 1998; Huws 1999; Kinnie et al. 2000a, 2000b; Knights and McCabe 1998, 2001; Marshall and Richardson 1996; Richardson and Marshall 1996; Stanworth 1998, 2000; Taylor and Bain 1999.)

18 See Salzinger (2002).

19 In exploring the links between exploitation and commodification of women's sexuality, derived from notions of black women bought and sold on the slave market, Collins has written that 'current portrayals of Black women in popular [American] culture – reducing Black women to butts – works to reinscribe these commodified body parts' and as such control and regulate women's sexuality (Collins 1990: 133).

20 Data collected from NCall for this research project indicate that the number of women employed in call centre and data entry work is on the rise, with women making up approximately 65 per cent of NCall's employees.

21 Soft skills include: listening skills, regional comprehension skills, empathetic skills, customer service skills, and persuasion skills, to name a few.

22 See Banerjee 1990, 1996; Baud 1991, 1992; Mies 1982.

23 Internationally, some writers have suggested that access to the export market and labour processes based on computers, technology and manual dexterity have been advantageous for women, as they have opened up new areas of employment (Freeman 2000; Pearson, 1993) and opportunities for 'cyber feminism' (Gajjala and Mamidipudi 1999), with others arguing that the technology has resulted in deskilling, sub-contracting, increased homeworking and increases in temporary employment (Reardon 1999). Certainly there has been an increase in women's employment in Asian economies as trends towards the decentralization of production processes from industrialized countries to newly industrialized countries have continued. Competition amongst Indian companies who specialize in outsourced work has led to an increase in sub-contracting, also known as 'outsourced Indian companies' (Mitter 1999) or 'third party service providers' (Taylor and Bain 2003a), which sometimes operates in the clandestine economy, and this has had an impact on the number of women working in the formal sector. Malaysia has experienced structural economic changes through the introduction of computers

and the liberalization of its telecommunications industry. Vietnam has also experienced changes in its telecommunications industry, as women now comprise 50 per cent of the total telecommunications labour force, as opposed to the small numbers that once represented women's participation in the labour market (Mitter and Banerjee 1999). In the Caribbean, Freeman (2000) has looked at sub-cultures emerging as a result of the cultural and class divides of those working in informatics and data processing, focussing on similar issues to those explored in this book such as identity, clothing, and 'pink collar' work. Although the proportion of women administrators or managers tends to be low in developing nations, Reardon and Ng have argued that there is nothing uniquely Asian about this as gender inequalities exist virtually everywhere (Reardon 1999: 12).

24 It reads: 'Women can not be exempted from the requirement that the maximum working day for adults is 9 hours, and can not work in factories between the hours of 6am and 7pm (unless the factory falls within a specific exemption, but in any case, not between the hours of 10pm and 5am). In relation to women, there must not be a change of shifts except after a weekly or other holiday. However, note that State governments can change these requirements in the fish curing and canning industries' (Factories Act 1948).

25 Also reported by Barua (2002).

26 Izzat is the Hindi, Punjabi and Urdu word for honour.

27 The 'general rule of thumb' in protecting the identity of research participants lies with anonymizing the interviews; however, all of the interviewees elected to use their own names, therefore to preserve a sense of ownership the call centres have been anonymized instead.

28 A point also made by Spivak (1988), when she argues that representations of Third World women have obscured their subjectivity while promoting the interests of the authors (see Jagger 2000: 5).

29 For a discussion of this, see Skeggs (2002: 361).

30 For examples of this in other studies, see Bolak (1996), Beoku-Betts (1994), De Andrade (2000).

31 For another example, see Bhattacharyya (1997).

32 For a greater discussion of this, see Wolf (1996).

33 For another example of this, see Beoku-Betts (1994: 429).

34 Although clothing will be discussed later in this book, I use 'acceptable' here to indicate observation of local customs where women cover most of their bodies and do not wear shorts or vest tops.

35 For another example, see Sherif (2001).

36 Shurmer-Smith notes the ambivalence around the return of non-resident Indians: 'people can be scathing about the opportunism of those who leave … and feel hurt by the condescending attitudes they seem to display when they visit'. Moreover, she notes characterizations of them as 'nervously returning Indians' and 'not really Indians' (Shurmer-Smith 2000: 178–79). I would also add to this list from my fieldwork 'non-reliable Indians' as a term often used to describe non-resident Indians.

37 For a discussion on clothing and the role of the researcher, see also Sherif (2001), Henry (2003), Mookherjee (2001).

38 Ghosh and Wang (2003) note similar transitions and transformations in airport lounges as women transformed from 'mems', or Westerners, to 'desis', or Indians.

39 Of her research in India, Henry writes, 'I spent most mornings deciding to wear a salwaar kamiz only to end up in the company of those wearing Western dress and feeling like an anthropological poser or, other days, showing up in a blouse and skirt and feeling very conspicuous amongst the saris' (Henry 2003: 234). Like Henry, although I belong to the Indian diaspora I was not returning 'home', and this created a sense of 'double consciousness' (Henry 2003). Given my own dislocated

sense of identity as a British born, Canadian raised Indian recently returned to Britain, I struggled with my own sense of identity and with the degrees of 'Indianness' that I felt. Questions regarding my background, parents, ancestral village, relationships with men (of Indian and non-Indian origin) forced me to articulate and construct an identity from which the research participants judged my level of authenticity and, as with Henry, my legitimacy as a researcher.

40 NCall is a fictitious name given to one of the call centres that form the basis of this study.

41 Cowie (2007) conducted research while similarly providing voice and accent training at a call centre in Bangalore.

42 Similarly to research on call centre case studies by Mulholland (2002) and work on gender and the informatics industry by Freeman (2000), the use of grounded theory (Glaser and Strauss 1967) allowed for the generation of theory through 'constant comparative' analysis (Strauss and Corbin 1994: 273), particularly in determining which theories and concepts are practical and useful in examining the research questions.

43 A 'thick' description allows for a more nuanced, cultural and historical analysis, contrasted with a 'thin' description that is simply factual.

44 Hereafter, the term 'identity' is used in this way.

45 Denzin (1995) contends that the postmodern self has interiorized the cinematic investigative voyeur's gaze, wherein which the gaze is an exercise of power generally deployed in a narrative structure with a male hero and a woman as the object of investigative activity, a structure often used in Bollywood films. In this way women simply lack the powerful gaze as they are always the object.

46 Castells' 'legitimizing, resistance, and project identities' (Castells 1997) situate identity within a matrix of economic, social and cultural global and local power relations. Similarly to Appadurai (1996), he views 'global cultural flows' as much more complex than a local/global dialectic.

47 Lawler argues that narratives are social products, 'they are not transparent carriers of [an] experience ... rather they are interpretive devices, through which people represent themselves ... furthermore, narratives do not originate with the individual: rather they circulate culturally to produce a repertoire from which people can produce their own stories' (Lawler 2002: 243).

48 Giddens' work, though highly influential and significant for social theorists, remains somewhat limited in moving beyond the local/global dialectic. Though his contributions to the understanding of agency and reflexivity are useful, as Lash and Urry (1994) suggest, his notions of self and identity are not embodied enough and as such are limited in engaging with how identity is discursively produced.

49 For discussions on transnational mobility, see Ong (1999).

50 Brah has argued that 'diaspora offers a critique of discourses of fixed origins, while taking account of a "homing desire" (not the same thing as desire for a "homeland")'. Far from a fixed or stable concept, Brah suggests that diasporic journeys are constituted through multiple journeys via a confluence of narratives 'as it [the jouney] is lived, and re-lived, produced, reproduced, and transformed through individual as well as collective memory and re-memory ... it is within this confluence of narrativity that "diasporic community" is differently imagined under different historical circumstances' (Brah 2003: 617).

51 In his discussion of new ethnicities, Hall writes that the diaspora experiences 'a process of unsettling, recombination, hybridization, and "cut-and-mix" – in short, the process of cultural diaspor-ization' (Hall 1996a: 447).

52 Hall is referring to the British Empire as opposed to Hardt and Negri's (2000) theoretical concept of 'Empire'.

53 Based on Yegenoglu's (2005: 123) reading of Hardt and Negri's *Empire* (2000). Furthermore, Ong (1999: 23) argues that transnationality is not detrimental to the

nation-state; rather, what is much more profound is the way in which the state regulates the agency and identity of displaced subjects.

54 Hybridity can also be read as a 'rubbing' of cultures (Griffin 2000: 194), a theory of 'fuzziness and melange, cut-and-mix, crisscross and crossover', or as a narrative trope that is only really useful as a critique of essentialism (Pieterse 1995: 55–64).

55 This is in reference to Kant's 1784 essay titled 'Idea for a Universal History from a Cosmopolitan Point of View'.

56 For a more thorough discussion of this, see Beck (2004).

57 Previously, to be cosmopolitan meant disengagement from nationalist discourses and participation in an order that was wider than nationalism (Delanty 1999: 366), sharing three basic tenets: individualism, universality and generality (Bowden 2003: 241).

58 A conventional understanding sees the cosmopolitan as 'a universal citizen, mobile, autonomous, and [who] chooses to be transnational. The cosmopolitan has no sense of self and therefore no notion of other ... and has no feeling for a world which he or she has voluntarily abandoned' (Delanty 1999: 368).

59 See Rundell (2004: 86).

60 Bhabha (1994) writes that the 'Third Space', which exists between the You and the I, represents both the general condition of the language and the specific implication of the utterance in a performative and institutional strategy of which it cannot 'in itself' be conscious.

2 Globalizing India: the rise of the call centre and BPO industries

1 These processes include: industrialization; urbanization; commodification; rationalization; differentiation; bureaucratization; the expansion of the division of labour; the growth of individualism and state formation processes (Featherstone 1995: 87).

2 Habitus is Bourdieu's understanding of the way in which individuals become themselves, develop attitudes and dispositions, and the way in which they engage in those practices (Bourdieu 1984).

3 Classem and Howes, quoted in Banerjee and Linstead (2001: 699).

4 There is an extensive literature on Indian cinema and Bollywood films that is not cited here. For a discussion of national identity in Indian cinema, see Chakravarty (1998).

5 One-third of the revenue derived from Bollywood movies is from NRI takings (Shurmer-Smith 2000: 175–77).

6 Denzin proposes that the cinematic apparatus introduced into American society a pragmatism and a pragmatic epistemology which taught Americans to be scientific and furtive in their daily investigative activities, something which is also prevalent in Indian society. Denzin cites examples such as Alan Pakula's *All The President's Men* (1976) and Oliver Stone's *JFK* (1991) as examples of films which cultivated a sense of pragmatism in investigative activities. He further proposes that Hollywood incorporated the voyeur into its own cinematic apparatus, developing the genre of reflexive-voyeur films, which violated the codes of film, disrupting traditional narrative cinema and disorienting the viewer. The voyeur's films deployed an investigative narrative structure with a (usually male) hero in search of truth-connoting action defined in male terms, a woman as the object of investigative activity, or a romantic triangle with women treated either as femmes fatales or wives and long-suffering girlfriends, a narrative structure nearly always used in Bollywood films. Denzin notes a gendering of the gaze, stating that women on screen simply lack a powerful gaze as they are almost always the object of the gaze (Denzin 1995: 58–59).

7 Mahatma Gandhi led a series of protests during the 'Quit India' campaign against the importing of British cotton goods into India. Gandhi called on Indians to make their own home-spun cloth called khadi.

8 Singhal and Rogers (2001: 192) suggest that this comes out of two distinctive processes, the first being the colonial development of services, such as the telegraph and postal services, which the British rulers managed with tight control; the second being Jawaharlal Nehru's post-independence socialist policies committed to state-run, state-owned monopolies in various sectors; both of which accompanied narrations of the nation.

9 The term 'brain drain' is often used by the Indian media and government to refer to the large numbers of IT graduates emigrating to places such as the United States, Canada, Australia and parts of Europe (mainly the UK, France and Germany) (Khadria 2001). Beginning in 2000 with the rapid increase of call centre work and IT work available in India, the numbers of IT graduates seeking employment outside India began to dwindle. Increased wages, knowledge gained from working abroad and the return of many Indians from the US post-11 September 2001 were celebrated at the first annual Pravasi Bharatiya Divas, where Shri Yashwant Sinha, Minister of External Affairs, commented that fears about India's 'brain drain' were now giving way to claims of India's 'brain gain'.

10 Spectramind is a Delhi based call centre and data entry site.

11 See Mitter 1995; Mitter 1999; Irani et al. 1999; Irani 1999; Khadria 1999, 2001; Rajan 1999; Ramani 1999; Sinha 1996.

12 In the mid-1990s Spectramind established itself as the first base call centre site inviting TNCs from outside to invest with them.

13 Interview transcript dated 26 June 2003, Gurgaon.

14 See Singhal and Rogers (2001) for an extensive discussion of the 'television revolution' in India.

15 Data gathered from interviews and NCall in 2003 confirmed that a call centre starting wage ranges from 500 to 700 Indian rupees per month, approximately from USD100 to £100 Sterling per month.

16 Wages for call centre employees start at Rs140,000 per annum (£1,845.43) for those engaged with routing calls and duties; Rs184,000 per annum (£2,425.42) for more complex calls and duties; Rs279,000 per annum (£3,677.68) for operations team leaders; Rs433,000 per annum (£5,707.64) for customer service team leaders; Rs646,000 per annum (£8,515.33) for managers; Rs1,362,000 per annum (£17,953.37) for senior managers; and Rs1,532,000 per annum (£20,194.24) for head of operations (Taylor and Bain 2003a). Taylor and Bain (2003a) use a US$ to Indian rupee conversion rate of 1:47.12 and a £ Sterling rate to US$ rate of 1:1.61. Using these figures £1 is equal to Rs75.8632.

17 Along with globalization, a major social transformation influencing the development of the call centre industry is the process of urbanization; the movement of people from rural to urban areas for education and employment opportunities has been a significant factor in the changing social world. India's population shift from rural to urban is demonstrated by the number of 'million-plus' cities rising from five in 1951 to thirty-five in 2001 (Dyson and Visaria 2004). The 2001 census shows that, of Indian cities, Delhi is third, with a population of 12.8 million, behind Mumbai, with a population of 16.4 million, and Kolkata, with 13.2 million. Dyson and Visaria (2004: 123) argue that this is because people can migrate to Delhi from many directions and that the city too can expand in many directions, which cannot happen in Mumbai due to its coastal location.

18 Examples of these include American Express, HSBC, Dell, AOL, Hewlett Packard and most prominently GE Capital, which employed 12,000 people at its Gurgaon site in 2003.

19 From 2003, examples include Tata Consultancy Services (24,000), HCL (24,000, including subsidiaries), Wipro (21,000), Infosys (17,000 employees worldwide), VCustomer (6,000 employees globally) and EXL (5,000). The smaller firms include Progeon (850 employees worldwide), Wipro Spectramind (6,500), ICICIoneSource

(2,200) and Daksh (3,500), which similarly bid for outsourcing contracts from major multinationals (Taylor and Bain 2003a).

20 Individual clients for each of the companies are too numerous to list here but include Microsoft, Lucent Technologies, Apple Computers, Monsanto, Reebok, Toshiba, Gap, Dell, J. Sainsbury, J.C. Penny, Adidas, HP, Nationwide, Boeing, Ericsson, IBM, Thames Water, Royal Bank of Scotland, Johnson and Johnson, Kellogg's, American Express, Deutsche Bank, GE, BT, Northwest Airlines, Singapore Airlines and Harrods. All these companies have listed some of the same corporations as clients, indicating that some transnational corporations outsource work to more than one call centre.

21 Taylor and Bain (2003a) show that there is some disagreement on the size of Indian call centres, with some reports reporting an average size of approximately 191 employees per call centre. Figures for the proportion of women in IT enabled services ranged from 25–30 per cent of the total workforce (Poster 2001), through 38 per cent of the total workforce (Ramesh 2004), to 51 per cent of the total workforce (Taylor and Bain, 2003a). Prior to this book few studies have been conducted with an explicit focus on gender. Of notable exception is that by Singh and Pandey (2005), though many of the other studies conducted reported an increase or likely increase in the number of women employed in call centres due to factors such as the changing social acceptance of night shifts.

22 Interview transcript dated 16 April 2003, Delhi.

23 Interview transcript dated 26 June 2003, Gurgaon.

24 Interview transcript dated 26 June 2003, Gurgaon.

25 This concurs with Taylor and Bain's (2003a) findings.

26 Thompson et al. (2004: 136) showed that in their study of an Australian call centre phrases such as 'right attitude' and 'cultural baggage' became euphemisms for a managerial preference for employees who showed little interest in or history of trade union membership. They show that an elaborate interview process was designed to identify young, enthusiastic and committed recruits; however, they were also intended to exclude staff who had come from corporate backgrounds where trade unionism was strong.

27 The suburbanization of call centres that tapped into the pool of married women looking for part-time work (Stanworth 1998) and those actively recruiting women for call centre work (Thompson et al. 2004: 135) has created traditional female employment ghettos (Belt 2002a, 2002b). Many have argued that this feminization of the call centre labour process has become increasingly evident (Baldry et al. 1998; Breathnach 2000; Lankshear et al. 2001: Russell 2002; Richardson and Marshall 1996; Zapf et al. 2003). Belt (2002a, 2002b) and others (Belt et al. 2000, 2002) agree with Stanworth (1998) that a growing number of women are employed in lower levels of call centre work involving voice-to-voice contact and are rarely promoted to more senior positions. They contend that companies recruit women for their 'soft skills', 'bubbly or lively personalities' and their 'natural' ability to perform emotional labour and 'smile down the phone' (Richardson and Marshall 1996; Belt, 2002b; Belt et al. 2002). Further evidence (Belt 2002b: 139) showed how women had purposely developed a 'flirty way of selling'. Such 'feminine skills' were said by Richardson and Marshall (1996) to include compassion and a caring, genuine desire to serve the customer, echoing the early arguments that the definition of skill is 'saturated with sex' (Phillips and Taylor 1980). Although, in theory, the rise of women working in fields that involve emotional labour could represent an important shift in the established gender order, challenging the existing patterns of female disadvantage in the labour force, studies point towards continuities in rather than disruptions to gender inequality (Belt 2002b).

28 Ng and Mitter (2005) also note that attrition is 30–35 per cent.

29 One UK study found that management put considerable effort into organizing social and recreational gatherings, with regular outings organized and certificates, awards, gift vouchers and movie tickets routinely given out (Thompson et al. 2004: 142).

30 The 'Panopticon', originally conceived as a blueprint for a prison by Jeremy Bentham, allows all prisoners to be observed without their knowledge while the observer remains unseen. Foucault likened this brightly lit prison design to our everyday lives and the discursive production of power, arguing that through this chimera of visibility modern society exercised its controlling systems of power. The 'Panopticon' also provides a potent metaphor to discuss crucial issues of power, control, surveillance and resistance in feminist research (Wolf 1996: 2), and in the analysis of call centre labour processes due to the layout of the work environment and the mechanized nature of the work (Fernie and Metcalf 1998; Taylor and Bain 1999). Moreover, it serves in a discussion of power, control, surveillance and resistance as they relate to women and women's sexuality in urban centres in India (Gedalof 1999). Power is not in an exterior position with respect to other relationships; rather it is the immediate effect of divisions and inequalities. Moreover, power comes from below and, as such, 'where there is power there is also resistance' (Foucault 1979: 94). Foucault's work is problematic for some feminists in that he does not directly account for women's experiences or a gendered subjectivity (Ramazanoglu 1993). However, Foucault offers feminist theory many entry points for a deconstructive analysis of the way in which power manifests and is utilized through racialized and sexualized discourses, particularly in his conception of resistance (Gedalof 1999).

31 Performance measures used to appraise agents and customer satisfaction include: politeness towards customers; length of calls; adherence to set procedures; call taping/review; adherence to script; content of calls; satisfaction measures; quality audit; and time between calls. Sigma 6 is one such quality control measure and was found to be used in call centres in this study.

32 Taylor and Bain quote a mortgage company manager who put the issue in stark terms, stating, 'there is a call centre in the UK that knows when their staff have diarrhoea, because they monitor toilet visits' (Taylor and Bain 1999: 110).

33 In a study of an Australian call centre, Thompson et al. (2004: 143) show that employees' families were occasionally invited to visit the workplace to get a sense of where they worked and what they did.

34 Research by Taylor and Bain (2005; Bain and Taylor 2008) and Mirchandani (2004a, 2004b) shows acts of individual resistance, including: agents pretending to be on calls when they were not; disengaging from the waiting queue of calls; and influencing the calculations of output, thereby affecting bonus payments. In a newspaper article, Siddhartha Deb provides an account of his experience posing as an agent who, when stressed with difficult customers and high call volumes, tells a customer that Chandigarh 'is near Tennessee, but you need to take a right before you come to Tennessee' (Deb 2004). Mirchandani (2004b) found that another strategy for resistance when customers were particularly irate or issues were complicated was for agents to give the customer a 'talla' or hoax solution knowing that it was highly unlikely that an agent would get the same customer twice.

35 Interview transcript dated 18 January 2003.

36 NCall is a fictitious name given by the author to the call centre that forms the basis of this study.

37 NOIDA stands for New Okhla Industrial Development Authority.

38 Approximately 300 employees worked on this particular process. Of the 300 survey questionnaires administered, 113 were completed in full and returned.

39 At the time of data collection, £1 Sterling was equivalent to 75 Indian rupees. The salaries at NCall, therefore, ranged from just under £100 per month up to £200 per month.

40 An Indian expression usually meant to indicate a way to pass time.

3 Pinking and rethinking professional identities: the construction of women's work identities

1 Sanskritization is the process of vertical mobility by which low-caste Hindus or tribals change their customs, ritual, ideology and way of life in the direction of a high and, frequently, 'twice-born' caste (Mies 1979: 39; Mazumdar 1994: 250).
2 An argument made by Mies (1979: 162–74) three decades earlier.
3 In 2005 the *Observer* reported irate customers as the primary reason for staff turnover in India, with agents complaining of rudeness, sexual harassment, fury at unsolicited sales calls and open racism (Gentleman 2005).
4 For a greater discussion of how corruption operates politically and culturally in India, see Pavarala (1996).
5 A report in the *Guardian* discussed unionization as the next issue for Indian call centres (Cooke 2005).
6 Informal discussions with NCall employees, Noida, 5 July 2003.
7 Informal discussions with NCall employees, Noida, 5 July 2003; and with NCall HR managers, 29 June 2003.
8 Much of this information comes from formal and informal discussions with call centre workers and key informants throughout the research process. Furthermore, this lack of non-vegetarian food was not limited to NCall as employees from other companies discussed similar issues.
9 This echoes Mies' (1979) earlier arguments of a similar nature.
10 In a study of men and women working as managers in Australia, Wajcman and Martin (2002) found that women rejected career narratives in narratives of identity in favour of domestic life.
11 Based on participant observation at NCall, June–August 2003.
12 Banerjee and Linstead (2001) state that globalization is just 'global colonialism' executing the objectives of colonialism with greater efficiency and rationalism and 'global culture' simply marks the transformation to cultures of consumption.

4 BTMs in BPOs: using sartorial strategies to establish patterns of identification and recognition

1 Abraham (2004: 213) draws upon the popular Hindu text *The Ramayana*, in which Lakshman, the brother of Ram, draws a circle around Sita, Ram's wife, to protect her from the dangers of the forest. For Indians, the circle symbolizes the confinement of Sita and the 'idealised confinement of the chaste Indian woman'. Sita becomes the quintessence of wifely devotion idealizing sacrifice for one's husband (Abraham 2004: 213). The second popular myth is that of Drapudi, the wife of one of the Pandavas, whose clothing was forcibly removed after she was lost to the winners of a gambling match. However, with the intervention of Lord Krishna, as her sari was removed it became longer, thus Drapudi remained fully clothed. This story is a part of an epic myth which includes the Bhagvad Gita, the most sacred text in the Hindu religion, and is thus very well known throughout India, prompting some feminists to question whether 'eve-teasing', a euphemism for sexual harassment, is rooted in Hindu mythology (R.S. Rajan 1999).
2 Although some feminists have drawn attention to how nationalist movements such as Hindutva have enabled an articulate, fighting individualism for women, others have argued that no feminist can suggest that a fundamentalist movement with uncompromising orthodox compulsions can contribute anything to the broad rights of women (Chaudhuri 2004: xxiv).
3 For an extensive discussion of Indian film and Bollywood, see Chakravarty (1998).
4 On many occasions I witnessed Bollywood inspired dancing in the five-star hotel nightclubs, complete with choreographed moves and lip-synching. The dancing was usually done by couples, with the men performing the roles with greater flair than

the women; however, some of the music, in particular the soundtrack to *Dil Chahta Hai* (2001), spoke to both genders equally and whole dance floors would fill, as in scenes in the film itself.

5 Rupert Murdoch's STAR-TV revolutionized Indian society and culture and, far from embracing Western ideals, Indians demanded more local productions, as a 'wired-in middle class' forced the indigenization of programming on Western channels such as MTV (Banerjee 2003; Cullity 2002; Juluri 2002; Kumar and Curtin 2002; McMillin 2001). For a socio-historic look at cultural change and its links to television, see Butcher (2003).

6 The Indian Government's recent High Level Committee report on the Indian diaspora estimates that almost 20 million people of Indian origin live overseas (Walton-Roberts 2004).

7 Cultural cosmopolitanism is defined as cosmopolitanism which strengthens ethnic nationalism.

8 Discussions with key informants, Delhi, 2002–03.

9 Beginning during the colonial period, the Revolt of 1857 marks the key moment in the evolution of a national Indian identity, as Hindus and Muslims were united against the British and a range of romantic figures had been thrown up, including Rhani of Jhansi (Jhansi Rani), a heroine who defended her fortress from the British and was later canonized. Rhani of Jhansi became goddess and national spirit all at once, thus giving birth to the 'woman as defender of the Motherland' myth, and the Hindu Indian woman was no longer someone to idealize but became the human face of the nation (Mazumdar 1994: 256). For a historical overview of the origins of the women's movement in India, see Jaywardena (1986: 73–108).

10 Hindu mythology holds the belief that women are in possession of dangerous powers, maya and shakti, and that if not controlled in everyday life, female sexuality will take a dangerous and destructive form (Abraham 2004: 212).

11 In comparison with the larger data set from the short survey questionnaire administered to NCall employees, my sample group shows a higher percentage of women with boyfriends and women engaged to be married and a lower percentage of married women. These number are shown as ratios of the percentages, sample group:NCall: single women 56:58, women with boyfriends 25:17, women engaged 9:1, women married 9:23.

12 In theorizing clothing and dress, various terms have been employed and, according to Entwistle (2000: 40), there has been little consensus on their definition and how they are to be used. For the purposes of this discussion, the term 'clothing' shall refer to the everyday dressing of the body as it occurs within the boundaries of cultural norms, various social milieus and office dress codes. Terms such as 'costume' or 'adornment' will be avoided and instead terms such as 'dress', 'ethnic', 'authentic' or 'traditional' clothing will be used to signify traditional Indian clothing. Furthermore, the term 'fashion' will be used according to Entwistle's definition as 'a particular system of dress found under particular social circumstances' (Entwistle 2000: 44).

13 Widely regarded as one of the earliest theorists on fashion, Georg Simmel argued that fashion was a strategy used by the higher stratum of society to distinguish itself from the lower stratum. He claims fashions would be abandoned by the higher stratum as soon the lower stratum began to appropriate them and that fashion works as a way to hold a particular social circle together whilst keeping others out (cited in Crane 2000: 189); within the working classes, Bourdieu (1984) argued, fashion and clothing were practices of 'distinction' and 'habitus'.

14 However, this accusation of ethnocentrism in fashion theory has been refuted by Entwistle (2000), who points out that the lack of definition in terminology and the focus on power as the key feature is limiting and perhaps ethnocentric in itself. Entwistle suggests that the study of fashion as a system of dress be historically and

geographically specific but that there be three essential features in that society under consideration: first, that social mobility is possible; second, that it has its own particular relations of production and consumption; and, third, that it be characterized by logic of regular and systemic change (Entwistle 2000: 47–48).

15 Freeman's findings connect with Bourdieu's theories (1984: 205–60) on the link between clothing and chances of material or symbolic profit.

16 Foucault (1979) did not specifically discuss clothing; however, his theories regarding power are used in examining gendered notions of dress, although his failure to acknowledge embodiment and agency presents a critical flaw in understanding how identity is negotiated and expressed (Entwistle 2000: 17).

17 The use of clothing to express one's social standing or political beliefs has a long history in India. Cohn (1989) suggests that Indian dress during the period of British rule acted as a way through which the British reinforced their separateness from the Indians. This was done through strict adherence to a British standard of dress by the colonials and through encouraging the Indians to dress 'in an oriental manner'. Cohn's second critical argument is that the dress codes were inextricably linked with notions of modesty, honour and respect. Bayly (cited in Tarlo 1996) goes on to argue that these beliefs were rekindled by Gandhi during the 'Quit India' campaign when he encouraged Indians to wear khadi or home-spun cloth, the use of which was meant to symbolically unite all classes against the 'divide and rule' tactics of the British colonial government (Legg 2003: 20). Gandhi's influences on Indian notions of dress and identity are hugely important, as he, along with Nehru, was one of a growing number of individuals who left for schooling in Britain only to return to India as a part of the 'England-returneds' (Tarlo 1996: 44). Much of his political ideology was expressed through clothing. His rejection of the suit and adoption of the loincloth symbolize his anxiety with this sartorial juggling and a desire to locate an 'authentic self' (Entwistle 2000: 73).

18 'Izzat' meaning honour related to family and culture; see (Moghadam 1994: 13).

19 Desi refers to someone from the 'desh', or homeland.

20 Based on my ethnographic observations, kurtis were worn by the young, upwardly mobile middle-class living in urban centres. Kurtis worn with trousers were rarely, if at all, seen outside major cities.

21 'Ethnic chic' exploded in the fashion industry in 2003, driven by Bollywood and fuelled by the imagination of consumers (Appadurai 1996). As one article reads, 'Sporting the latest Bollywood trend was never this easy and pocket-friendly. With kurtis making a cool statement on screen – from Shah Rukh Khan in *Chalte Chalte* to Akshay Kumar in *Andaaz* – any guy next door can now dress up like a Bollywood stud. Simply hop over to *Janpath, Sarojini Nagar Market, or Lajpat Nagar Market* and shell out a few bucks' (Arora 2003). All three markets mentioned (in italics) are in Delhi and popular with call centre employees due to their location near fast food places, cafés and cinemas.

22 See Figure 2.1, showing two women on their coffee break. One woman is dressed in traditional Indian clothing and the other is dressed in Western clothing.

23 Chummeries were bachelor quarters allocated to junior Raj officials in colonial India.

5 Techs and the city: challenging patriarchal norms through spatial practice

1 Hanson and Pratt (1995: 16) draw on the work of feminist art historian Griselda Pollock to look at 'containment stories', noting 'the male gaze' and the way in which women's bodies were the medium through which class and gender relations were represented and reworked. In particular, they write, Pollock's view that 'the practice of painting is itself a site for the inscription of sexual differences' suggests that the subjectivity of women is continuously inscribed and reinscribed through

discourses, cultural representations and everyday practices (Hanson and Pratt 1995: 16–17).

2 Drawing upon Yuval-Davis and Anthias, Legg (2003: 10) discusses at length the participation within rather than representation of women in nationalist projects, moving beyond the focus on women as simply representations of the nationalist movement and looking at the way in which women participated in nationalist struggles in India (Legg 2003). Beginning with his 'Quit India' campaign (1939–44), Gandhi insisted on women's active involvement in the struggle for independence, despite his belief that women's natural place was in the home. In this way Gandhi reimagined the home as a space in which women could be protected from the 'evil eye' and still participate in the movement by making home-spun cloth (khadi) and by being involved in the 'swadeshi' movement (self-made). This was accomplished by integrating women's participation in the movement into their religious duties. Legg argues that by crowning women as 'Queens of the household' Gandhi sought to meet a compromise between the need for women's agency and the forceful demands of an emergent 'new patriarchy' (Legg 2003: 13–14). Historically, Delhi remained independent of British rule until 1803 and was only systematically reorganized after 1857. Thus it remained under the Muslim influence of the Mughal Emperors and the tradition of purdah (segregation of women and men) was strong throughout the middle and upper classes (Legg 2003: 15). Gandhi's concept of 'spatially limited agency' for women wishing to participate in the nationalist struggle allowed for the political workforce to increase as well as for male Indian nationalists to strengthen claims to civility without actually threatening the security of their home lives (Legg 2003: 14).

3 Mies (1979) sought to contextualize the way in which women's roles were constructed in India and provided a historical and anthropological context to the social expectations of women as mothers and wives, referring to religious texts as the basis for these role expectations. Evidence points to the way in which patriarchal structures determined not only the way women experienced and accessed the domestic and public realm but also that motherhood was and is expected of Indian women. Mitter has written that by becoming a mother the Hindu woman 'redeems her stock, improves her standing at home and in society, confirms her cultural status, and gains some degree of freedom, especially if she has produced sons' (Mitter 1991: 90). Women's confinement to the domestic realm in this way can work to produce much more positive relations and a much more positive way of relating to the home. Thus home has the potential to be liberating and can serve as a valuable base for personal and cultural identity (Legg 2003:19).

4 Prime Minister Vajpayee's speech at the first annual Pravasi Bharatiya Divas on 9 January 2003 included a focus on and commitment to women's literacy. Furthermore, the age of consent was raised from 16 to 18 and the legal age of marriage for women was raised from 18 to 21, encouraging women to remain in school and pursue further education.

5 Elsewhere, Patel has written that 'although the presence of middle-class women in the urban nightscape represents a break in traditional norms, their mobility and spatial access is based on regimes of control and surveillance' (Patel 2006: 14).

6 The term 'exploitation' is an incredibly subjective one in this discussion as in this particular analysis it is meant to describe the exploitative relations between the UK and India, an idea strenuously objected to by Indian women workers in the call centres. Their understanding of exploitation is one of 'sexual exploitation', particularly the way in which men exploit women with the promise of job opportunities, pay rises and, in some cases, the threat of losing their job.

7 The Head of Human Resources at NCall pointed towards planned, monthly work parties that encouraged informal relations amongst employees as an employee retention strategy, something which many Indian call centres claim to do.

8 This data is from throughout 2003.

9 For a more in-depth look at Shiv Sena, see Banerjee (2000).

10 Chatterjee writes that the modern city occupies an ambivalent place in the imagination of middle-class Indians due to their lack of agency in thinking about it. He suggests that the industrial city was a product of modernity and that the colonial city was a product of imperialism to which Indians adapted. As the extended family crumbled under the pressure of economic changes, middle-class Indians proceeded to extend its moral influence over urban institutions. An imagined morphology of the Indian metropolis is characterized by a central business district with advanced transport, telecommunications and business facilities, producing technocratic elites (Baviskar 2003: 80–81).

11 Boyer is writing about women in twentieth-century Montreal.

12 All descriptions of Zaika are based on fieldnotes from from January to August 2003.

13 This description is based on the visits that I made to Zaika, at night and during the day, with call centre workers, as well as interviews with both men and women who frequented the restaurant at least twice a week.

14 Based on ethnographic observations and informal interviews.

6 Conclusion: agency and identity

1 'Globalization is just "global colonialism" executing the objectives of colonialism with greater efficiency and rationalism and "global culture" simply marks the transformation to cultures of consumption' (Banerjee and Linstead 2001: 683).

Bibliography

Abraham, L. (2004) 'Redrawing the *Lakshman Rekha*: Gender Differences and Cultural Constructions in Youth Sexuality in Urban India', in Srivastava, S. (ed.) *Sexual Sites, Seminal Attitudes*. New Delhi: Sage Publications, pp. 209–41.

Adams, P. and Ghose, R. (2003) 'India.com: The Construction of a Space Between', *Progress in Human Geography*, Vol. 27(4), pp. 414–37.

Adkins, L. (2002) *Revisions: Gender and Sexuality in Late Modernity*. Milton Keynes: Open University Press.

Afshar, H. and Barrientos, S. (1999) 'Introduction: Women, Globalization, and Fragmentation', in Afshar, H. and Barrientos, S. (eds) *Women, Globalization and Fragmentation in the Developing World*. London: Macmillan Press Ltd, pp. 1–17.

'After Hours Accent' (2003) *Times of India*, 7 October.

Ahmad, I. and Reifeld, H. (2003) 'Introduction', in Ahmad, I. and Reifeld, H. (eds) *Middle Class Values in India and Western Europe*. New Delhi: Social Science Press, pp. 1–18.

Alcoff, L. and Potter, E. (eds) (1991) *Feminist Epistemologies*. New York and London: Routledge.

Annamalai, E. (2004) 'Nativization of English in India and Its Effects on Multilingualism', *Journal of Language and Politics*, Vol. 3(1), pp. 151–62.

Anthias, F. (2001) 'New Hybridities, Old Concepts: The Limits of "Culture"', *Ethnic and Racial Studies*, Vol. 24(4), pp. 619–41.

Anthias, F. (2002) 'Where Do I Belong? Narrating Collective Identity and Translocational Positionality', *Ethnicities*, Vol. 2(4), pp. 491–514.

Anzaldua, G. (1999) *Borderlands La Frontera: The New Mestiza*, 2nd edition. San Francisco: Aunt Lute Books.

Appadurai, A. (1996) *Modernity at Large: Cultural Dimensions of Globalization*. Minneapolis and London: University of Minnesota.

Appadurai, A. (1999) 'Globalization and the Research Imagination', *International Social Science Journal*, Vol. 51(2), pp. 229–38.

Appadurai, A. (2001) 'Grassroots Globalization and the Research Imagination', in Appadurai, A. (ed.) *Globalization*. Durham, NC and London: Duke University Press, pp. 1–21.

Arabindoo, P. (2005) 'A Class Act: Bourgeois Ordering of Public Spaces in Chennai', paper presented at BASAS Annual Conference, University of Leeds, Leeds, 30 March–1 April.

Armstrong, N.J. (1999) 'Flexible Work in the Virtual Workplace: Discourses and Implications of Teleworking', in Felstead, A. and Jewson, N. (eds) *Global Trends in Flexible Labour*. London: Macmillan Business Press, pp. 43–61.

Arora (2003) 'Cool Kurtis Flaunt 'Em As Shah Rukh Does!', *Hindustan Times*, 12 June.

Arun, S., Heeks, R. and Morgan, S. (2004) *ICT Initiatives, Women and Work in Developing Countries: Reinforcing or Changing Gender Inequalities in South India?*, Development Informatics Working Paper Series. Manchester: Institute for Development Policy and Management.

Athreya, M.B. (1996) 'India's Telecommunications Policy: A Paradigm Shift', *Telecommunications Policy*, Vol. 20(1), pp. 11–22.

Atkinson, R. and Flint, J. (2001) 'Accessing Hidden and Hard-to-Reach Populations: Snowball Research Strategies', *Social Research Update*, Issue 33, pp. 1–6.

Bagnara, S. (2000) 'Towards Telework in Call Centres', *Euro-Telework*. Available at: http://www.euro-telework.org (accessed 25 September 2008).

Bain, P. and Taylor, P. (2000) 'Entrapped by the "Electronic Panopticon"? Worker Resistance in the Call Centre', *New Technology, Work and Employment*, Vol. 15(1), pp. 2–18.

Bain, P. and Taylor, P. (2008) 'No Passage to India? Initial Responses of UK Trade Unions to Call Centre Offshoring', *Industrial Relations Journal*, Vol. 39(1), pp. 5–23.

Baldry, C., Bain, P. and Taylor, P. (1998) '"Bright Satanic Offices" Intensification, Control, and Team Taylorism', in Thompson, P. and Warhurst, C. (eds) *Workplaces of the Future*. London: Macmillan, pp. 163–83.

Ballard, R. (ed.) (1994) *Desh Pardesh: The South Asian Presence in Britain*. London: Hurst and Company.

Bamzai, K. and Doshi, A. (2005) 'Single and Unsafe', *India Today*, 13 June, pp. 26–33.

Banerjee, K. (1999) 'Gender Stratification and the Contemporary Marriage Market in India', *Journal of Family Issues*, Vol. 20(5), pp. 648–76.

Banerjee, M. (2003) 'Travelling Barbies and Rolling Blackouts: Images of Mobility in Mira Nair's Monsoon Wedding', *Comparative American Studies*, Vol. 1(4), pp. 448–70.

Banerjee, M. and Miller, D. (2003) *The Sari*. Oxford: Berg.

Banerjee, N. (ed.) (1990) *Indian Women in a Changing Industrial Society*. New Delhi: Sage Publications.

Banerjee, N. (1996) 'The Structural Adjustment Programme and Women's Economic Empowerment', in Rao, N., Rurup, L. and Sudarshan, R. (eds) *Sites of Change: The Structural Context for Empowering Women in India*. New Delhi: Tulika, pp. 133–45.

Banerjee, S. (2000) *Warriors in Politics: Hindu Nationalism, Violence, and the Shiv Sena in India*. Boulder, CO: Westview Press.

Banerjee, S.B. and Linstead, S. (2001) 'Globalization, Multiculturalism and Other Fictions: Colonialism for the New Millenium?', *Organization*, Vol. 8(4), pp. 683–722.

Bannister, N. (2001) 'Call Centres Blamed for Acoustic Shock', *Guardian*, 13 February.

Barber, B. (1995 [2004]) 'Jihad vs McWorld', in Lechner, F. and Boli, J. (eds) *The Globalization Reader*, 2nd edition. Oxford: Blackwell Publishing, pp. 29–35.

Barsamian, D. (2004) *The Checkbook and the Cruise Missile: Conversations with Arundhati Roy*. Cambridge, MA: Southend Press.

Barua, V. (2002) 'Call Centres May Get Wake-up Call over Shops Act', *Financial Express*, 2 December.

Baud, I.S.A. (1991) 'In All Its Manifestations: The Impact of Changing Technology on the Gender Division of Labour', in Banerjee, N. (ed.) *Indian Women in a Changing Industrial Scenario*. New Delhi: Sage Publications, pp. 33–132.

Baud, I.S.A. (1992) *Forms of Production and Women's Labour: Gender Aspects of Industrialisation in India and Mexico*. New Delhi and London: Sage Publications.

Bauman, Z. (1998) *Globalization: The Human Consequences*. Cambridge: Polity.

Baviskar, A. (2003) 'Between Violence and Desire: Space, Power, and Identity in the Making of Metropolitan Delhi', *International Social Science Journal*, Vol. 175, pp. 89–98.

Beck, U. (1992) *Risk Society: Towards a New Modernity*, trans. M. Ritter. London: Sage Publications.

Beck, U. (2004) 'Cosmopolitical Realism: On the Distinction between Cosmopolitanism in Philosophy and the Social Sciences', *Global Networks*, Vol. 4(2), pp. 131–56.

Belt, V. (2002a) 'A Female Ghetto: Women's Careers in Call Centres', *Human Resource Management Journal*, Vol. 12(4), pp. 51–66.

Belt, V. (2002b) 'Capitalising on Femininity: Gender and the Utilisation of Social Skills in Telephone Call Centres', in Holtgrewe, U., Kerst, C. and Shire, K. (eds) *Re-Organising Service Work: Call Centres in Germany and Britain*. Aldershot: Ashgate, pp. 123–45.

Belt, V., Richardson, R. and Webster, J. (2000) 'Women's Work in the Information Economy', *Information, Communication, and Society*, Vol. 3(3), pp. 336–85.

Belt, V., Richardson, R. and Webster, J. (2002) 'Women, Social Skill, and Interactive Service Work in Telephone Call Centres', *New Technology, Work and Employment*, Vol. 17(1), pp. 20–34.

Beoku-Betts, J. (1994) 'When Black Is Not Enough: Doing Field Research amongst Gullah Women', *NWSA Journal*, Vol. 6(3), pp. 413–33.

Bhabha, H. (1994) *The Location of Culture*. London and New York: Routledge.

Bhachu, P. (2004) *Dangerous Designs: Asian Women Fashion the Diaspora Economies*. New York and London: Routledge.

Bhatia, N. (2003) 'Fashioning Women in Colonial India', *Fashion Theory*, Vol. 7(3/4), pp. 327–44.

Bhattacharyya, D. (1997) 'Mediating India: An Analysis of a Guidebook', *Annals of Tourism Research*, Vol. 24(2), pp. 371–89.

Bhopal, K. (2001) 'Researching South Asian Women: Issues of Sameness and Difference in the Research Process', *Journal of Gender Studies*, Vol. 10(3), pp. 279–86.

Blaikie, N (2000) *Designing Social Research*. Cambridge: Polity Press.

Bocock, R. (1992) 'Consumption and Lifestyles', in Bocock, R. and Thompson, K. (eds) *Social and Cultural Forms of Modernity*. Cambridge: Open University Press, pp. 119–68.

Bolak, H.C. (1996) 'Studying One's Own in the Middle East: Negotiating Gender and Self–Other Dynamics in the Field', *Qualitative Sociology*, Vol. 19(1), pp. 107–30.

Bolton, S.C. (2000) 'Emotion Here, Emotion There, Emotional Organizations Everywhere', *Critical Perspectives on Accounting*, Vol. 11, pp. 155–71.

Bondi, L. (1990) 'Feminism, Postmodernism, and Geography: Space for Women?', in McDowell, L. and Sharp, J. (eds) *Space, Gender, Knowledge*. London: Arnold.

Bondi, L. and Rose, G. (2003) 'Constructing Gender, Constructing the Urban: A Review of Anglo-American Feminist Urban Geography', *Gender, Place and Culture*, Vol. 10(3), pp. 229–45.

'Boomtime for Call Centre Trainers' (2002) *Times of India*, 18 February.

Bourdieu, P. (1984) *Distinction: A Social Critique of the Judgement of Taste*, trans. R. Nice. Cambridge, MA: Harvard University Press.

Bowden, B. (2003) 'Nationalism and Cosmopolitanism: Irreconcilable Differences or Possible Bedfellows', *National Identities*, Vol. 5(3), pp. 235–49.

Boyer, K. (1998) 'Place and the Politics of Virtue: Clerical Work, Corporate Anxiety, and the Changing Meanings of Public Womanhood in Early Twentieth-Century Montreal', *Gender, Place, and Culture*, Vol. 5(3), pp. 261–76.

Brah, A. (1996) *Cartographies of the Diaspora*. London and New York: Routledge.

Brah, A. (2003) 'Diaspora, Border, and Transnational Identities', Lewis, R. and Mills, S. (eds) *Feminist Postcolonial Theory: A Reader*. Edinburgh: Edinburgh University Press, pp. 613–34.

Breathnach, P. (2000) 'Globalisation, Information Technology, and the Emergence of Niche Transnational Cities: The Growth of the Call Centre Sector in Dublin', *Social Science Quarterly*, Vol. 31(4), pp. 477–85.

BT Martlesham Reports (1992) *An Overview of Teleworking: A Report by BT Research Laboratories*. London: British Telecommunications.

Budhwar, P.S., Varma, A., Singh, V. and Dhar, R. (2006) 'HRM Systems of Indian Call Centres: An Exploratory Study', *International Journal of Human Resource Management*, Vol. 17(5), pp. 881–97.

'Bullying Still Rife in Call Centre "Sweat Shops"' (2001) *Guardian*, 20 February.

Butcher, M. (2003) *Transnational Television, Cultural Identity and Change: When STAR Came to India*. New Delhi: Sage Publications.

Butler, J. (1990) *Gender Trouble: Feminism and the Subversion of Identity*. New York: Routledge.

'Call Centres Usher in Lingo Revolution' (2003) *Times of India*, 27 September.

Callaghan, G. and Thompson, P. (2001) 'Edwards Revisited: Technical Control and Call Centres', *Economic and Industrial Democracy*, Vol. 22(1), pp. 13–37.

Cameron, A. and Palan, R. (2004) *The Imagined Economies of Globalization*. London: Sage Publications.

Castells, M. (1996 [2000]) *The Rise of the Network Society*, 2nd edition. Oxford: Blackwell Publishing.

Castells, M. (1997 [2000]) *The Power of Identity*, 2nd edition. Oxford: Blackwell Publishing.

Castells, M. (1998 [2000]) *End of Millenium*, 2nd edition. Oxford: Blackwell Publishing.

Caulkin, S. (2002) 'Is There Anybody on the Line?', *Guardian*, 25 August.

Centre for Contemporary Cultural Studies (1982) *The Empire Strikes Back*. London: Hutchinson.

Chakravarty, S.S. (1998) *National Identity in Indian Popular Cinema: 1947–1987*. Delhi: Oxford University Press.

Chadhuri, M. (2001) 'Gender and Advertisements: The Rhetoric of Globalization', *Women's Studies International Forum*, Vol. 24(3/4), pp. 373–85.

Chanda, I. (2004) 'Birthing Terrible Beauties: Feminisms and "Women's Magazines"', in Chaudhuri, M. (ed.) *Feminism in India*. New Delhi: Kali for Women, pp. 228–45.

Chanda, R. (2002) *Globalization of Services: India's Opportunities and Constraints*. Oxford: Oxford University Press.

Chatterjee, P. (2003) 'Are Indian Cities Becoming Bourgeois at Last?', in Chandrasekhar, I. and Seel, P.S. (eds) *Body.City: Siting Contemporary Culture in India*. New Delhi: Tulika Books, pp. 170–85.

Chaudhary, N. and Sriram, S. (2001) 'Dialogues of the Self', *Culture and Psychology*, Vol. 7(3), pp. 379–92.

Chaudhuri, M. (2004) 'Introduction', in Chaudhuri, M. (ed.) *Feminism in India*. New Delhi: Kali for Women, pp. xi–xlv.

Chengappa, R. and Goyal, M. (2002) 'Housekeepers to the World', *India Today*, 18 November, pp. 36–48.

Chowdary, T.H. (1998) 'Politics and Economics of Telecom Liberalization in India', *Telecommunications Policy*, Vol. 22(1), pp. 9–22.

Clifford, J. and Marcus, G. (1986) *Writing Culture: The Poetics and Politics of Ethnography*. Berkeley and London: University of California Press.

Code, L. (1993) 'Taking Subjectivity into Account', in Alcoff, L. and Potter, E. (eds) *Feminist Epistemologies*. New York and London: Routledge, pp. 15–48.

Coffey, A. (2002) 'Ethnography and the Self: Reflections and Representations', in May, T. (ed.) *Qualitative Research in Action*. London: Sage Publications, pp. 313–31.

Cohen, L and El-Sawad, A. (2007) 'Lived Experiences of Offshoring: An Examination of UK and Indian Financial Service Employees' Accounts of Themselves and One Another', *Human Relations*, Vol. 60(8), pp. 1235–62.

Cohn, B. (1989) 'Cloth, Clothes and Colonialism: India in the Nineteenth Century', in Weiner, A. and Schneider, J. (eds) *Cloth and Human Experience*. Washington, DC: Smithsonian Institution Press.

Collins, P.H. (1990 [2000]) *Black Feminist Thought: Knowledge, Consciousness, and the Politics of Empowerment*, 2nd edition. New York and London: Routledge.

Collins, P.H. (1994) 'The Social Construction of Black Feminist Thought', in Evans, M. (ed.) *The Woman Question*, 2nd edition. London: Sage Publications, pp. 82–103.

Cooke, M. (2005) 'Britain Should Export Unions as Well as Jobs', *Guardian*, 2 April.

Cowie, C. (2007) 'The Accents of Outsourcing: The Meanings of "Neutral" in the Indian Call Centre Industry', *World Englishes*, Vol. 26(3), pp. 316–30.

Craik, J. (1994) *The Face of Fashion: Cultural Studies in Fashion*. London: Routledge.

Crane, D. (2000) *Fashion and Its Social Agendas: Class, Gender, and Identity in Clothing*. Chicago: University of Chicago Press.

Crang, M. and Thrift, N. (2000) 'Introduction', in Crang, M. and Thrift, N. (eds) *Thinking Space*. London and New York: Routledge, pp. 1–30.

Cullity, J. (2002) 'The Global Desi: Cultural Nationalism on MTV', *Journal of Communication Inquiry*, Vol. 26(4), pp. 408–25.

'Cyber Coolies or Cyber Sahibs' (2003) *Times of India*, 7 September.

D'Cruz, P. and Noronha, E. (2006) 'Being Professional: Organizational Control in Indian Call Centres', *Social Science Computer Review*, Vol. 24(3), pp. 342–61.

Das, G. (2000) *India Unbound: From Independence to the Global Information Age*. New Delhi: Penguin Books.

Das, G. (2003) 'Cyber Coolies or Cyber Sahibs', *Times of India*, 7 September. Available at: http://timesofindia.indiatimes.com/cms.dll/html/uncomp/articleshow?msid=169677 (accessed September 2008).

Das Gupta, B. (2000) 'India's Adjustment Experience: 1991 to 1999', in Damodaran, V. and Unnithan-Kumar, M. (eds) *Postcolonial India: History, Politics, and Culture*. New Delhi: Manohar, pp. 173–202.

Datta, R.C. (2003) 'Worker and Work – A Case Study of an International Call Centre in India', unpublished.

De Andrade, L. (2000) 'Negotiating from the Inside: Constructing Racial and Ethnic Identity in Qualitative Research', *Journal of Contemporary Ethnography*, Vol. 29(3), pp. 268–90.

de la Haye, A. and Wilson, E. (eds) (1999) *Defining Dress: Dress as Object, Meaning, and Identity*. Manchester: Manchester University Press.

Dear, M. and Flusty, S. (1999) 'The Postmodern Urban Condition', in Featherstone, M. and Lash, S. (eds) *Spaces of Culture: City, Nation, World*. London: Sage Publications, pp. 64–85.

Deb, S. (2004) 'Call Me', *Guardian Weekend*, 3 April.

Deery, S. and Kinnie, N. (2002) 'Call Centres and Beyond: A Thematic Evaluation', *Human Resource Management Journal*, Vol. 12(4), pp. 3–13.

Deery, S., Iverson, R. and Walsh, J. (2002) 'Work Relationships in Telephone Call Centres: Understanding Emotional Exhaustion and Employee Withdrawal', in *Journal of Management Studies*, Vol. 39(4), pp. 471–96.

Delanty, G. (1999) 'Self, Other and World: Discourses of Nationalism and Cosmoplitanism', *Cultural Values*, Vol. 3(3), pp. 365–75.

Delhi Government (2004) 'Making Women More Secure in Delhi: Towards Confidence Building and Tackling Sexual Harassment'. Available at: http://socialwelfare.delhigovt.nic.in/Pdf/compendium.PDF (accessed 25 September 2008).

Denny, C. (2003a) 'Call for Calm as World of Employment Tilts', *Guardian*, 17 November.

Denny, C. (2003b) 'Profits of Loss', *Guardian*, 25 November.

Denzin, N. (1995) *The Cinematic Society: The Voyeur's Gaze*. London: Sage Publications.

Derne, S. (1999) 'Making Sex Violent: Love as a Force in Recent Hindi Films', *Violence Against Women*, Vol. 5(5), pp. 548–75.

Desai, N. (1996) 'Women's Employment and Their Familial Role in India', in Shah, A.H., Baviskar, B.S. and Ramaswamy, E.A. (eds) *Social Structure and Change, Volume 2: Women in Indian Society*. New Delhi: Sage Publications, pp. 98–112.

Dhillon, A. (2008) 'Dating Site Brings Indian Call Centre Workers Closer', *The Telegraph*, 10 August.

Dokeniya, A. (1999) 'Re-forming the State: Telecom Liberalization in India', *Telecommunications Policy*, No. 23, pp. 105–28.

Dyson, T. and Visaria, P. (2004) 'Migration and Urbanization: Retrospect and Prospects', in Dyson, T., Cassen, R. and Visaria, L. (eds) *Twenty First Century India: Population, Economy, Human Development, and the Environment*. Oxford: Oxford University Press, pp. 108–29.

Economist (2000a) 'The Wiring of India', 25 May.

Economist (2000b) 'When India Wires Up', 20 July.

Ehrenreich, B. and Hochschild, A.R. (eds) (2002) *Global Woman: Nannies, Maids, and Sex Workers in the New Economy*. London: Granta Books.

Elson, D. (1995) 'Male Bias in the Development Process: An Overview', in Diane Elson (ed.) *Male Bias in the Development Process*, 2nd edition. Manchester: Manchester University Press, pp. 1–28.

Elson, D. and Pearson, R. (1981a) '"Nimble Fingers Make Cheap Workers": An Analysis of Women's Employment in Third World Export Manufacturing', *Feminist Review*, No. 7, pp. 87–107.

Elson, D. and Pearson, R. (1981b) 'The Subordination of Women and the Internationalisation of Factory Production', in Young, K., Wolkowitz, C. and McCullagh, R. (eds) *Of Marriage and Market*. London: CSE Books, pp. 144–66.

Elson, D. and Pearson, R. (1989) *Women's Employment and Multinationals in Europe*. London: Macmillan Press.

Entwistle, J. (2000) *The Fashioned Body: Fashion, Dress, and Modern Social Theory*. Cambridge: Polity Press.

Entwistle, J. (2001) *Body Dressing*. Oxford and New York: Berg.

Factories Act (1948) Available at: http://www.ilo.org/public/english/employment/gems/eeo/law/india/facto.htm (accessed 25 September 2008).

Faulkner, W. and Arnold, E. (1985) *Smothered by Invention*. London: Pluto Press.

Featherstone, M. (1995) *Undoing Culture: Globalization, Postmodernism and Identity*. London: Sage Publications.

Featherstone, M. and Lash, S. (1995) 'Globalization, Modernity, and the Spatialization of Social Theory: An Introduction', in Featherstone, M., Lash, S. and Robertson, R. (eds) *Global Modernities*. London: Sage Publications, pp. 1–24.

Fernandez, L. (2000) 'Nationalizing "The Global": Media Images, Cultural Politics and the Middle Class in India', *Media, Culture, and Society*, Vol. 22, pp. 611–28.

Fernie, S. and Metcalf, D. (1998) *(Not) Hanging on the Telephone: Payment Systems in the New Sweatshops*. London: Centre for Economic Performance, London School of Economics.

Finch, J. (2003) 'In India, It's Service with a Compulsory Smile', *Guardian*, 17 November.

Flanagan, P. (2003) 'The Empire Strikes Back', *Daily Express*, 3 December.

Foucault, M. (1972) *The Archaeology of Knowledge*, trans. A.M. Sheridan Smith. London: Tavistock.

Foucault, M. (1977) *Discipline and Punish: The Birth of the Prison*, trans. A.M. Sheridan. London: Penguin.

Foucault, M. (1979) *The History of Sexuality: Volume 1*, trans R. Hurley. London: Penguin.

Freeman, C. (1993) 'Designing Women: Corporate Discipline and Barbados's Off-Shore Pink Collar Sector', *Cultural Anthropology*, Vol. 8(2), pp. 169–86.

Freeman, C. (2000) *HighTech and High Heels: Women, Work, and Pink Collar Identities in the Caribbean*. Durham, NC and London: Duke University Press.

Freeman, C. (2001) 'Is Local:Global as Feminine:Masculine? Rethinking the Gender of Globalization', *Signs*, Vol. 26(4), pp. 1007–37.

Frenkel, S. J., Tam, M., Korczynski, M. and Shire, K. (1998) 'Beyond Bureaucracy? Work Organization in Call Centres', *International Journal of Human Resource Management*, Vol. 9(6), pp. 957–79.

Friedman, J. (1995) 'Global System, Globalization and the Parameters of Modernity', in Featherstone, M., Lash, S. and Robertson, R. (eds) *Global Modernities*. London: Sage Publications, pp. 69–90.

Friedman, J. (1999) 'The Hybridization of Roots and the Abhorrence of the Bush', in Featherstone, M. and Lash, S. (eds) *Spaces of Culture: City, Nation, World*. London: Sage Publications, pp. 230–56.

Gahlaut, K. (2005) 'India in Fashion', *India Today*, 9 May.

Gajjala, R. (2004) *Cyber Selves: Feminist Ethnographies of South Asian Women*. Walnut Creek, CA: AltaMira Press.

Gajjala, R. and Mamidipudi, A. (1999) 'Cyberfeminism, Technology, and International Development', *Gender and Development*, Vol. 7(2), pp. 8–16.

Gary, K. and Townsend-Gault, E. (2004) 'Factory Made: The Role of Vocational Training in Migrant Women Workers' Negotiations with the Globalized Market Place', paper presented at the Gender, Development, and Public Policy in an Era of Globalization Conference, Asian Institute of Technology, Bangkok, 17–18 May.

Gedalof, I. (1999) *Against Purity: Rethinking Identity with Indian and Western Feminisms*. London and New York: Routledge.

Geertz, C. (1973) *The Interpretation of Cultures: Selected Essays*. New York: Basic Books.

Gentleman, A. (2005) 'Indian Call Staff Quit over Abuse on the Line', *Observer*, 29 May.

Gerson, K. and Horowitz, R. (2002) 'Observation and Interviewing: Options and Choices in Qualitative Research', in May, T. (ed.) *Qualitative Research in Action*. London: Sage Publications, pp. 199–224.

Ghosh, S. and Wang, L. (2003) 'Transnationalism and Identity: A Tale of Two Faces and Multiple Lives', *Canadian Geographer*, Vol. 47(3), pp. 269–82.

Giddens, A. (1984) *The Constitution of Society: Outline of the Theory of Structuration.* Cambridge: Polity Press.

Giddens, A. (1990) *The Consequences of Modernity.* Cambridge: Polity Press.

Giddens, A. (1991) *Modernity and Self-Identity: Self and Society in the Late Modern Age.* Cambridge: Polity Press.

Gillespie, M. and Cheesman, T. (2002) 'Media Cultures in India and the South Asia Diaspora', *Contemporary South Asia*, Vol. 11(2), pp. 127–33.

Glaser, B. and Strauss, A. (1967) *The Discovery of Grounded Theory: Strategies for Qualitative Research.* New York: Aldine de Gruyter.

Goss, J. (1997) 'The "Magic of the Mall": An Analysis of Form, Function, and Meaning in the Contemporary Retail Built Environment', in McDowell, L. (ed.) *Undoing Place.* London: Arnold, pp. 265–84.

Gottfried, H. (1992) 'In the Margins: Flexibility as a Mode of Regulation in the Temporary Help Service Industry', *Work, Employment and Society*, Vol. 6(3), pp 443–60.

Grebner, S., Semmer, N.K., Lo Faso, L., Gut, S., Kalin, W. and Elfering, A. (2003) 'Working Conditions, Well-Being, and Job-Related Attitudes among Call Centre Agents', *European Journal of Work and Organizational Psychology*, Vol. 12(4), pp. 341–65.

Greenbaum, J. (1998) 'The Times They Are a'Changing: Dividing and Recombining Labour through Computer Systems', in Thompson, P. and Warhurst, C. (eds) *Workplaces of the Future.* London: Macmillan, pp. 124–41.

Grewal, I. and Kaplan, C. (1994) 'Introduction: Transnational Feminist Practices and Questions of Postmodernity', in Grewal, I. and Kaplan, C. (eds) *Scattered Hegemonies: Postmodernity and Transnational Feminist Practices.* Minneapolis: University of Minnesota Press, pp. 1–33.

Griffin, K. (2000) 'Culture and Economic Growth: The State and Globalization', in Pieterse, J.N. (ed.) *Global Futures: Shaping Globalization.* London and New York: Zed Books, pp. 189–202.

Grosz, E. (1995 [1999]) 'Bodies-Cities', in Price, J. and Shildrick, M. (eds) *Feminist Theory and the Body: A Reader.* Edinburgh: Edinburgh University Press, pp. 381–7.

Hall, E.J. (1993) 'Smiling, Deferring, and Flirting: Doing Gender by Giving Good Service', *Work and Occupations*, Vol. 20(4), pp. 452–71.

Hall, S. (1992a) 'The Question of Cultural Identity', in Hall, S., Held, D. and McGrew, T. (eds) *Modernity and Its Futures.* Cambridge: Polity Press, pp. 274–325.

Hall, S. (1992b) 'The West and the Rest', in Hall, S. and Gieben, B. (eds) *Formations of Modernity.* London: Polity Press, pp. 275–331.

Hall, S. (1993) 'Cultural Identity and Diaspora', in Williams, P. and Chrisman, L. (eds) *Colonial Discourse and Postcolonial Theory: A Reader.* London: Harvester Wheatsheaf, pp. 392–403.

Hall, S. (1995) 'New Cultures for Old', in Massey, D. and Jess, P. (eds) *A Place in the World?* Milton Keynes: Open University Press, pp. 174–214.

Hall, S. (1996a) 'New Ethnicities', in Morley, D. and Chen, K. (eds) *Critical Dialogues in Cultural Studies.* London: Routledge, pp. 441–9.

Hall, S. (1996b) 'Who Needs Identity?' in Hall, S. and du Gay, P. (eds) *Questions of Cultural Identity.* London: Sage Publications, pp. 1–17.

Hall, S. (2001) 'Nappy Threat to Call Centre Staff', *Guardian*, 21 February.

Hannerz, U. (1992 [2004]) 'The Global Ecumene', in Lechner, F. and Boli, J. (eds) *The Globalization Reader*, 2nd edition. Oxford: Blackwell Publishing, pp. 109–19.

Hansen, K.T. (1999) 'Second-Hand Clothing Encounters in Zambia: Global Discourses, Western Commodities, and Local Histories', *Africa*, Vol. 69(3), pp. 343–65.

Hanson, S. and Pratt, G. (1995) *Gender, Work, and Space*. London and New York: Routledge.

Haraway, D. (1991) *Simians, Cyborgs, and Women: The Reinvention of Nature*. New York: Routledge.

Harding, L. (2001) 'Delhi Calling', *Guardian*, 9 March.

Harding, S. (1986) *The Science Question in Feminism*. Milton Keynes: Open University Press.

Harding, S. (1987a) 'Introduction', in Harding, S. (ed.) *Feminism and Methodology: Social Science Issues*. Milton Keynes: Open University Press, pp. 1–14.

Harding, S. (1987b) 'Conclusion', in Harding, S. (ed.) *Feminism and Methodology: Social Science Issues*. Milton Keynes: Open University Press, pp. 181–90.

Harding, S. (1991) *Whose Science? Whose Knowledge? Thinking From Women's Lives*. Milton Keynes: Open University Press.

Harding, S. (1993) 'Rethinking Standpoint Epistemology: What Is Strong Objectivity?', in Alcoff, L. and Potter, E. (eds) *Feminist Epistemologies*. New York and London: Routledge, pp. 49–82.

Harding, S. (1994) 'Feminism and Theories of Scientific Knowledge', in Evans, M. (ed.) *The Woman Question*, 2nd edition. London: Sage Publications, pp. 104–13.

Hardt, M. and Negri, A. (2000) *Empire*. Cambridge, MA and London: Harvard University Press.

Heeks, R. (1996) *India's Software Industry: State, Policy, Liberalisation, and Industrial Development*. New Delhi and London: Sage Publications.

Henry, M.G. (2003) '"Where Are You Really From?": Representation, Identity, and Power in the Fieldwork Experiences of a South Asian Diasporic', *Qualitative Research*, Vol. 3(2), pp. 229–42.

Hilpern, K. (2000) 'A Call for Change', *Guardian*, 19 February.

Hislop, J. and Arbor, S. (2003) 'Sleepers Wake! The Gendered Nature of Sleep Disruption among Mid-Life Women', in *Sociology*, Vol. 37(4), pp. 695–711.

Holman, D. (2002) 'Employee Wellbeing in Call Centres', *Human Resource Management Journal*, Vol. 12(4), pp. 35–50.

Holman, D. and Fernie, S. (2000) 'Can I Help You? Call Centre Jobs and Job Satisfaction', *Centrepiece*, Vol. 5(1), London School of Economics.

Hochschild, A.R. (1983) *The Managed Heart*. Berkeley and Los Angeles: University of California Press.

hooks, b. (1990) 'Marginality as Site of Resistance', in Ferguson, R., Gever, M., Minh-ha, Trinh T. and West, C. (eds) *Out There: Marginalization and Contemporary Cultures*. New York: The New Museum of Contemporary Art; Cambridge, MA: The MIT Press.

hooks, b. (1991) *Yearning: Race, Gender, and Cultural Politics*, UK edition. Toronto: Between the Lines Press.

Houdart-Blazy, V. (1996) *The Information Society: A Challenge For Women*, Issue 44. Brussels: The Women of Europe Dossier.

Houlihan, M. (2002) 'Tensions and Variations in Call Centre Management Strategies', *Human Resource Management Journal*, Vol. 12(4), pp. 67–85.

Howe, L.K. (1977) *Pink Collar Workers: Inside the World of Women's Work*. New York: G.P. Putnam's Sons.

Howland, M. (1993) 'Technological Change and the Spatial Restructuring of Data Entry and Processing Services', *Technological Forecasting and Social Change*, Vol. 43, pp. 185–96.

Hsiung, P. (1996) 'Between Bosses and Workers: The Dilemma of a Keen Observer and a Vocal Feminist', in Wolf, D. (ed.) *Feminist Dilemmas in Fieldwork*. Oxford: Westview Press, pp. 122–37.

Hubbard, P., Kitchin, R. and Valentine, G. (2004) *Key Thinkers on Space and Place*. London: Sage Publications.

Huntington, S.P. (1993 [2004]) 'The Clash of Civilizations', in Lechner, F. and Boli, J. (eds) *The Globalization Reader*, 2nd edition. Oxford: Blackwell Publishing, pp. 36–43.

Huws, U. (1999) 'Material World: The Myth of the Weightless Economy', in Panitch, L. and Leys, C. (eds) *Socialist Register 1999*. Suffolk: Merlin Press, pp. 29–55.

Huws, U, Korte, W.B. and Robinson, S. (1990) *Telework: Towards the Elusive Office*. Chichester: John Wiley and Sons Ltd.

IDS (1997) *Pay and Conditions in Call Centres*, London: Incomes Data Services.

IDS (2001) *Pay and Conditions in Call Centres*, London: Incomes Data Services.

IDS (2004) *Pay and Conditions in Call Centres*, London: Incomes Data Services.

ILO (1990) *Conditions of Work Digest: Telework*, Vol. 9(1) ILO: Geneva.

Irani, A. (ed.) (1999) *Proceedings of the Workshop on Telework, Teletrade, and Sustainable Development*. Maastricht, Netherlands: UNU/INTECH.

Irani, A., Gothoskar, S. and Sharma, J.C. (1999) *Potential and Prevalence of Teleworking: A Survey of Mumbai City*. Maastricht, Netherlands: UNU/INTECH.

Jagger, A. (2000) 'Globalizing Feminist Ethics', in Narayan, U. and Harding, S. (eds) *Decentering the Center: Philosophy for a Multicultural, Postcolonial, and Feminist World*. Bloomington and Indianapolis: Indiana University Press, pp. 1–25.

Jaywardena, K. (1986) *Feminism and Nationalism in the Third World*. London and Delhi: Zed Books.

Jelsoft Enterprises (2005) 'Is Your Job Going Offshore?' Available at: www.yourjobisgo ingtoindia.com (accessed 25 September 2008).

Jowell, T. (2003) 'Masala Pudding', *Hindustan Times*, 10 March.

Juluri, V. (1999) 'Global Weds Local: The Reception of Hum Aapke Hain Koun', *European Journal of Cultural Studies*, Vol. 2(2), pp. 231–48.

Juluri, V. (2002) 'Music Television and the Invention of Youth Culture in India', *Television and New Media*, Vol. 3(4), pp. 367–86.

Kabeer, N. (2000) *The Power to Choose: Bangladeshi Women and Labour Market Decisions in London and Dhaka*. London and New York: Verso.

Kakar, S. (1988) 'Feminine Identity in India', in Ghadially, R. (ed.) *Women in Indian Society: A Reader*. New Delhi: Sage Publications, pp. 44–68.

Kakar, S. (1989) *Intimate Relations: Exploring Indian Sexuality*. Chicago: University of Chicago Press.

Kandiyoti, D. (1988) 'Bargaining with Patriarchy', *Gender and Society*, Vol. 2(3), pp. 274–90.

Kanter, R.M. (1977) *Men and Women of the Corporation*. New York: Basic Books.

Kapur, R. (2000) 'Too Hot to Handle: The Cultural Politics of Fire', *Feminist Review*, No. 64, pp. 53–64.

Karam, A.M. (2000) 'Feminist Futures', in Pieterse, J.N. (ed.) *Global Futures: Shaping Globalization*. London and New York: Zed Books, pp. 175–86.

Kaviraj, S. (2005) 'An Outline of a Revisionist Theory of Modernity', paper presented at the British Association of South Asian Studies Annual Conference, University of Leeds, Leeds, UK, 30 March–1 April.

Keniston, K. (2004) 'Introduction: The Four Digital Divides', in *IT Experience in India: Bridging the Digital Divide*. New Delhi: Sage Publications, pp. 11–36.

Khadria, B. (1999) *The Migration of Knowledge Workers*. New Delhi: Sage Publications.

Khadria, B. (2001) 'Shifting Paradigms of Globalization: The Twenty-First Century Transition towards Generics in Skilled Migration from India', *International Migration*, Vol. 39(5), pp. 45–71.

King, A.D. (2000) 'Cities: Contradictory Utopias', in Pieterse, J.N. (ed.) *Global Futures: Shaping Globalization*. London and New York: Zed Books, pp. 224–41.

Kingdon, G., Cassen, R., McNay, K. and Visaria, L. (2004) 'Education and Literacy', in Dyson, T., Cassen, R. and Visaria, L. (eds) *Twenty First Century India: Population, Economy, Human Development, and the Environment*. Oxford: Oxford University Press, pp. 130–57.

Kinnie, N., Hutchinson, S. and Purcell, J. (2000a) 'Fun and Surveillance: The Paradox of High Commitment Management in Call Centres', *International Journal of Human Resource Management*, Vol. 11(5), pp. 967–85.

Kinnie, N., Purcell, J. and Hutchinson, S. (2000b) 'Managing the Employment Relationship in Telephone Call Centres', in Purcell, K. (ed.) *Changing Boundaries in Employment*. Bristol: British Academic Press, pp. 133–59.

Kishwar, M. (2004) 'A Horror of "Isms": Why I Do Not Call Myself a Feminist', in Chaudhuri, M. (ed.) *Feminism in India*. New Delhi: Kali for Women, pp. 26–51.

Kjellerup, N. (1999) 'The Toxic Call Centre', *Call Centre Management*. Available at: http://www.callcentres.com.au/toxic_call_center.htm (accessed 25 September 2008).

Klopper, S. (2000) 'Redressing the Past: The Africanisation of Sartorial Style in Contemporary South Africa', in Brah, A. and Coombs, A.E. (eds) *Hybridity and Its Discontents: Politics, Science, Culture*. London and New York: Routledge, pp. 216–31.

Knights, D. and McCabe, D. (1998) '"What Happens When the Phone Goes Wild?": Staff, Stress, and Spaces for Escape in a BPR Telephone Banking Work Regime', *Journal of Management Studies*, Vol. 35(2), pp. 163–94.

Knights, D. and McCabe, D. (2001) '"A Different World": Shifting Masculinities in the Transition to Call Centres', *Organization*, Vol. 8(4), pp. 619–45.

Kobayashi-Hilary, M. (2004) *Outsourcing to India: The Offshore Advantage*. London: Springer.

Kofman, E. (2005) 'Figures of the Cosmopolitan: Privileged Nationals and National Outsiders', *Innovation*, Vol.18(1), pp. 83–97.

Korczynski, M. (2003) 'Communities of Coping: Collective Emotional Labour in Service Work', *Organization*, Vol. 10(1), pp. 55–79.

Koskela, H. (1997) '"Bold Walk and Breakings": Women's Spatial Confidence Versus Fear of Violence', *Gender, Place, and Culture*, Vol. 4(3), pp. 301–19.

Kraidy, M. (2002) 'The Global, The Local, and the Hybrid: A Native Ethnography of Globalization', in Taylor, S. (ed.) *Ethnographic Research: A Reader*, London: Sage Publications, pp. 187–209.

Kumar, K. (1995) 'Fordism and Post-Fordism', in *From Post-Industrial to Post Modern Society*. Oxford: Blackwell, pp. 36–65.

Kumar, R. (2000) 'Confucian Pragmatism vs Brahmanical Idealism: Understanding the Divergent Roots of Indian and Chinese Economic Performance', *Journal of Asian Business Studies*, Vol. 16(2), pp. 49–69.

Kumar, S. and Curtin, M. (2002) '"Made in India": In Between Music Television and Patriarchy', *Television and New Media*, Vol. 3(4), pp. 345–66.

Kusakabe, K. and Wah, H. (2004) 'Expansion of Relational Spaces of Burman Migrants in the Border Town of Tachilek Myanmar', paper presented at the Gender, Development, and Public Policy in an Era of Globalization Conference, Asian Institute of Technology, Bangkok, 17–18 May.

Lal, J. (1996) 'Situating Locations: The Politics of Self, Identity, and "Other" in Living and Writing the Text', in Wolf, D. (ed.) *Feminist Dilemmas in Fieldwork*. Oxford: Westview Press, pp. 185–214.

Lankshear, G., Cook, P., Mason, D., Coates, S. and Button, G. (2001) 'Call Centre Employees' Responses to Electronic Monitoring: Some Research Findings', *Work, Employment, and Society*, Vol. 15(3), pp. 595–605.

Lash, S. and Urry, J. (1994) *Economies and Signs and Space*. London: Sage Publications.

Lawler, S. (2002) 'Narrative in Social Research', in May, T. (ed.) *Qualitative Research in Action*. London: Sage Publications, pp. 242–58.

Legg, S. (2003) 'Gendered Politics and Nationalized Homes: Women and the Anti-Colonial Struggle in Delhi, 1930–47', *Gender, Place, and Culture*, Vol. 10(1), pp. 7–27.

Leshkowich, A.M. and Jones, C. (2003) 'What Happens When Asian Chic Becomes Chic in Asia', *Fashion Theory*, Vol. 7(3/4), pp. 281–300.

Lewig, K.A. and Dollard, M.F. (2003) 'Emotional Dissonance, Emotional Exhaustion and Job Satisfaction in Call Centre Workers', *European Journal of Work and Organizational Psychology*, Vol. 12(4), pp. 366–92.

Lewis, R. and Mills, S. (eds) (2003) *Feminist Postcolonial Theory: A Reader*. Edinburgh: Edinburgh University Press.

Lim, L. (1990) 'Women's Work in Export Factories: The Politics of a Cause', in Tinker, I. (ed.) *Persistent Inequalities*. New York: Oxford University Press, pp. 101–22.

Lorde, A. (1984) *Sister Outsider: Essays and Speeches*. Freedom, CA: Crossing Press.

Luke, T.W. (1999) 'Simulated Sovereignty, Telematic Territoriality: The Political Economy of Cyberspace', in Featherstone, M. and Lash, S. (eds) *Spaces of Culture: City, Nation, World*. London: Sage Publications, pp. 27–48.

Macalister, T. and Clark, A. (2003) 'MPs to Attack Transfer of Rail Inquiries to India', *Guardian*, 10 November.

Macaulay, T.B. (1835) 'Macaulay's Minute on Education'. Available at http://www.geocities.com/bororissa/mac.html (accessed 8 January 2009).

McDonald, I. (1999) '"Psychological Patriots"? The Politics of Physical Culture and Hindu Nationalism in India', *International Review for the Sociology of Sport*, Vol. 34(4), pp. 343–58.

McDowell, L. (1999) *Gender, Identity, and Place: Understanding Feminist Geographies*. Minneapolis: University of Minnesota Press.

Mackintosh, M. (1981) 'Gender and Economics: The Sexual Division of Labour and the Subordination of Women', in Young, K., Wolkowitz, C. and McCullagh, R. (eds) *Of Marriage and the Market*. London: CSE Books.

McMillin, D.C. (2001) 'Localizing the Global: Television and Hybrid Programming in India', *International Journal of Cultural Studies*, Vol. 4(1), pp. 45–68.

McMillin, D. (2006) 'Outsourcing Identities: Call Centres and Cultural Transformations in India', *Economic and Political Weekly*, 21 January, pp. 235–41.

McNay, K., Unni, J. and Cassen, R. (2004) 'Employment', in Dyson, T., Cassen, R. and Visaria, L. (eds) *Twenty First Century India: Population, Economy, Human Development, and the Environment*. Oxford: Oxford University Press, pp. 158–77.

McWilliams, S. (1991) 'Tsitsi Dangarembga's Nervous Condition: At the Crossroads of Feminism and Post-Colonialism', *World Literature Written in English*, Vol. 31(1), pp. 103–12.

'The Male Gaze' (2002) *Sunday Times of India*, 8 December.

Malik, K.N. (1997) *India and the United Kingdom: Change and Continuity in the 1980's*. New Delhi: Sage Publications.

Mandeville, P. (2003) 'Towards a Different Cosmopolitanism – Or, the "I" Dislocated', *Global Society*, Vol. 17(2), pp. 209–21.

Mani, B. (2003) 'Undressing the Diaspora', in Puwar, N. and Raghuram, P. (eds) *South Asian Women in the Diaspora*. Oxford: Berg.

Marshall, J.N. and Richardson, R. (1996) 'The Impact of Telemediated Services on Corporate Structures: The Example of Branchless Retail Banking in Britain', *Environment and Planning A*, Vol. 28, pp. 1843–58.

Mason, J. (1996) *Qualitative Researching*. London: Sage Publications.

Mason, J. (2002) 'Qualitative Interviewing: Asking, Listening, and Interpreting', in May, T. (ed.) *Qualitative Research in Action*. London: Sage Publications, pp. 225–41.

Massey, D. (1994) *Space, Place and Gender*. Cambridge: Polity Press.

Massey, D. and Jess, P. (eds) (1995) *A Place in The World?* Milton Keynes: Open University Press.

May, T. (2001) *Social Research: Issues, Methods and Process*. Milton Keynes: Open University Press.

Mazumdar, S. (1994) 'Moving away from a Secular Vision? Women, Nation, and the Cultural Construction of Hindu India', in Moghadam, V. (ed.) *Identity Politics and Women*. Oxford: Westview Press, pp. 243–73.

Menon, O. (2001) *Gender and Politics in India*. Oxford: Oxford University Press.

Mies, M. (1979) *Indian Women and Patriarchy: Conflicts and Dilemmas of Students and Working Women*. New Delhi: Concept Publishing.

Mies, M. (1982) *The Lace Makers of Narsapur: Indian Housewives Produce for the World Market*. London: Zed Books.

Mies, M. (1983) 'Towards a Methodology for Feminist Research', in Bowles, G. and R. Duelli Klein (eds) *Theories of Women's Studies*. London: Routledge, pp. 117–39.

Milgram, B.L. (2005) '"Ukay-Ukay" Chic: Tales of Second Hand Clothing Fashion and Trade in the Philippine Cordillera', in Palmer, A. and Clark, H. (eds) *Old Clothes, New Looks*. New York: Berg, pp. 134–54.

Mirchandani, K. (2004a) 'Practices of Global Capital: Gaps, Cracks, and Ironies in Transnational Call Centres in India', in *Global Networks*, Vol. 4(4), pp. 355–73.

Mirchandani, K. (2004b) 'Webs of Resistance in Transnational Call Centres: Strategic Agents, Service Providers and Customers', in Thomas, R., Mills, A.J. and Helms Mills, J. (eds) *Identity Politics at Work: Resisting Gender, Gendering Resistance*. London and New York: Routledge, pp. 179–95.

Mitter, S. (1986) 'Women and the Changing Structure of Employment', in *Common Fate: Common Bond: Women in the Global Economy*. London: Pluto Press, pp. 1–55.

Mitter, S. (1991) *Dharma's Daughters*. New Brunswick, NJ: Rutgers University Press.

Mitter, S. (1995) 'Beyond the Politics of Difference: An Introduction', in Mitter, S. and Rowbotham, S. (eds) *Women Encounter Technology*. London and New York: UNU/INTECH, pp. 1–18.

Mitter, S. (1999) *Telework and Teletrade in India: Combining Diverse Perspectives and Visions*. Maastricht, Netherlands: UNU/INTECH.

Mitter, S. and Banerjee, N. (eds) (1999) *Gender Technology and Development*, Vol. 3, No. 1.

Mitter, S. and Rowbotham, S. (1995) *Women Encounter Technology*. London and New York: Routledge.

Mitter, S., Fernandez, G. and Varghese, S. (2004) 'On the Threshold of Informalization: Women Call Centre Workers in India', in Carr, M. (ed.) *Chains of Fortune: Linking Women Producers and Workers with Global Markets*. London: Commonwealth Secretariat, pp. 165–83.

'Mobiles, CDs, Parties: Call of a New World' (2003) *Times of India*, 14 November.

Moghadam, V. (1994) 'Introduction: Women and Identity Politics in Theoretical and Comparative Perspective', in Moghadam, V. (ed.) *Identity Politics and Women*. Oxford: Westview Press, pp. 3–26.

Moghadam, V. (2000) 'Transnational Feminist Networks: Collective Action in an Era of Globalization', *International Sociology*, Vol. 15(1), pp. 57–85.

Mohanty, C. (1991a) 'Introduction', in Mohanty, C. Russo, A. and Torres, L. (eds) *Third World Women and the Politics of Feminism*. Bloomington and Indianapolis: Indiana University Press, pp. 1–50.

Mohanty, C. (1991b) 'Under Western Eyes: Feminist Scholarship and Colonial Discourses', in Mohanty, C. Russo, A. and Torres, L. (eds) *Third World Women and the Politics of Feminism*. Bloomington and Indianapolis: Indiana University Press, pp. 51–80.

Mohanty, C., Russo, A. and Torres, L. (1991) *Third World Women and the Politics of Feminism*. Bloomington and Indianapolis: Indiana University Press.

Monbiot, G. (2003) 'The Flight to India', *Guardian*, 21 October.

Mookherjee, N. (2001) 'Dressed for Fieldwork: Sartorial Borders and Negotiations', *Anthropology Matters*. Available at: http://www.anthropologymatters.com/journal/2001/mookherjee_2001_dressed.htm (accessed 25 September 2008).

Mulholland, K. (2002) 'Gender, Emotional Labour, and Teamworking in a Call Centre', *Personnel Review*, Vol. 31(3), pp. 283–303.

Mulvey, L. (1975) 'Visual Pleasure and Narrative Cinema', *Screen*, Vol. 16(3), pp. 6–18.

Nagar, R. (2002) 'Footloose Researchers, "Travelling" Theories, and the Politics of Transnational Feminist Praxis', *Gender, Place, and Culture*, Vol. 9(2), pp. 179–86.

Nagar, R. (2003) 'Collaboration across Borders: Moving Beyond Positionality', *Singapore Journal of Tropical Geography*, Vol. 24(3), pp. 356–72.

Nagrath, S. (2003) '(En)countering Orientalism in High Fashion: A Review of India Fashion Week 2002', *Fashion Theory*, Vol. 7(3/4), pp. 361–75.

Nakamuro, L. (2002) *Cybertypes: Race, Ethnicity, and Identity on the Internet*. New York and London: Routledge.

Narayan, U. (2000) 'Essence of Culture and a Sense of History: A Feminist Critique of Cultural Essentialism', in Narayan, U. and Harding, S. (eds) *Decentering the Center: Philosophy for a Multicultural, Postcolonial, and Feminist World*. Bloomington and Indianapolis: Indiana University Press, pp. 80–100.

Natarajan, N. (1994) 'Women, Nation, and Narration in Midnight's Children', in Grewal, I. and Kaplan, C. (eds) *Scattered Hegemonies: Postmodernity and Transnational Feminist Practices*. London and Minneapolis: University of Minnesota Press, pp. 76–89.

Nelson, L. (1999) 'Bodies (and Spaces) Do Matter: The Limits of Performativity', *Gender, Place, and Culture*, Vol. 6, pp. 331–53.

Ng, C. and Mitter, S. (2005) 'Valuing Women's Voices: Call Centre Workers in Malaysia and India', *Gender Technology and Development*, Vol. 9(2), pp. 209–33.

Ng Choon Sim, C. (1999) 'Making Women's Voices Heard: Technological Change and Women's Employment in Malaysia', *Gender Technology and Development*, Vol. 3(1), pp. 19–42.

Oakley, A. (1981) 'Interviewing Women: A Contradiction in Terms', in Roberts, H. (ed.) *Doing Feminist Research*. London: Routledge and Kegan Paul, pp. 30–61.

Olivera, R. (2003) 'Women Make the Right Call', *Times of India*, 4 November.

Ong, A. (1999) *Flexible Citizenship: The Cultural Logics of Transnationality*. Durham, NC and London: Duke University Press.

Ong, A. (2004) 'Cyberpublics and Diaspora Politics among Transnational Chinese', *Interventions*, Vol. 5(1): 82–100.

Pain, R. (1991) 'Space, Sexual Violence and Social Control: Integrating Geographical and Feminist Analyses of Women's Fear of Crime', *Progress in Human Geography*, Vol. 15(4), pp. 415–31.

Pain, R. (1997) 'Social Geographies of Women's Fear of Crime', *Transactions of the Institutes of British Geographers*, NS 22, pp. 231–44.

Palan, R. (2004) 'Constructivism and Globalisation: From Units to Encounters in International Affairs', *Cambridge Review of International Affairs*, Vol. 17(1), pp. 11–23.

Pande, R. (2005) 'Looking at Information Technology for a Gender Perspective: The Call Centres in India', in *Asian Centre for Women's Studies*, Vol. 11(1), pp. 58–82.

Pandurang, M. (2003) 'Conceptualizing Emigrant Indian Female Subjectivity: Possible Entry Points', in Puwar, N. and Raghuram, P. (eds) *South Asian Women in the Diaspora*. Oxford: Berg, pp. 87–98.

Papola, T.S. and Sharma, A.N. (eds) (1999) *Gender and Employment in India*. New Delhi: Vikas Publishing.

Parker-Talwar, J. (2004) 'Work and the Commodity Culture in the Third World City: A Focus on Transforming Labour Relations in New Delhi, India', unpublished.

Patel, R. (2006) 'Working the Night Shift: Gender and the Global Economy', *ACME: An International E-Journal for Critical Geographies*, Vol. 5(1), pp. 9–27.

Pavarala, V. (1996) *Interpreting Corruption: Elite Perspectives in India*. New Delhi and London: Sage Publications.

Pearson, R (1993) 'Gender and New Technology in the Caribbean: New Work for Women?', in J. Momsen (ed.) *Women and Change in the Caribbean: A Pan-Caribbean Perspective*, Bloomington: Indiana University Press, pp. 287–95.

Pearson, R. (1994) 'Office Automation: An International Perspective', in Ng, C. and Munro-Kua, A. (eds) *Keying into the Future: The Impact of Computerization on Office Workers*, Kuala Lumpur: WDC Publishing.

Pearson, R. (1998) 'Nimble Fingers Revisited: Reflections on Women and Third World Industrialisation in the Late Twentieth Century', in Jackson, C. and Pearson, R. (eds) *Feminist Visions of Development: Gender, Analysis and Policy*. London: Routledge, pp. 171–86.

Pearson, R. (2000) 'Moving the Goal Posts: Gender and Development in the 21st Century', *Gender and Development*, Vol. 8(1), pp. 10–19.

Perrons, D. (2004) *Globalization and Social Change: People and Places in a Divided World*. London and New York: Routledge.

Petrazzini, B.A. (1996) 'Telecommunications Policy in India: The Political Under-pinnings of Reform', *Telecommunications Policy*, Vol. 20(1), pp. 39–51.

Phillips, A. (2002) 'What It Was Like, What Happened, and What It's Like Now: Developments in Telecommunications over Recent Decades', *Journal of Regulatory Economics*, Vol. 21(1), pp. 57–78.

Phillips, A. and Taylor, B. (1980) 'Sex and Skill: Notes Towards a Feminist Economics', *Feminist Review*, No. 6, pp. 79–88.

Phizacklea, A. and Wolkowitz, C. (1995) *Homeworking Women: Gender, Racism, Class at Work*. London: Sage Publications.

Pieterse, J.N. (1995) 'Globalization as Hybridization', in Featherstone, M., Lash, S. and Robertson, R. (eds) *Global Modernities*. London: Sage Publications, pp. 45–68.

Pieterse, J.N. (2000) 'Shaping Globalization', in Pieterse, J.N. (ed.) *Global Futures: Shaping Globalization*. London and New York: Zed Books, pp. 1–20.

Pink, D.H. (2004) 'The New Face of the Silicon Valley', *Wired*, February, pp. 94–8.

Poster, W. (1998) 'Globalization, Gender, and the Workplace: Women and Men in an American Corporation in India', *Journal of Developing Societies*, Vol. 14(1), pp. 40–65.

Poster, W. (2001) 'Dangerous Places and Nimble Fingers: Discourses of Gender Discrimination and Rights in Global Corporations', *International Journal of Politics Culture and Society*, Vol. 15(1), pp. 77–105.

Poster, W. (2007) 'Who's on the Line? Indian Call Centre Agents Pose as Americans for U.S.-Outsourced Firms', *Industrial Relations*, Vol. 46(2), pp. 271–304.

Poynton, C. (1993) 'Naming Women's Workplace Skills', in Probert, B. and Wilson, B. (eds) *Pink Collar Blues: Work, Gender, and Technology*. Malaysia: Melbourne University Press, pp. 85–100.

Pringle, R. (1989) *Secretaries Talk: Sexuality, Power and Work*. London: Verso.

Probert, B. and Wilson, B.P. (1993) 'Gendered Work', in Probert, B. and Wilson, B.P (eds) *Pink Collar Blues: Work, Gender, and Technology*. London: Melbourne University Press, pp. 1–19.

Pronk, J. (2000) 'Globalization: A Developmental Approach', in Pieterse, J.N. (ed.) *Global Futures: Shaping Globalization*. London and New York: Zed Books, pp. 40–52.

Puri, J. (1999) *Woman, Body, Desire, in Post-Colonial India: Narratives of Gender and Sexuality*. New York: Routldege.

Puwar, N. (2003) 'Melodramatic Postures and Constructions', in Puwar, N. and Raghuram, P. (eds) *South Asian Women in the Diaspora*. Oxford: Berg, pp. 21–41.

Puwar, N. and Raghuram, P. (2003) 'Dislocating South Asian Women in the Academy', in Puwar, N. and Raghuram, P. (eds) *South Asian Women in the Diaspora*. Oxford: Berg, pp. 1–20.

Raghuram, P. (2003) 'Fashioning the South Asian Diaspora', in Puwar, N. and Raghuram, P. (eds) *South Asian Women in the Diaspora*. Oxford: Berg, pp. 67–86.

Rajan, P. (1999) *Teleworking: Training and Education Need*. Maastricht, Netherlands: UNU/INTECH.

Rajan, R.S. (1999) 'Reading the Story of Draupadi's Disrobing: Meanings for Our Times', in Rajan, R.S. (ed.) *Signposts: Gender Issues in Post-Independence India*. Delhi: Kali for Women Press, pp. 331–58.

Rajgopal, A. (1999) 'Thinking about the New Middle Class', in Rajan, R.S. (ed.) *Signposts: Gender Issues in Post-Independence India*. Delhi: Kali for Women Press, pp. 57–100.

Ramani, S. (1999) *IT-Enabled Services: A Growing Form of Telework*. Maastricht, Netherlands: UNU/INTECH.

Ramazanoglu, C. (ed.) (1993) *Up against Foucault: Explorations of Some Tensions Between Foucault and Feminism*. London: Routledge.

Ramazanoglu, C. and Holland, J. (2002) *Feminist Methodology: Challenges and Choices*. London: Sage Publications.

Remesh, B. (2004) *Cyber Coolies in BPO*. V.V. Giri National Labour Institute.

Rao, S. (1999) 'Woman as Symbol: The Intersection of Identity Politics, Gender, and Indian Nationalism', *Women's Studies International Forum*, Vol. 22(3), pp. 317–28.

Rath, S. (2004) 'Post/past-"Orientalism": Orientalism and its dis/re-orientation', *Comparative American Studies*, Vol. 2(3), pp. 342–59.

Rathi, N.T. (2002) 'The Night Is Always YOUNG', *India Today*, 18 November.

Reardon, G. (1999) *Globalisation, Technological Change, and Women Workers in Asia.* Maastricht, Netherlands: UNU/INTECH.

Reddy, S. (2003) 'Sari, Wrong Number', *Outlook*, 27 January.

Richardson, R. and Marshall, J.N. (1996) 'The Growth of Telephone Call Centres in Peripheral Areas of Britain', *Area*, Vol. 28(3), pp. 308–17.

Robertson, R. (1995) 'Glocalization: Time–Space and Homogeneity–Heterogeneity', in Featherstone, M., Lash, S. and Robertson, R. (eds) *Global Modernities.* London: Sage Publications, pp. 25–44.

Robins, D. (1991) *The Work of Pierre Bourdieu: Recognizing Society.* Boulder, CO: Westview Press.

Rose, G. (1993) *Feminism and Geography.* Cambridge: Polity Press.

Roseneil, S. (1993) 'Greenham Revisited: Researching Myself and My Sisters', in Hobbs, D. and May, T. (eds) *Interpreting the Field: Accounts of Ethnography.* Oxford: Clarendon Press, pp. 177–208.

Roseneil, S. (1995) 'The Coming of Age of Feminist Sociology: Some Issues of Practice and Theory for the Next Twenty Years', *British Journal of Sociology*, Vol. 46(2) (June), pp. 191–207.

Roseneil, S. (1999) 'Postmodern Feminist Politics: The Art of the (Im)Possible', *European Journal of Women's Studies*, Vol. 6(2), pp. 161–82.

Roseneil, S. and Seymour, J (1999) 'Practising Identities: Power and Resistance', in Roseneil, S. and Seymour, J. (eds) *Practising Identities: Power and Resistance.* Basingstoke: Macmillan Press, pp. 1–10.

Roy, A. (2001) *The Algebra of Infinite Justice.* New Delhi: Penguin.

Roy, A. (2004) *The Ordinary Person's Guide to Empire.* London: HarperCollins.

Rundell, J. (2004) 'Strangers, Citizens and Outsiders: Otherness, Multiculturalism and the Cosmopolitan Imaginary in Mobile Societies', *Thesis Eleven*, No. 78, pp. 85–101.

Runkle, S. (2004) 'Making Miss India: Constructing Gender, Power, and the Nation', *South Asian Popular Culture*, Vol. 2(2), pp. 145–59.

Russell, B. (2002) 'The Talk Shop and Shop Talk: Employment and Work in a Call Centre', *Journal of Industrial Relations*, Vol. 44(4), pp. 467–90.

Said, E.W. (1978 [2003]) *Orientalism.* London: Routledge Kegan Paul.

Said, E.W. (1993) *Culture and Imperialism.* London: Chatto and Windus.

Saldanha, A. (2002) 'Music, Space, Identity: Geographies of Youth Culture in Bangalore', *Cultural Studies*, Vol. 16(3), pp. 337–50.

Salzinger, L. (2002) 'Manufacturing Sexual Subjects: "Harassment", Desire and Discipline on a Maquiladora Shopfloor', in Taylor, S. (ed.) *Ethnographic Research: A Reader*, London: Sage Publications, pp. 115–37.

Sampson, H. (2003) 'Transnational Drifters or Hyperspace Dwellers: An Exploration of the Lives of Filipino Seafarers Aboard and Ashore', *Ethnic and Racial Studies*, Vol. 26(2), pp. 253–77.

Sangari, K. (2003) 'New Patriotisms: Beauty and the Bomb', in Chandrasekhar, I. and Seel, P.S. (eds) *Body.City: Siting Contemporary Culture in India.* New Delhi: Tulika Books, pp. 198–217.

Sangari, K. and Vaid, S. (1989) 'Recasting Women: An Introduction', in Sangari, K. and Vaid, S. (eds) *Recasting Women: Essays in Colonial History.* New Delhi: Kali for Women, pp. 1–26.

Sarantakos, S. (1993) *Social Research.* Basingstoke: Macmillan Press.

Sarkar, S. and Niyogi De, E. (2002) *Trans-Status Subjects.* Durham, NC and London: Duke University Press.

Sassen, S. (1998) *Globalization and Its Discontents*. New York: New Press.

Sassen, S. (1999) 'Digital Networks and Power', in Featherstone, M. and Lash, S. (eds) *Spaces of Culture: City, Nation, World*. London: Sage Publications, pp. 49–63.

Sassen, S. (2001a) 'Spatialities and Temporalities of the Global: Elements for Theorization', in Appadurai, A. (ed.) *Globalization*. Durham, NC and London: Duke University Press, pp. 260–78.

Sassen, S. (2001b) *The Global City: New York, London, and Tokyo*, 2nd edition. Princeton and Oxford: Princeton University Press.

Sassen, S. (2002) 'Introduction: Locating Cities on Global Circuits', in Sassen, S. (ed.) *Global Networks, Linked Cities*. New York and London: Routledge, pp. 1–37.

Sassen, S. (2003) 'Globalization or Denationalization?', *Review of International Political Economy*, Vol. 10(1), pp. 1–22.

Seabrook, J. (2003) 'Progress on Hold', *Guardian*, 24 October.

Seale, C. (1999) *The Quality of Qualitative Research*. London: Sage Publications.

Secor, A.J. (2002) 'The Veil and Urban Space in Istanbul: Women's Dress, Mobility, and Islamic Knowledge', *Gender, Place, and Culture*, Vol. 9(1), pp. 5–22.

Shah, N., Gothoskar, S., Ghandi, N. and Chhachi, A. (2001) 'Structural Adjustment, Feminisation of Labour Force and Organisational Strategies', in Menon, N. (ed.) *Gender and Politics in India*. New Delhi: Oxford University Press, pp. 145–47.

Sherif, B. (2001) 'The Ambiguity of Boundaries in the Fieldwork Experience: Establishing Rapport and Negotiating Insider/Outsider Status', *Qualitative Inquiry*, Vol. 7(4), pp. 436–47.

Shire, K., Hotgrewe, U. and Kerst, C. (2002) 'Re-Organising Customer Service Work: An Introduction', in Holtgrewe, U., Kerst, C., and Shire, K. (eds) *Re-Organising Service Work: Call Centres in Germany and Britain*. Aldershot: Ashgate, pp. 1–16.

Shome, R. (2006) 'Thinking through the Diaspora: Call Centres, India, and a New Politics of Hybridity', *International Journal of Cultural Studies*, Vol. 9(1), pp. 105–24.

Shukla, A. (2003) 'Sena Sounds V-Day Threat', *Hindustan Times*, 13 February.

Shurmer-Smith, P. (2000) *India: Globalization and Change*. London: Arnold.

Simpson, D., Love, J. and Walker, J. (1987) *The Challenge of New Technology*. Brighton: Wheatsheaf Books.

Singh, P. and Pandey, A. (2005) 'Women in Call Centres', *Economic and Political Weekly*, 12 February.

Singhal, A. and Rogers, E.M. (2001) *India's Communication Revolution: From Bullock Carts to Cyber Marts*. New Delhi: Sage Publications.

Sinha, N. (1996) 'The Political Economy of India's Telecommunications Reforms', *Telecommunications Policy*, Vol. 20(1), pp. 23–38.

Skeggs, B. (1994) 'Situating the Production of Feminist Ethnography', in Maynard, M. and Purvis, J. (eds) *Researching Women's Lives from a Feminist Perspective*. London: Taylor and Francis, pp. 72–92.

Skeggs, B. (2002) 'Techniques for Telling the Reflexive Self', in May, T. (ed.) *Qualitative Research in Action*. London: Sage Publications, pp. 349–74.

Smelser, N.J. (2003) 'On Comparative Analysis, Interdisciplinarity and Internationalization in Sociology', *International Sociology*, Vol. 18(4), pp. 643–57.

Smith, D.E. (2002) 'Institutional Ethnography', in May, T. (ed.) *Qualitative Research in Action*. London: Sage Publications, pp. 17–52.

Sonwalker, P. (2001) 'India: Makings of Little Cultural/Media Imperialism', *Gazette*, Vol. 63(6), pp. 505–19.

Spivak, G. (1986) 'Imperialism and Sexual Difference', *Oxford Literary Review*, Vol. 8 (1–2), pp. 225–40.

Spivak, G. (1988) 'Can the Subaltern Speak?', in Nelson, C. and Grossberg, L. (eds) *Marxism and the Interpretation of Culture*, London: Macmillan, pp. 1–43.

Spivak, G. (1999) *A Critique of Postcolonial Reason: Toward a History of the Vanishing Present*. Cambridge, MA and London: Harvard University Press.

Srinivas, L. (2002) 'The Active Audience: Spectatorship, Social Relations and the Experience of Cinema in India', *Media, Culture, and Society*, Vol. 24, pp. 155–73.

Srivastava, S. (2004) 'Introduction: Semen, History, Desire, and Theory', in Srivastava, S. (ed.) *Sexual Sites, Seminal Attitudes*. New Delhi: Sage Publications, pp. 11–48.

Standing, G. (1989) 'Global Feminization through Flexible Labour', *World Development*, Vol. 17(7), pp. 1077–95.

Stanley, L. and Wise, S. (1993) *Breaking out Again: Feminist Ontology and Epistemology*, 2nd edition. London and New York: Routledge.

Stanworth, C. (1998) 'Telework and the Information Age', *New Technology, Work and Employment*, Vol. 13(1), pp. 51–62.

Stanworth, C. (2000) 'Women and Work in the Information Age', *Gender, Work, and Organization*, Vol. 7(1), pp. 20–32.

Stone-Mediatore, S. (2000) 'Chandra Mohanty and the Revaluing of "Experience"', in Narayan, U. and Harding, S. (eds) *Decentering the Center: Philosophy for a Multicultural, Postcolonial, and Feminist World*. Bloomington and Indianapolis: Indiana University Press, pp. 110–27.

Strauss, A. and Corbin, J. (1994) 'Grounded Theory Methodology: An Overview', in Denzin, N.K. and Lincoln, Y.S. (eds) *Handbook of Qualitative Research.*, 3rd edition, London: Sage, pp. 507–36.

Szerszynski, B. and Urry, J. (2002) 'Cultures of Cosmopolitanism', *Sociological Review*, Vol. 50(4), pp. 461–81.

Tarlo, E. (1996) *Clothing Matters: Dress and Identity in India*. London: Hurst and Company.

Taylor, F.W. (1913) *The Principles of Scientific Management*. New York: Harper.

Taylor, P. and Bain, P. (1999) 'An "Assembly Line in the Head": Work and Employee Relations in the Call Centre', *Industrial Relations Journal*, Vol. 30(2), pp. 101–17.

Taylor, P. and Bain, P. (2003a) *Call Centres in Scotland and Outsourced Competition from India*. Stirling: Scotecon Network.

Taylor, P. and Bain, P. (2003b) '"Subterranean Worksick Blues": Humour as Subversion in Two Call Centres', *Organization Studies*, Vol. 24(9), pp. 1487–509.

Taylor, P. and Bain, P. (2005) '"India Calling to the Far Away Towns": The Call Centre Labour Process and Globalisation', *Work, Employment, and Society*, Vol. 19(2), pp. 261–82.

Taylor, P. and Bain, P. (2008) 'United by a Common Language? Trade Union Responses in the UK and India to Call Centre Offshoring', *Antipode*, Vol. 40(1), pp. 131–54.

Taylor, P., Mulvey, G., Hyman, J. and Bain, P. (2002) 'Work Organization, Control, and the Experience of Work in Call Centres', *Work, Employment, and Society*, Vol. 16(1), pp. 133–50.

Taylor, S. (1998) 'Emotional Labour and the New Workplace', in Thompson, P. and Warhurst, C. (eds) *Workplaces of the Future*. London: Macmillan, pp. 85–103.

Thapan, M. (1997) 'Femininity and Its Discontents: The Woman's Body in Intimate Relationships', in Thapan, M. (ed.) *Embodiment: Essays on Gender and Identity*. Delhi: Oxford University Press, pp. 172–93.

Thapan, M. (2001) 'Adolescence, Embodiment and Gender Identity In Contemporary India: Elite Women in a Changing Society', *Women's Studies International Forum*, Vol. 24(3/4), pp. 359–71.

Thompson, P., Callaghan, G. and van den Broek, D. (2004) 'Keeping up Appearances: Recruitment, Skills and Normative Control in Call Centres', in Deery, S. and Kinnie, N. (eds) *Call Centres and Human Resource Management: A Cross-National Perspective*. Basingstoke: Palgrave, pp. 129–52.

Toffler, A. (1980) *The Third Wave*. London: Collins.

Toor, S. (2000) 'Indo-Chic: The Cultural Politics of Consumption in Post-Liberalization India', *SOAS Literary Review* 2 (July). Available at: www.soas.ac.uk/soaslit/issue2/TOOR.PDF (accessed 25 September 2008).

Treanor, J. (2002) 'Bank Chief's Cold Call for British Staff', *Guardian*, 6 August.

Truong, Thanh-Dam (1999) 'The Underbelly of the Tiger: Gender and the Demystification of the Asian Miracle', *Review of International Political Economy*, Vol. 6(2) (Summer), pp. 133–65.

Tulloch, C. (1999) 'That Little Magic Touch: The Headtie', in de la Haye, A. and Wilson, E. (eds) *Defining Dress: Dress as Object, Meaning, and Identity*. Manchester: Manchester University Press, pp. 63–78.

Tuyen, N.N. (1999) 'Transitional Economy, Technological Change and Women's Employment: The Case of Vietnam', *Gender Technology and Development*, Vol. 3(1), pp. 43–64.

Tyler, M. and Hancock, P. (2001) 'Flight Attendants and the Management of Gendered "Organizational Bodies"', in Backett-Milburn, K. and McKie, L. (eds) *Constructing Gendered Bodies*. Basingstoke: Palgrave, pp. 25–38.

Tyrell, H. (1999 [2004]) 'Bollywood versus Hollywood: Battle of the Dream Factories', in Lechner, F. and Boli, J. (eds) *The Globalization Reader*, 2nd edition. Oxford: Blackwell Publishing, pp. 312–18.

Urry, J. (1999) 'Mobile Cultures', Lancaster: Department of Sociology, Lancaster University. Available at: http://www.comp.lancs.ac.uk/sociology/papers/Urry-Mobile-Cultures.pdf (accessed 25 September 2008).

Valentine, G. (1989) 'The Geography of Women's Fear', *Area*, Vol. 21(4), pp. 385–90.

Valentine, G. (1992) 'Images of Danger: Women's Sources of Information about the Spatial Distribution of Male Violence', *Area*, Vol. 24(1), pp. 22–29.

Varma, P.K. (1998) *The Great Indian Middle Class*. New Delhi: Penguin Books.

Varma, P.K. (2004) *Being Indian*. New Delhi: Penguin Books.

Wajcman, J. (1991) *Feminism Confronts Technology*. Cambridge: Polity Press.

Wajcman, J. and Martin, B. (2002) 'Narratives of Identity in Modern Management: The Corrosion of Gender Difference?', *Sociology*, Vol. 36(4), pp. 985–1002.

Walby, S. (1988) *Gender Segregation at Work*. Milton Keynes: Open University Press.

Walby, S. (1990) *Theorizing Patriarchy*. Oxford: Wiley Blackwell.

Wallace, J. (1998) 'What Does It Mean to be a Woman?', *The Times Higher Education Supplement*, 8 May. Available at: www.thes.co.uk. (accessed 25 September 2008).

Walton-Roberts, M. (2004) 'Globalization, National Autonomy, and Non-Resident Indians', *Contemporary South Asia*, Vol. 13(1), pp. 53–69.

Webb, J., Schirato, T. and Danaher, G. (eds) (2002) *Understanding Bourdieu*. London: Sage Publications.

Webster, J. (1990) *Office Automation: The Labour Process and Women's Work in Britain*. Hemel Hempstead: Harvester Wheatsheaf.

Webster, J. (1993) 'Women's Skills and Word Processors', in Probert, B. and Wilson, B.P. (eds) *Pink Collar Blues: Work, Gender, and Technology*. London: Melbourne University Press, pp. 41–59.

Welsch, W. (1999) 'Transculturality: The Puzzling Form of Cultures Today', in Featherstone, M. and Lash, S. (eds) *Spaces of Culture: City, Nation, World*. London: Sage Publications, pp. 194–213.

Whelan, J., Whelan, M. and Henderson, K. (2002) 'Improvisational Choreography in Teleservice Work', *British Journal of Sociology*, Vol. 53(2), pp. 239–58.

Williams, B.F. (1996) 'Skinfolk, Not Kinfolk', in Wolf, D. (ed.) *Feminist Dilemmas in Fieldwork*. Oxford: Westview Press, pp. 71–95.

Witz, A. (2000) 'Whose Body Matters? Feminist Sociology and the Corporeal Turn in Sociology and Feminism', *Body and Society*, Vol. 6(2), pp. 1–24.

Witz, A., Warhurst, C. and Nickson, D. (2003) 'The Labour of Aesthetics and the Aesthetics of Organization', *Organization*, Vol. 10(1), pp. 33–54.

Wolf, D. (1996) 'Situating Feminist Dilemmas in Fieldwork', in Wolf, D. (ed.) *Feminist Dilemmas in Fieldwork*. Oxford: Westview Press, pp. 1–55.

'Women Make the Right Call' (2003) *Times of India*, 4 November.

Wray, R. (2003) 'If They Don't Want Us, I Don't Want Them', *Guardian*, 17 November.

Wyatt, A. (2005) '(Re)imagining the Indian (Inter)national Economy', *New Political Economy*, Vol. 10(2), pp. 163–79.

Yegenoglu, M. (2005) 'Cosmopolitanism and Nationalism in a Globalized World', *Ethnic and Racial Studies*, Vol. 28(1), pp. 103–31.

Yeoh, B. and Yeow, P. (1997) 'Where Women Fear to Tread: Images of Danger and the Effects of Fear and Crime in Singapore', *GeoJournal*, Vol. 43(3), pp. 273–86.

Yeoh, B., Willis, K. and Fakhri, A. (2003) 'Transnational Edges Introduction: Transnationalism and Its Edges', *Ethnic and Racial Studies*, Vol. 26(2), pp. 207–17.

Yuval-Davis, N. (1994) 'Identity Politics and Women's Ethnicity', in Moghadam, V. (ed.) *Identity Politics and Women*. Oxford: Westview Press, pp. 408–24.

Young, K., Wolkowitz, C. and McCullagh, R. (eds) (1981) *Of Marriage and Market*. London: CSE Books.

Zapf, D., Isic, A., Bechtoldt, M. and Blau, P. (2003) 'What Is Typical for Call Centre Jobs? Job Characteristics, and Service Interactions in Different Call Centres', *European Journal of Work and Organizational Psychology*, Vol. 12(4), pp. 311–40.

Films

Chalte Chalte (2003) Directed by Aziz Mirza. India.

Dil Chahta Hai (2001) Directed by Farhan Akhtar. India.

Hum Aapke Hain Koun (Who Am I To You?) (1994) Directed by Ram Laxman. India.

Mother India (Bharat Mata) (1967) Directed by Mehboob Khan. India.

Yasmin (2005) Directed by Kenneth Glenaan. UK.

Websites

NASSCOM, National Association of Software and Services Companies. Available at: www.nasscom.in (accessed September 2008).

No Jobs for India, No Jobs for India. Available at: www.nojobsforindia.com (accessed 25 September 2008).

Index

agency 1, 145, 159; agency/structure dynamic 2, 8, 9; call centre 2, 164; consumption 32–33; identity 2, 7, 8, 23, 26, 162, 172 (construction 2, 7, 23, 162); women 3, 7, 15, 83, 102, 106, 109, 116, 130, 134, 148, 155, 159, 160, 162, 180; *see also* women

Asia: information technology (IT) 13, 170–71; women 13, 170–71

Australia 174, 177; call centre industry 43, 55, 175, 176

Bollywood 33–34, 95, 99, 144; *Andaaz* 179; audience 99, 177–78; *Chalte Chalte* 122, 179; clothing 122, 179; India: cinematic society 22, 33–34, 99, 143, 145; *Mother India* 9, 34, 169; national identity 33, 99, 133, 173, 177–78; 'rhetoric of danger and threat' 152–53; women 9, 22, 34, 120, 172, 169, 173; *see also* India; media

call centre industry 1, 6, 23, 39, 170; Australia 43, 55, 175, 176; definition 39; 'global feminization of labour' 9–10; health 44, 45, 50–51; Information Technology Enabled Services-Business Process Outsourcing (ITES–BPO) 42, 104, 164; transnationalism 23, 31, 35; United Kingdom 1, 39, 47, 49, 52, 65, 86–87, 91–92; *see also* call centre industry, India; globalization; information communications technology (ICT); information technology (IT); telecommunications; women in Indian call centres

call centre industry, India 1, 3, 4, 5–7, 8–11, 13–15, 28–55, 144, 160, 168–69;

accent change 6, 16, 23, 47, 68, 87, 89, 107, 161; age 43, 46, 52, 55 (discrimination 12, 45–46); aliases/name changes 6, 16, 47, 57, 86–89, 161, 168, 171; beginnings 40–41; class dimensions 96–98, 163; clients 43, 174–75; clothing 60, 107, 109, 111, 116–20, 123–31, 137–38, 140–41, 162, 179; college-like atmosphere 12–13, 75, 75, 78–79, 129, 145, 158, 163; consumerism 33, 60, 94, 123, 146–47, 179; cosmopolitanism 3, 24–26, 89, 101, 107–11, 116, 127, 143, 173; customer service 68–69; Delhi 43, 51, 94–95, 117, 154, 159, 162, 163, 168–69, 174, 179, 182 (Delhi as a 'global city' 94, 132, 145–51); discussions on 1–2, 15, 16, 28, 41, 48–50, 160; education 55, 59, 92, 93; exploitation 5, 6, 11, 16, 72, 79, 160, 180; GE 40, 41, 174; globalization 27, 28, 30, 34, 89, 161, 163, 164, 174; Gurgaon 51, 159, 146, 149, 150, 155, 162, 168; emotional labour 57, 65–69; employment 43, 175; facilities 44–45, 52–53, 75, 77, 177; gendering 61–63, 66, 69; health and safety 44, 45, 50–51, 56, 73–74, 76, 84–85, 93, 102, 140, 143, 151, 152–54, 162; identity 4, 6, 8–11, 16, 23, 26, 29–30, 34, 82, 86–89, 108, 159, 163, 168 (construction 2, 3, 7, 11, 82, 101, 128–31, 147, 159–60; 'global colonial' identities 89; Indian identity 32, 100, 107–8, 133, 159–60, 161; 'locational masking' 86, 87, 108; transnational 31–32); incentives 42, 44, 46, 72–74, 76–77, 84, 117, 176, 180; labour process and management 47–48,

eBooks – at www.eBookstore.tandf.co.uk

A library at your fingertips!

eBooks are electronic versions of printed books. You can store them on your PC/laptop or browse them online.

They have advantages for anyone needing rapid access to a wide variety of published, copyright information.

eBooks can help your research by enabling you to bookmark chapters, annotate text and use instant searches to find specific words or phrases. Several eBook files would fit on even a small laptop or PDA.

NEW: Save money by eSubscribing: cheap, online access to any eBook for as long as you need it.

Annual subscription packages

We now offer special low-cost bulk subscriptions to packages of eBooks in certain subject areas. These are available to libraries or to individuals.

For more information please contact webmaster.ebooks@tandf.co.uk

We're continually developing the eBook concept, so keep up to date by visiting the website.

www.eBookstore.tandf.co.uk